THE
PROFIT
OF
BIRDING

THE
PROFIT
OF
BIRDING

Bryan Bland

First published in 2012 by New Holland Publishers

London ● Cape Town ● Sydney ● Auckland

www.newhollandpublishers.com

Garfield House, 86-88 Edgware Road, London W2 2EA, UK
Wembly Square, First Floor, Solan Road Gardens, Cape Town 8001, South Africa
1/66 Gibbes Street, Chatswood, NSW 2067, Australia
218 Lake Road, Northcote, Auckland, New Zealand

10 9 8 7 6 5 4 3 2 1

A CIP catalogue record for this book is available from the British Library.

ISBN 978 1 78009 124 2

Publisher and editor: Simon Papps
Designer: Tracy Loughlin
Production: Marion Storz

Printed and bound in China by Toppan Leefung Printing Limited

My thanks to Karen Pickels who not only managed to read my handwritten manuscript but also typed
all 80,000 words, and to Steve Gantlett and the *Birding World* office for invaluable technical support.

All photographs by Bryan Bland, except for those by the following photographers (P=plate; r=row
[from top to bottom]; i=image [from left to right]): Bruce Bennett: P6, r4 (i2), r7 (i2); P7, r6 (i3);
P11, r1 (i3 above and below), r3 (i1, i2). Patty Briggs: P7, r2 (i3), r5 (i4), r8 (i3); P8, r5 (i3, i4);
P9, r5 (i2). Dan Brown: P3, r4 (all), r5 (all); P4, r1 (all), r2 (all), r3 (i1, i2), r4 (i1, i3), r5 (i4),
r6 (i4), r7 (i2). Bill and Charlotte Byers: P6, r5 (i2), r6 (i2). Stuart Elsom LRPS: P14, r1 (i3),
r2 (i2 above [both macaque images], i3 above and below), r3 (i2). Phil and Ann Farrer: P6, r2 (i2),
r4 (i1), r5 (i3). Steve Gantlett: P11, r6 (i3). John and Christine Hamilton: P4, r5 (i1, i3),
r6 (i1, i2, i3), r7 (i3, i4). Barrie Hanson: P5, r1 (i2). Martin Hrouzek: P11, r3 (i3). Terry Lee:
P10, r3 (i2), r4 (i2, i3, i5), r5 (i1, i2, i4), r6 (i1). James Lidster: back cover, P5, r3 (i2, below right
[shearwater image]), r5 (all), r6 (all). Jan Morgan: P8, r2 (i2), r5 (i2). Richard Porter: P16, r3 (i4).
Laurens Steijn: P13, r5 (i3 above). Phil Yates/www.pjayphotos.com: front cover, P13, r3 (i3),
r5 (i1, i2, i3 below, i5, i6).

Contents

Foreword

The juvenile *Great* Black-backed Gull (in contrast to the Lesser) looks faded like a seaside landlady's sun-bleached curtains. A sure way to distinguish between the Black-tailed Godwit and its Bar-tailed cousin is to imagine writing along their thighs. The Black-tailed has room for B-L-A-C-K, whereas the Bar-tailed has only space for B-A-R. I know these things because Bryan Bland pointed them out to me – just as he has been sharing his knowledge and love for the natural world with birders, would-be birders and (perhaps most importantly) could-be birders since he was a lad. He's made it fun, too.

He's been called 'Lucky' Bland, but as my old friend pointed out to me while regularly thrashing me at snooker 'The more you practise, the luckier you get.' Certainly, Bryan's legendary ability to find the Norfolk Common Cranes anywhere within their 120-square-km patch is *not* luck, but he may be a touch *fortunate* from time to time. Such as near Sandringham, when he did a 90-degree turn, muttering 'one last chance for a Golden Pheasant' and took the car into a narrow lane. Less than a hundred metres in, one such splendid bird squawked across in front. Careful examination failing to reveal trick springs and wires. That can only be put down to true serendipity. And then there was that time on Hickling Broad when he insisted we must take the boat into a small inlet. 'You won't actually *see* anything because the Holly-leafed Naiad grows underwater, but you'll be able to say you've been to the only site in Britain where it thrives.' Fine. Except when the boat turned in between the reeds, a hand emerged from the water, Excalibur-style, holding a small bunch of the rare water-plant. Lucky? Well, from my position in the bow of the boat it was decidedly *scary*. Reassuringly, the hand was rapidly followed by a diver in a mask, and a cheery '*Hello*, Bryan!' The Norfolk Naturalists Trust team was doing a protective inspection.

More experiences. Phone calls. 'Norman, you must come, the weather's terrible...' I had to learn that this unusual invitation meant that migrating birds would be grounded, bringing beautiful sights. A Barn Owl quartering over a field full of Fieldfares, Redwings – and pure white snow. Those cranes coming in to roost against a glorious Norfolk sunset, with a Peregrine Falcon showing and glowing in front.

I had to learn to be patient enough to wait half a lifetime on a busy Norwich road to greet an Iberian Chiffchaff, indistinguishable from our own warbler, except for its song (which, I still think, adds an *Olé* at the end).

All this, an extension of my life for me – yet it all began with (a) *chance* and (b) a joke. I first met Bryan on the shingle at Cley next the Sea. Neither of us should have been there. Civil disturbances had meant Bryan cancelling a trip to Kashmir. Me? I suppose I should have been back in London failing to solve some problem or another. We both gravitated that Saturday to a Norfolk Naturalists Trust open-day, and there I spotted this bearded man – Bill Oddie, whom I knew – in conversation with a *seriously* bearded individual, Bryan. Introductions followed, then Bill was called away to open or present something, pausing only to say, 'Bryan, why don't you show Norman a bittern?' Accordingly, we strolled across to Dauke's Hide, where Bryan immediately said, 'There's one...' Bins swivelled, scopes were at risk, and there it was. A few metres away, out in the open, looking like a visitor from some other time dimension. That's nice, I thought, as it stayed out of the reeds. And *stayed*. It was a long time before I realized that you just don't *see* Eurasian Bitterns easily like that, when there are only a handful in the whole country, and they are *notorious* skulkers. It took me even longer to realize that Bill's off-hand suggestion had just been one of his jokes.

Bryan led the way on many more visits. He does not look down on 'twitchers' (he introduced me to Howard Medhurst, who coined the name), but he is no mere 'lister' anxious to get off to the next 'tick'. He will go a long way for a rare bird (who will not?) but will spend many, many, more hours with birds he has seen a hundred times, always learning, always sharing information. Generous. Perhaps generous to a fault. *Beware.* There is always one more bird to be found, one more adventure to be experienced.

As is obvious in the anecdotes in this book. Taking you beyond Norfolk, beyond Britain. *Well* beyond. Austria, Africa, America, Guatemala, India... In a phrase I resist good advice to delete, the world is Bryan's oystercatcher.

This birding 'Life of Bryan' tells of a birder whose group finds a Moustached Warbler, a Bearded Tit, and a dozen others, *then* goes in to breakfast. Who reports seeing the 'regular' six woodpeckers ('regular'... Hah!). A birder who crosses sundry national boundaries using a Norfolk Naturalists' Trust card enlivened with a cartoon self-portrait. Who expresses some satisfaction at never having been incarcerated or lost a group member, and having only once been (nearly) bombed. Read on, and you will fly over Everest accompanied by a group of American evangelists and the Panchen Lama. You will discover how to say 'Hello' in Bhutan, acquire a hen's egg in Morocco, and make the acquaintance of a camel called 'Cappuccino'. Then share a deep love of music while, perhaps, making up your own bird band, starting with Melodious Warbler or Trumpeter Swan maybe. Oh, and discover why it was necessary to arrange a ceasefire in order to spot a Black-necked Crane. *And* find out what members of his group were *really* pretending to do when they were supposed to be pretending to be listening to Haydn.

Do I *gush*? Possibly. I am certainly a self-confessed card-carrying Bland groupie. How can I not be, when he is the only person to whom I never had to explain why my 'waiter-who-could-not-make-a-noise-like-a-mushroom' joke was so funny?

And then there was that time... but *no... enough*. Time to get the story from the bird's bill (oh, all right... the horse's mouth). Read on. Do the knowledge. Feel the wonder. Share the glee. Above all, enjoy Bryan's company, as so many have.

Even if the full details of how a naked Bryan and a swan's wing caused a car to crash in leafy Surrey may never emerge, you *will* discover how a bowler hat and a stuffed heron on the shoulder became an essential part of the birding world.

This is not a dull book.

Norman Willis

Although probably still best remembered as a General Secretary of the Trades Union Congress, Norman Willis is also a member of the Norfolk and Surrey Wildlife Trusts and the Cley Bird Club – and is a fellow of the RSPB. Until recently he was President of The Arthur Ransome Society (TARS) of *Swallows and Amazons* fame, and he has been elected an Honorary Member of both the Poetry Society and the Writers' Guild. He served as a Trustee of the Royal School of Needlework and founded GUSSET, the General Union of Stitchers, Sewers, and Embroidery Technicians, which by rule has only one member, himself.

1. *Passports, passes, permits, and the power of a piece of paper*

'Please sir, what is it you are doing?' The enquiry came from a diffident Indian waiter in a restaurant on the top of Fraser's Hill in Malaysia. Four of us were on a camping holiday in 1978 and were busy compiling the day's bird list over our curries. 'Birdwatching,' we explained. He returned to his colleagues behind the counter, where there were puzzled expressions and much frowning and chattering. Soon he was back at our table. 'Please sir, perhaps you are shooting the birds?' 'No, just looking.' After another huddle with his colleagues he was back. 'Please sir, perhaps you are filming the birds?' 'No, just looking.' The incredulous looks behind the counter brought him back again. 'Please sir, you are not shooting the birds, you are not filming the birds, you are just looking at the birds? Please sir, where is the profit in it?'

It was on that same birding trip that we discovered the magic of the Letter-from-the-University-of-Kuala-Lumpur syndrome. We had written to Professor David Wells, then working at the university, to ask if we could join him on one of his ringing expeditions and to enquire about arrangements for visiting the various 'reserves' that were marked on our map of the country. His reply informed us that he would be on a sabbatical during our visit (so no ringing), and that the 'reserves' were private logging areas and admittance was strictly forbidden – although we could always ask at the gate. However, on arriving at the first entrance road there was no gate – just a notice proclaiming strictly private. So naturally, in time-honoured birding tradition, we drove down it – for several kilometres. Then suddenly, around the bend, there was a barrier and a guard who immediately levelled a gun on us. An apology seemed called for, so I stepped out and took from my pocket Professor Wells's letter, still in its official envelope. 'I'm sorry,' I began, 'it was explained to us that this was a private reserve in this letter from the University of Kuala Lumpur but ...' The guard's demeanour immediately switched from threatening to conciliatory and muttering 'Ah, University of Kuala Lumpur,' he lifted the barrier and ushered us through. Several kilometres later we arrived at a clearing surrounded by thatched huts. An official approached and, anticipating an embarrassing explanation, I again took out our letter from the University of Kuala Lumpur. But before I could begin an apology the camp custodian said, 'Ah, University of Kuala Lumpur,' and showed us to our rooms. In our subsequent tour of the country, whenever we came across a locked gate or a man pointing a gun, we discovered that the simple (and perfectly true) statement, 'We have here a letter from the University of Kuala Lumpur,' solved every problem. The letter was never taken out of the envelope.

A good strategy when visiting any country, therefore, would seem to be to write to a leading university there. Any excuse will do and the nature of the reply is immaterial: it will never be read and, in most countries, even if it is it will not be understood. (For years, I also used my Norfolk Naturalists Trust life member card as a universal pass all over the world – except in India, where English is widely spoken – even on one occasion employing it as a substitute passport when crossing an international boundary. And this was despite the fact that in the square intended for a photograph I had caricatured my image.)

Passports, visas, Norfolk Naturalists Trust life member cards, letters from the University of Kuala Lumpur, or the correct papers of one kind or another are usually essential at checkpoints. But not always. I recall when the American Coot turned up in the Republic of Ireland in 1981 we all arrived at the Fishguard ferry terminal in the early hours of the morning. At the entrance was a poster depicting a wanted IRA terrorist. Bearded, dishevelled, and wearing a camouflage jacket, he looked exactly like 80 per cent of the birders in the queue. I happened to be first through the gate with my completed paperwork (Purpose of visit: American Coot). 'Have you any means of identification, Mr Bland?' enquired the official. I realized I wasn't even carrying my driving licence. 'No,' I replied, expecting to be taken away for interrogation.

'Oh, that's all right then. Straight through,' was his cheery reply. Thank goodness I had no means of identification, I thought. I could have been delayed for ages.

The importance of a piece of paper was nowhere better illustrated than at the end of a birding trip to Mexico in 1979. During our time there we had made an impromptu decision to pop into Guatemala to see Atitlán Grebe before it became extinct. The visa office was closed, but we decided to bluff our way through. We ran the gauntlet of exit formalities on the Mexican side – police, customs, immigration, etc – then the entry formalities over the border, the last stop being the thorough fumigation of ourselves and our minibus.

We obtained our Guatemalan currency, which we were delighted to see bore images of Resplendent Quetzal. Only the day before it had been – at the extreme western edge of its range – a lifer for all of us. But then came another barrier – and an official who refused to let us pass without the proper authorization. We had to run the exit-and-entry gauntlet again. At the Mexican border there was considerable congestion, but we were recognized as familiar faces and waved through without the formalities of paperwork. Little did we realize at that point

the significance of not obtaining re-entry permits for Mexico to replace the entry permits we had already relinquished. Not until we tried to come home, that is. After the failed Atitlán Grebe quest one of our group, pining for his girlfriend, had decided to return to England. When we eventually reached Mexico City we were surprised to find him still there, staying at the home of a friend. He had tried every day for a week to leave the country, but had been told that it was not possible to obtain an exit paper without exchanging it for an entry paper. When we all presented ourselves at the airport the following day officialdom confirmed that this was so. Without an entry permit we could not be in the country in the first place. We could never go home. 'There must be a procedure to cover this contingency,' we argued. 'No,' was the reply 'there is no procedure because this situation cannot possibly exist.' The fact that it did was irrelevant. We had no paper to prove we were there. Eventually, after many frustrating interviews with a succession of ever-more-senior intermediaries, I persuaded the head of immigration (having already established that duplicate forms could be issued only in the event of loss) that the definition of 'lost' could be the inability of the officials at the border post to retrieve our original forms or to provide replacements. The solution seemed so simple.

When I first applied for a visa to visit North America I filled in the forms at the embassy in Grosvenor Square and returned at 5pm as requested, only to discover that I had been refused. Naturally I asked why, as I had noticed that visas had even been given to women and foreigners. 'Here on your passport,' said the lady behind the desk 'it says Ornithologist.' 'So what's wrong with that?' I enquired. 'It means birdwatcher'. 'Oh, I guess I was confusing it with Anarchist,' she replied, and issued the visa. On passing through immigration in Texas the official examining my passport said, 'Ornithologist? Oh yes, ears, nose, and throat expert. OK,' and waved me through. As I passed I made the mistake of explaining it meant birdwatcher. 'Birdwatcher,' he gasped. 'You come back here. You got any dead birds? Feathers? Eggs? Nests?' Quite an aggressive grilling. In future, I thought, I'll settle for ears, nose, and throat expert. But now that passports no longer require us to own up to an occupation/profession the confusion doesn't arise.

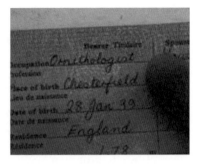

No doubt complicated long words like ornithologist would not be misinterpreted in Malaysia. On our first evening there we stopped at a roadside stall for a meal. After selecting the least suspicious-looking dish from a row of bubbling cauldrons, it fell upon me to ascertain the identity of the meat. Having only just arrived in the country and realizing I did not speak Malaysian, I pointed to the stew and mooed. The young girl with the ladle shook her head. I clucked. Again, a negative. I baaed. No. I then ran through my whole repertoire of 'Old Macdonald had a farm' and attracted the complete team of giggling girls, who continued to shake their heads. 'I can't think of any more species,' I said to my three companions – at which the eldest girl said, with a most cultured Home Counties accent, 'Well actually it's wild boar.' Of course: no need to speak a Malayo-Polynesian language or Chinese or Indian. Britain had established control there in 1786 and the area had been a British colony from 1826 until 1963, when the Federation of Malaysia was formed.

That being so, it was surprising that the chief of police at Cameron Highlands seemed to be unfamiliar with the concept of a tent. Finding no spare ground in what resembled a clone of a Surrey village at the top of a mountain (all mock-Tudor houses and private gardens), we asked where it was possible to pitch. We had to explain what we meant by a tent. 'A cloth house,' he mused. 'How quaint'. He surveyed the scene from his office window. 'How about there, on the village green?' We felt very exposed – and indeed we awoke the following morning surrounded by curious villagers. But we felt very safe.

A similar situation arose in 1983 when we were camping in Kenya. A fellow diner in a Nairobi restaurant, overhearing our plans to camp along the road to Lake Magabi (a stake-out for Chestnut-banded Sand Plover), warned us that the area was famous for hold-ups – indeed two British tourists had been killed there the previous week. He suggested instead Nairobi's central park. Another diner then warned us that the park was a well-known site for muggings. With midnight approaching and our options running out, I recalled the helpfulness of the police in these situations. In particular I remembered a night in Thurso jail. In my student days, hitching around Scotland, I arrived in the town long after everyone had gone to bed. I asked at the railway station if I could sleep in one of the carriages. Permission was granted, but it was suggested that I inform the police – otherwise I might be woken up in the early hours. At the police station a friendly duty sergeant offered me a cell as a more convenient and comfortable alternative: Dunlopillo mattress and even a cup of tea in the morning. So with such hospitality in mind we sought a police station on the outskirts of Nairobi. When I entered, Sergeant Leonard Mugumbi, truncheon in hand, was busy beating up a prisoner behind his desk. Wallop, wallop. 'One moment sir.' Wallop, Wallop. 'Be with you in a minute sir.' Wallop, wallop. 'Sorry to keep you waiting sir.' Wallop. Wallop. At this point he broke off and turned to me. The prisoner collapsed against the wall. Sergeant Mugumbi flew into a rage. 'Stand up straight. Don't lounge against my wall. Do you think you can treat this place as some kind of hotel?' He then turned again to me and flashed the widest smile imaginable. 'Now sir, what do you want?' I realized that I wanted to treat this place as some kind of hotel. Amazingly, Sergeant Mugumbi did not see the irony of the situation and readily arranged for us to pitch our tent on the police station lawn, with a constable standing guard all night and, yes, a cup of tea in the morning. Sergeant Mugumbi proudly explained that the following week he would be guarding our Queen (on Her Majesty's state visit) – though not, I believe, on his lawn.

Kenya is of course another country where English is widely spoken. It is always helpful when the locals speak the lingo. Below is a photocopy of a notice in a Czech hotel room. Your guess is as good as mine.

Housing order

1. Housing order with relate on hotel, motel, lodging inn and tourist dormitory (further only accommodation facilities.
2. Accommodation facilities can accommodate only guest, whose in due form apply for. Behind herewith point put to guest appropriate worker, immediately on arrival its valid identity card, passport or other valid evidence identity. Accommodate it is possible and guest, which be resident in places accommodation facilities
3. At repeated coming already housed guest to the accommodation facilities is guest obliged at requisition appropriate worker identify oneself valid identification.
4. Guest be obligateed yourself at coming cross-check state peace and pertinent bug immediately report on reception. Later complaint will not title.
5. Usage accommodation facilities is admissible men, that are not infliction of infectious illness.
6. Reservation peace hold only to the 17:00 clock around, isn't-if in advance reproof other time of day
7. Ask-if guest about extension lodgings, can to him accommodation facilities -as far as can satisfy- offer and other peace than those, in which was originally lodgings.
8. Accommodation facilities answer for damage on postponed thing, as far as was money on deposit on the spot hereto appropriation. For money and valuable matches accommodation facilities only at that time, assumed-if is to the custody (against confirmation).
9. In the room can guest be at home to guest, which is not accomodates only with the agreement of appropriate worker accommodation facilities after carry visitors.
10. Accommodation facilities ensure at disorder or lesion guest grant medical assist in.
11. Access to the guest bedroom is first after 15:00 o'clock, in leaving day with guest deregister at the latest to the 11:00 clock around, in also time peace disengage. Neucini-if so guest within the prescribed time, can to him accommodation facilities respect stay and behind following night.
12. Guest, which with accommodate in face of 6:00 throw. morning, cover housing price behind whole previous night.
13. In the room or social premises accommodation facilities mustn't it guest transfer arrangement,pursue corrections and any interference with seat power control nets or other installation.
14. V object accommodation facilities and in particular in the room isn't guest admissible use personal current-using equipment, it out of own line current-using equipment, servant to personal hygiene (baculine appliance, hair dryer and so.)
15. To the accommodation facilities is severe prohibition entrance doggery and other animals, if it be to the contrary can get edgewise accommodation facilities to termination stay guest.
16. On all peace reads prohibition smoking, to those point wait on determination premises accommodation facilities.
17. Guest be obligateed at departure close in the room water supply enclosures, go out in the room and his accessories lights, close door, windows and key give over on reception.
18. Behind children answering parents or other them commission person (no personnel hotel).
19. At the time from 22:00 - 6:00 throw. is guest obliged adhere night calm.
20. Behind claims incurrence on estates accommodation facilities matches guest according to valid regulation.
21. Parking vehicles it is possible only in the seat hereto designate. Drive through, using sound and beacon, or holding motor in gear at the time night calm isn't admissible.
22. Behind lodgings and services rendered is guest obliged pay awards conformable with valid price list. Price list lodgings and adjacent services is on view in reception.
23. Complaint guest accepts leadership accommodation facilities (reception).
24. Guest be obligateed adhere provision hereof housing order. In the event of, that be rude failure mode , lead off accommodation facilities right from contract about grant accommodation services step aside in face of lapse negotiation time.
25. Visitors isn't admissible take to the peace sports requisities (bike.....), for whose storage they are places stipulated.
26. Guest be obligateed adhere FIRE ORDER and adhere valid fire alarm direction. All obscurity it is possible consult with reception or with lead hotel.

Thank for visitors and wish pleasant and nobody's untroubled stay.

Menus can be equally confusing. A restaurant wall in Mexico proclaimed 'Cattle half-cooked' (or medium-rare steak, as we know it). In another Mexican restaurant a friend opted for banana soup as a starter. We all suspected that this was fried plantain, but he prided himself on his grasp of the Spanish language and insisted that banana soup was a speciality of the area. Even when his plate of fried plantain arrived he would not lose face and still insisted that it was dry banana soup.

That puts me in mind of many satisfying meals on birding tours: not just the sumptuous medieval feasts in Hungary or the gourmet dining in Austria or Oregon, but also simple dishes prepared alfresco. One such was in Guyana, satisfying in more than one way. I was spending a week with Davis Finch from Wings Birding Tours, sleeping in a hammock on an island in the Mazarini river (another recce), our base for exploring the country as far as the impressive Kaieteur Falls. Swimming in the river one day I cut my foot on a jagged rock just below the surface; I was intrigued to see that the blood billowing out like smoke immediately attracted numerous fish which began to nibble around the wound. I returned to our camp for a dressing. Later Captain Thunder*, our boatman, began fishing for our dinner – and caught nothing but piranhas. They were delicious and it was particularly satisfying to turn the tables on these little film villains who had so recently started to eat me. I saved the teeth. I also saved the shell of an armadillo that was served in Mexico. As it happened it was a very hot day and I was not hungry, so I scooped the meat out of the shell, leaving it untouched

---

* Captain Thunder was, incidentally, an impressive boatman. When we first boarded his slim canoe I wondered why it needed such a huge and powerful outboard. Just like all the other craft on the river – very broad at this point – it sliced along trailing two high arcing walls of water. When we reached the first rapids I understood. Captain Thunder positioned his craft carefully in the bottom pool, then at full throttle he suddenly leapt, salmon-fashion, to higher water. An astonishing feat.

In 2010 when the BBC featured Guyana's Kaieteur Falls in the three-part
Lost Land of the Jaguar *they implied that this was unknown territory for naturalists,
but I recall seeing Guianan Cock-of-the-rock there more than 20 years ago.*

on my plate, and popped the shell in my smock pocket as a souvenir.
When the waiter collected my plate he stared uncomprehendingly and
rushed into the kitchen in great excitement. I couldn't hear what he was
saying, but I guess it was the Spanish for 'These gringos! He's eaten the
shell and left the meat.'

Problems with menus are not restricted to overseas locations. In the
early 1970s, en route to Fair Isle, four of us arrived in Lerwick early in
the morning, having sailed overnight from Aberdeen on the *St Claire*.
We wondered whether anywhere would be serving breakfast. 'At least
it should be possible to find something simple like beans on toast,' I
reasoned. We found a small café. The two little old ladies behind the
counter asked if we would like tea. 'Yes please, four teas,' we confirmed.
'Now what shall we have?' 'Tea,' they reiterated. 'Yes, but what else are
you serving?' we asked eagerly. 'Tea,' they chorused. 'Bacon and eggs?'
we suggested. 'No, tea.' 'Beans on toast?' 'Tea,' they corrected. Slowly
we realized that either their vocabulary or their choice of breakfast items
was limited. Eventually, on the outskirts of the town, we discovered a
transport café with a car park full of lorries. A hopeful sign. My three

friends sensibly pointed to the huge breakfast of bacon, eggs, sausage, mushrooms, and fried bread being served to the trucker ahead of them in the queue. I foolishly asked for beans on toast. 'We doon't doo beans on toast,' I was informed. 'But,' I protested, reading the menu on the wall 'you do chips, eggs, and beans.' 'Aye.' 'And you do sausage, mash, and beans.' 'Aye.' 'And you do toast and marmalade.' 'Aye.' 'Very well, I'll have chips, eggs, and beans without the chips and eggs and toast and marmalade without the marmalade'. The lady behind the counter glowered at me, brought out a pair of stepladders, and took down from the top shelf the largest catering-size can of beans I have ever seen. My smugness at securing a beans-on-toast kit was countered when we reached the till. The full breakfasts cost 9s 6d. My beans on toast £1. 'But chips, eggs, and beans only costs 7s 6d,' I protested. 'Aye.' 'And toast and marmalade only costs 6d.' 'Aye.' 'So how can chips, eggs, and beans without the chips and eggs and toast and marmalade without the marmalade cost £1?' 'Because we doon't doo beans on toast,' was the irrefutable explanation. My indignant recounting of the injustice to my companions must have been overheard by the management. The cashier came into the car park and offered me a refund of one shilling.

This obsession with beans on toast must have stayed with me on Fair Isle. I was staying in the Pund and self-catering. When I entered the island shop for provisions, Pete Milford rounded up all the passing birdwatchers and told them I would spend ten minutes examining everything on offer, then buy a tin of baked beans. The shop gradually filled with birders. When I eventually settled for a tin of beans I couldn't understand why there was such an irruption of laughter and applause. But I enjoyed another beans-on-toast breakfast.

Pund was the croft where Mary, Duchess of Bedford stayed on several occasions between 1910 and 1914 when she visited Shetland in her yacht *Sapphire*. In the 1970s Gordon Barnes generously permitted the more impoverished birders to stay there. One summer I was staying there alone and so enjoying the peace and the beautiful weather that I phoned my dear wife Betty and suggested she joined me. 'It will be like a second honeymoon,' I enthused. Unfortunately, by the time Betty had travelled by coach from Surrey, by the *St Clair* from Aberdeen to Lerwick, and by the *Good Shepherd* from Sumburgh to Fair Isle (a horrendous crossing in strong winds), the weather had changed. Betty also pointed out that Pund no longer had a door and that the ground floor was deep in sheep droppings – and indeed sheep. I can't understand why I hadn't noticed this. Moreover, as Betty's hammer toe prevented her from climbing the slats to the bunk, the ground floor was Betty's bedroom. Things had changed since the Duchess of Bedford's day. But for us it was indeed like a second honeymoon. Betty reminded me that the first one had been a disaster too.

In 1994 in Costa Rica we even had breakfast with the President. José Maria Figueres Olsen had just been elected by a landslide majority – as popular a choice as his father had been earlier that century (three times in fact – 1948-49, 1953-55, and 1970-74). His first act as President was quite remarkable. 'The civil service can continue running the country efficiently,' he announced. 'I am not going to take any decisions until I have spoken to everyone in the country to find out what they really want.' For his first three months in office he travelled to a different town or village every day and was available for non-stop interviews and meetings. By chance we found ourselves staying at the same hotel one day. He was so enthusiastic that he was eager to start at dawn. At that hour we birdwatchers were the only other people up and about.

Travelling to a different part of the world more than once every month throughout the 1980s it was perhaps inevitable in those pre-awareness days that I should develop deep-vein thrombosis. Foolishly I ignored this for years. I was lucky that the clot did not go to my lungs, but it did blow a valve in my left leg which swelled to twice normal size. By sleeping with the bottom of my bed propped up on a table I started each day with a reasonably matching pair, but by the evening the disparity was obvious once more. The left leg became so huge and blue that everyone suggested I should have it off and specialize in parrots (Arrrr Jim lad). Whilst sorting out photographs for this book I discovered a couple (taken in Israel and Morocco: see Plate 1, page 113) which reminded me that I even used to wear a surgical stocking, something that had completely slipped my memory. I now wear groin-to-toe elastic stockings on long flights – which is why I have taken to wearing trousers as the shorts-and-tights combination make me look as though I'm in an amateur production of *Richard III*.

Eventually I was sent to hospital for a venogram. I asked the nurse if that was like a gorillagram, but with a beautiful young woman instead of a hairy primate. I had a mental image of Botticelli's *The Birth of Venus* (or 'The Society of Marine Conchologists makes its greatest discovery' as Ronald Searle has it – try doing an image search on Google). 'Afraid not,' she said. 'You're the one who is going to be naked. Please disrobe and lie down over there.' The subsequent operation to strip out the main veins was swift and painless, and a credit to the National Health Service. 'You'll be walking in two weeks,' said the nurse. On the way home from the hospital there was a Thrush Nightingale at Gramborough Hill, only a few hundred metres from the car park at Salthouse. It provided a good test. The next day there was a Lesser Grey Shrike at Holme. It involved a slightly longer walk, but was still no problem. Then a Yellow-browed Warbler in Holkham Pines. Again the curative effect and instant healing qualities of birds in the bush proved efficacious. So the next day I went for my usual fortnight on the Isles of Scilly – with a matching pair of legs for the first time in years.

In 2004 I was immobilized for a little longer by a slipped disc and sciatica. It was a taste of things to come. First, on a visit to the British Museum a young lady offered me her seat on the Tube. Then, when I was trying to hobble a short distance from Titchwell car park, an old fellow who must have been in his 80s called me 'Sir' and asked if he could help. The final straw came when I was trying to cross the square from the Tube station to the opera house at Covent Garden and tripped on the cobbles: a beggar offered me his milk-crate to sit on as I obviously needed it more than him.

Then in 2006, when gangrene rendered all my toes black and grungy, I inadvertently ripped off a little toe in Libya and assumed I would be left with a stump forever. But curiously a few months and many dressings later it grew back. The doctor said I must be part amoeba or salamander and wanted to write an article for *The Lancet*.

However, all that sounds like the debit side of birding. So, to hark back to the opening paragraph, where is the profit in it? Well, quite apart from any financial considerations, the joy and satisfaction of 'just looking' at a bird cannot be fully explained. Birds have engaged man's attention since prehistoric times. These creatures that can live in our world then fly to the heavens have always been seen as the link between man and God, divine messengers, intermediaries (even our angels have birds' wings). In so many cultures they represent the soul. But without examining these deeper implications 'just looking' has opened my eyes to the wonders of nature and has taken me to 70 countries around the world – not a particularly impressive tally by many birdwatchers' reckoning, but a representative selection from all continents. Many of these I would never have otherwise visited. Betelgeuse may or may not go to supernova during our lifetime. But meanwhile the 92 chemical elements that make up our universe provide an endless variety of wonderful sights – the snow-clad Himalaya flushed flamingo pink at sunrise; the astonishing variability of Antarctic ice from glass-like transparency to summer-sky blue; the densely vegetated peaks and troughs of Gough Island rising abruptly from the South Atlantic, so invitingly mysterious (yet strictly forbidden territory) that it would be no surprise to see a Pterodactyl winging down a valley or a Stegosaurus emerging onto a rocky beach; the jungle-wrapped ruins of Tikal or Palenque or iconic Machu Picchu, Luxor, or Abu Simbel; volcano-fringed Lake Atitlán; vistas of empty beaches and dunes; skeins of Pink-footed Geese against a winter sunset; Scarlet Ibis petalling the mangroves; Great Bustards in full foam-bath display... the list really is endless. I have also enjoyed the company of like-minded clients and friends by leading over 1,000 tours – how wonderful to spend one's working life with the very people one would choose as holiday companions.

The bottom line is that, in a world which the media insist is full of sectarian hatred, religious and cultural division, weapons of mass destruction, pollution, climate change, global warming, and the imminent demise of our civilization and life as we know it, it is uplifting and necessary to spend time in the unchanged and unchanging natural world to enjoy life-affirming experiences and to interface with other cultures, where goodwill and a sense of bonding and common interest predominate, and where birds still fly to heaven and affirm by their colourful appearance and melodious vocalizations the joy of life. This has provided me with some memorable experiences and it is time to record them in a (slightly) less random and rambling order than the impromptu thoughts in this opening chapter.

2. *Man cannot live by birds alone*

In addition to leading many birds-only tours in various parts of the globe, I have been happy to pioneer several dual-interest holidays, notably birds and history and birds and music. Birds and bats, which I introduced in 1996 with Brian and Patty Briggs as co-leaders, did not find a permanent place in the tour calendar, despite being fully booked. There were plenty of birders interested in bats. But batters, it seems, are not interested in birds. Consequently, after a day's birding, the birders would come along for an hour or so after dinner to see some bats in the hand, then opt for bed with a cheery 'Goodnight Bryan. See you at dawn.' I would stay up all night with the batters, who would then hit the hay for a morning in bed just as the birders were rising. You can probably spot the flaw in that scenario. Also, the health and safety aspect became too complicated when a dozen batters with collecting bottles scurried along ancient rafters in every belfry for a 'droppings opportunity'.

The birds and history concept began when I first started leading tours to Mexico 30 years ago. I thought it a pity to treat the Mayan ruins at Palenque, Chichen Itza, and Uxmal merely as vantage points to obtain better views of Keel-billed Toucans. So I introduced brief lectures on Mayan history and culture. My colleagues considered this quaint and argued that these were birding trips and the clients were not interested in buildings. But obviously they were. And, after all, spending some moments to admire the magnificent carvings and architectural features did not deprive us of any bird species. I am happy to say that the Mexico tours now feature as 'official' birds and history experiences.

In those early days it was not possible to hire minibuses on Cozumel

*The Mayans built some excellent bird-observation centres, such
as this Keel-billed Toucan viewing tower at Palenque, Mexico.*

island – which we visited for endemics such as Cozumel Vireo and
Cozumel Thrasher – so we had to transport them on the little open
ferry from the Yucatán mainland. Surrounded by trucks filled with
bananas and pineapples we arrived one year at the Cozumel island port
alongside a Viking Olsen cruise-ship. 'Where y'all from?' enquired a
cruise passenger from the deck way above us. 'England,' we replied. 'Did
you sail across from England this morning?' (He obviously thought it
was the daily fresh fruit delivery.) 'No, just the other side.' 'The other
side of the island?' 'No, the Mexican mainland is just across the water
over there.' Despite being on a world cruise geography was obviously
not his strong point. The following day there was no sign of the cruise
ship. But the day after that it was back again. We assumed that the
captain was relying on the short attention span of his passengers and
putting out to sea every other day only to return to the same port on
alternate days and announce a different destination. ('OK. Buenos
Aries. Ten minutes on shore.')

Other tour leaders have discussed the cruise-ship mentality with me. 'Is there water all around this island?' and 'I never see the crew in the evenings. Do they sleep on the boat?' are typical questions. One lady on checking in to her cabin angrily complained that she had specifically requested a sea view and yet she was overlooking a car park. Realising that she was serious, the organizer assured her that as soon as the ship sailed he would rectify the matter. 'You'd better, young man, or your company will be hearing from me.'

Mayan history comes to life even more vividly on the Guatemala tours (see page 320). And history and Egypt are virtually synonymous. Significantly the birds and the buildings are often inextricably linked. This goes for India too (see page 29).

As for birds and music, the credit here must go in large part to my wife Betty. Even after 30 years of marriage to me, Betty had never become at all interested in birds, but we did share a love of music. So, to enable us to spend more time together co-leading overseas tours, I wrote a short paragraph in a Sunbird newsletter asking if there was anyone else who couldn't live by birds alone and if anyone was interested in a holiday combining birds and music. My fellow directors didn't expect a response, but by return of post the trip was potentially full, with 30 on the waiting list – and I hadn't even suggested a venue or a price. For the happy outcome, see Chapter 6.

Incidentally, Betty became well known for her succinct summaries of the birding world. 'I don't want to spend the rest of my life with people in woolly hats saying what's about?' was a memorable outburst. For a very intelligent woman she had a penchant for basic misconceptions. When I first contacted Caledonian MacBrayne to enquire how much it would cost to take a large coach on the ferry from Skye to the Outer Hebrides and was quoted a price of £12 per metre, Betty was outraged. 'Twelve pounds a metre,' she declared. 'That's outrageous. How far is it to the Outer Hebrides?' She proved a very popular co-leader.

It is surely no coincidence that the birds and music combination is a particularly happy (and healthy) one. The Bible tells us that 'when the evil spirit was upon Saul, David took a harp and played with his hand; so Saul was refreshed, and was well, and the evil spirit departed from him'. Handel's Water Music worked wonders for George I. Einstein's mother (when her child was classified as educationally sub-normal) discovered that the key to unlocking his genius was Bach and Mozart. Students' IQ tests reveal that listening to Mozart before or during testing significantly affects results. Mozart (particularly his clarinet quintet) is also important in treating children with conditions such as autism and Asperger's, and in reaching participants in a coma (since the autonomic nervous system remains responsive to music). Patients with coronary artery problems who listen to or play music, as well as doing graduated exercises during rehabilitation, recover better than those who only exercise, and have better memory, mood, and cognitive/intellectual ability, as well as greater exercise tolerance than those who are not exposed to music. Austrian wine producers insist their playing Mozart renders the grapes happier and healthier. Cows produce more milk if Strauss waltzes are played in the milking parlour. And hens lay more eggs. It is also interesting that rats can be trained to choose the type of music they prefer: pop or rock music is soon rejected in favour of classical or light music. Spiders also prefer classical, and build their webs as far as possible from rock or pop. If it's good enough for Einstein or a rat, it's good enough for a birder.

3. *Far Pavilions, close encounters*

Ancient Greece, ancient Rome, ancient Egypt, ancient China, the earliest civilizations in the Americas and Mesopotamia... all very significant cultures, but none of them bears much resemblance to the modern societies in those areas. By contrast, the cultural continuity between India's past and present is remarkably evident. In religious and philosophical beliefs, in Ayurveda (the ancient branch of medicine still widely practised today), and most noticeably in a respect for all life forms, the belief in non-harm to living beings – a central tenet of Buddhism, Jainism, and Hinduism – little has changed in 4,000 years. Mrs Ghandi's conservation efforts were so much more effective in a country where slogans such as 'Respect the Tiger: it may be you in your next life' and 'It could be your great grandmother' are meaningful. And the principle of non-violence, the passive resistance advocated by Mahatma Gandhi and that inspired Martin  Luther King, John F. Kennedy, Nelson Mandela, and Barack Obama, owes much to India's ancient culture. India is indeed living history.

The culture of this remarkable country really came to the fore in the 1980s with a succession of epic films and television series: *Gandhi*, *A Passage to India*, *The Jewel in the Crown*, *The Far Pavilions*... India became such a popular destination that Sunbird had to run three consecutive northern India tours every year combining Bharatpur (Keoladeo National Park), Corbett, and Nainital – plus an alternative offering more history and incorporating Bharatpur, Rajasthan, and the Thar Desert.

All these destinations remained hassle-free, and for over 30 years (occasionally three times a year) I have enjoyed many happy moments there. But border states (Assam, Sikkim, Kashmir, Ladakh), buffers as they are against communist China and areas of ethnic unrest, are always difficult places to visit, and in the 1980s permission to do so was not readily granted. There was a period in the late 1980s when I found myself in a different trouble spot every year, despite continually choosing different destinations. In 1987 the Bodos began fighting for a separate homeland. However, taking advantage of a temporary relaxation in restrictions, a trip to Assam was arranged in 1988 as an extension to our northern India tour. To ensure all went smoothly I travelled ahead of the group whilst Peter Grant guided it around Nainital and Corbett. After we had both completed the Assam segment I was due to meet another group for a tour of Sikkim, whilst Peter accompanied the first group home. I had to have special permission to be in Assam without a group and for more than a week – and under no circumstances could I prolong my stay beyond the date on my permit. Unfortunately I

Kaleej Pheasants are regular skulkers around Nainital.

never received the telex advising me not to fly to Bagdogra airport as a war had broken out in Darjeeling. The gurkas wanted an independent Gurkaland, and to make their point had blown up the hotel we were due to stay in, destroyed the bridges, and were shooting people in the streets. Bagdogra airport was under military control and my group was nowhere to be seen – and therefore neither were my permits allowing me to travel beyond Darjeeling. Ironically, the visa in my passport was merely stamped 'Valid for 14 days in Darjeeling' – which fortunately included Bagdogra airport. The army informed me that there were no telephones, so it was impossible to contact our ground agent in Delhi. I decided to go to the reserve scheduled for that night anyway and commissioned a local to drive me there in his vehicle, not realizing that as soon as I left the airport I was an illegal immigrant. I discovered this at the entrance gate to the reserve when, without the correct papers (my Norfolk Naturalists open-sesame card was completely ineffective here), I was refused admission and moved on. Frequent police checks made it clear that I would not be allowed to stay anywhere and would have to keep moving indefinitely. Finally we reached the Bhutan Gate and, fearing that I would spend the rest of my life living in his vehicle, my driver abandoned me. Entering Bhutan was not an option. The King, wisely believing GNH (Gross National Happiness) to be more important than GNP ('The happiness of the people should be the guiding goal of development': there is even a Ministry of Happiness), and not wanting his country to be corrupted by western capitalism and the consumer society, strictly limited the number of tourists and charged US$100 a day for a visa. Bhutan was also the first country not only to ban smoking in public but also to ban the sale of tobacco. We have so much to learn from Bhutan. My permit for Assam had expired. My permits for Bangladesh and Bengal had not arrived. It had been a tiring day. It was late. I was ready for bed. I called on the chief of police.

He was charming and most sympathetic, but explained he could not give me permission to stay as officially I could not be there. However, in exchange for my passport, he agreed to escort me (personally) to a hotel for one night whilst he considered the options. He even carried my case. 'Have you eaten?' he enquired as we stepped over the threshold, but as I was about to answer 'No' the stench from the kitchen hit me and I hurriedly changed the response to 'Yes'. I bought a huge bunch of bananas, slept in my clothes in a filthy little room, and decided the sensible course of action was to return to Bagdogra airport, the only place I was authorized to be, even if it was the epicentre of a war. The following morning I collected my passport from a police chief happy to hear that I was no longer his responsibility, discovered there was actually a service bus all the way to Bagdogra airport, and hidden amongst the 200 locals on board (or so it seemed) arrived there without once being asked to show my papers.

Reappearing at the airport I was greeted like a long-lost friend. I was given an office to work in, stayed at the staff hostel, and travelled in and out each day in the staff coach. I was even asked if I could teach them yoga 'because we are noticing how calm you are in this crisis'. But still it was difficult to get in touch with the outside world. A French journalist who had been reporting on the war was being flown to Delhi. I gave him a note to read out to our ground agents there and eventually, having reasoned with first a captain then a major that it was impossible to run a war without a telephone somewhere, was granted a 30-second incoming message: 'Group being sent to Kashmir instead of Sikkim. Try to fly to Srinagar'. Amazingly this proved to be possible and, together with a group of American evangelists and the Panchen Lama and his entourage, I found myself flying over Mount Everest. Never have I experienced such turbulence. The wings were bouncing so violently, the juddering was so extreme, that surely the plane was about to break into pieces. The oxygen masks came down. The evangelists were screaming. But presumably the Lama prayed us to a calm outcome and landing in Kashmir was like arriving in Paradise.

Truly, the Mogul emperors really did create heaven on Earth in the Vale of Kashmir with their formal gardens intersected by channels of cool water – 'pale hands I loved beside the Shalimar'. Staying on a cedar-wood houseboat on Dal Lake was then the most relaxing and peaceful experience imaginable.

Cedarwood houseboats on Dal Lake come with a Pied or White-throated Kingfisher on every post.

After a trouble-free week there and armed with fresh permits I returned with this new group to Assam. Again we visited Manas reserve on the Assam/Bhutan border. Just across the river from our lodgings at Mothanguri Rest House was the Bhutan Royal Hunting Lodge, the best place in the world to see Golden Langurs. But more significantly, the border fence on our side of the river was interrupted by a small gate announcing 'Bhutan. Keep Out.' No customs and immigration, no guard, no lock. No more intimidating than a 'Private' sign back home where, if challenged, a polite apology and the explanation 'I'm sorry, I thought that meant the general public,' is usually sufficient to appease the average gamekeeper. So naturally on our first visit we had opened the gate and walked into the land of the Thunder Dragon.

No repercussions. On this return visit we repeated the experience. Admittedly this time a Bhutanese guard crossed the river, but after a conversation with our lady Indian guide/interpreter he returned, apparently happy. We therefore decided that the next day, after a morning visit to the Hunting Lodge to see Golden Langurs, we would walk into deeper Bhutan as far as the first village. The plan seemed to work. We took a boat across the river. Again, a guard initially was turning us away – explaining that they were awaiting an important visitor at the Hunting Lodge. But the head man intervened, pointing out that The Visitor was not expected before midday, which gave us plenty of time to locate the langurs. 'Please take my guards with you and take my boat back when you are ready,' he said. I remarked to our interpreter on how courteous the Bhutanese were. Rather sheepishly she replied, 'I think I had better explain. Yesterday the guard came across the river to throw you out of Bhutan. But I told him that you had been here a fortnight ago and noticed the private path into Bhutan, so you had travelled to Bhutan Gate and met with your friend Jigme Singye Wangchuk who had given you permission to enter.' So that's why we were receiving such courteous treatment. How embarrassing. It was true that I had travelled to Bhutan Gate (under police escort). The meeting with my friend the King was an exaggeration. But there was now no opportunity to correct this falsification so off we went.

On my earliest walk up this jungle trail I had been frustrated that I could not make contact with any of the locals who passed us. I did not even know the Bhutanese for Hello. (It's *Kuzoo Zangpo*, by the way.) So I had spent my enforced stay in Bagdogra airport learning basic Bhutanese (Dzongkha, a Tibetan dialect) from a family also stranded there. The blank pages in my copy of *A Pictorial Guide to the Birds of the Indian Subcontinent* were festooned with phonetic phrases. I now tried them out on one of the succession of locals walking their little black pigs. This broke the ice instantly and his impassive expression changed into an endearing smile. In retrospect I guess I must have needed help with the interpretation of my next exchange. 'Are you taking your pigs to Barpeta Road market?' I asked. 'No,' came the reply. 'These are presents for our king who is coming to the hunting lodge today.' I now knew who The Visitor was. It was my mate. And no doubt by now he had been informed of my whereabouts. However, we did reach the nearest village, drank the local tea (laced with butter, not milk), admired the scenery (Bhutan must be one of the most beautiful countries in the world), and arrived back in India as the sun was setting. This was probably fortunate as parked by the river crossing were several Land-rovers flying the royal flag. At dinner some of our group who had opted out of the long walk observed that a party from the Bombay Natural History Society had been sent back to the Indian side of the border, whereas they had been given permission to continue birding on the Bhutan side and a general with lots of medals on his chest had bade them to have a nice day. We left for Kaziranga very early the next morning, no doubt leaving Jigme Singye Wangchuk still pondering the identity of his friend.

White-throated Laughingthrush is, for the eye and the ear,
one of the most striking Himalayan residents.

Sadly the following year Manas, just like Darjeeling, became a no-go area when the Bodos attacked, killed the rangers, and took control. In 1990 the Indian government imposed direct rule on Assam following separatist violence from the Marxist militant United Liberation Front of Assam, and in the following four months it was reported that the ULFA, operating from the jungles of Myanmar, had been involved in 97 killings, mainly of Congress politicians. But Srinagar had proved itself to be a heaven on Earth. What could go wrong there? So a new Sunbird tour was arranged coupling Kashmir and Ladakh. What could go wrong? Erudite readers might have already spotted a potential source of trouble. The population of Srinagar is largely Muslim – in fact fundamentalist Muslims, the most easterly followers of Ayatollah Khomeini in Iran. In 1988 Salman Rushdie published *The Satanic Verses*. In 1989 Ayatollah Khomeini called for Rushdie and his publishers to be killed. So given a scenario involving three groups – Kashmiri Fundamentalist Muslims, Ladakhi Buddhists, and Western Christians – who were the aggressors, who were the victims, and who were risking life and limb as the protectors? It is symptomatic of our brainwashing by the media that it comes as a surprise to most people that the Buddhists were attacking the Christians who were being protected by the Muslims.

It began when communist China, always keen to annexe Ladakh, convinced the majority Buddhist population that it was unfair for control to be in the hands of the Muslims. There had already been trouble in neighbouring Tibet. Pro-independence demonstrations erupted in Lhasa in September/October 1987 and continued throughout 1988 and until March 1989, when they were forcibly suppressed by Chinese troops. In May and October 1988 peacefully demonstrating monks and civilians were shot by police, and in 1989 many anti-China demonstrators were shot and all foreigners expelled. Against this background, fighting broke out in Leh, the capital of

Spotted Forktails breed on Himalayan streams from 3,000m down to 600m.

Ladakh and known as the rooftop of the world, shortly before our trip in 1990. So I flew out in advance to make sure it was safe.

From Srinagar there is only one road through Ladakh, winding up over the Greater Himalaya – one of the highest roads in the world – and so breathtakingly spectacular that a camera mounted on the vehicle and programmed to take a picture quite arbitrarily, every 30 seconds, would produce an unrivalled set of dramatic images (see Plate 2, page 114). Not only the mountain scenery, but also the cloud formations were gasp-inducing. Eastbound traffic only is permitted in the mornings, westbound in the afternoons, so narrow is the road, and teams of roadworkers are camped along its length undertaking non-stop repairs. Ali, the driver of my redoubtable Ambassador taxi, constantly stopped to scoop up handfuls of wet mud, which he packed around the engine and radiator to keep them cool. Regular curiously worded signs advised caution:

Better be mister late than late mister. Papa go slow, orphanage no no. Watch your nerves on my curves. All will wait, better be late. Drive slow and god with you, drive fast and you are on your own. Go man go, but go slow. Life is wonderful, ponder and think, why cut it short by speed and drink. Be cautious and avoid pregnancy and widowhood. Let life and love last, do not press fast. Go slowly and let your life be as long as this road. Start early, drive slowly, reach safely. Honeymoon should be long, so drive with song. Women tell him wake and drive slow for my sake. Do a good deed, control your speed. Alert today, alive tomorrow. Drive like hell, you will be there. If you are married, divorce speed.

Some of them had a sexual connotation:

My curves are gorgeous, go over them slowly. Don't kiss with mountain or river or any veh (sic).

The numbers of vehicles crumpled and rusting in the valley bottoms confirmed that these reminders to go slow were necessary. Even so, I could not help but think of the signs erected by the Nainital police, which are so much less specific, a typical example being: 'Praise loudly, chide softly'. (I was able to recycle this one at a police station in Trinidad when I was asked to suggest a thought for the day for its blackboard.) Speeding – indeed the very presence of motor vehicles – seemed completely at odds with a lifestyle in this land which otherwise represented Tibet 300 years ago: traditional agriculture, gompas, monasteries, prayer flags, roadside buddhas, monks, and the predominant sound in an otherwise silent and serene environment the cheery 'Pleased to meet you' refrain of Common Rosefinches.

And indeed all seemed peaceful in Leh. A curfew had been imposed but the fighting was over. Suitably reassured I began the return journey to Delhi to meet the group. It soon became obvious that something was different. Trickling streams that we had forded without regard were now wide raging torrents and rose above the wheels of our little Ambassador. Amazingly, with only me to push, Ali managed to cross river after river.

Apparently, during my days in Leh, violent thunderstorms had raged over the Himalaya. I recalled the dramatic clouds that had seemed so photogenic. We travelled 200km without seeing another vehicle. When we reached the Zojila Pass we discovered why. The road over the Greater Himalaya was blocked by 35 landslides and ahead of us was a queue of vehicles (mostly lorries with Sikh drivers) that stretched for miles. A barrier had been erected and the army was not letting anyone through. I was obliged to spend the night there. But the next day I had to be in Delhi to meet the group. So I decided to run over the Himalaya. I left my luggage with Ali and his taxi and presented myself (in smock and shorts) at the barrier, to be told that no one could pass. 'How far until the road starts again?' I enquired. 'Eighty kilometres.' 'Ah well, that's not so far for me. I'm British so it's only 50 miles.' 'But it rises to 4,000m.' 'No problem. I live in Norfolk' (I was banking on them not being familiar with Noel Coward's observation.) 'But it's still raining.' 'So I'll get wet.' 'But it's very cold.' I took off my smock and explained I was too hot anyway. (As it happens, a large sign behind me proclaimed that this was the coldest inhabited place on Earth with a recorded temperature of -60°C. There is a saying that in Ladakh anyone whose head is in the sun and feet are in the shade will endure both heatstroke and frostbite at the same time.) Eventually, the army relented and said: 'Very well. God go with you. Be careful of the falling rocks.' I genuinely believe that in India it is considered unfair or unlucky to thwart a madman. Ali wanted to give me his coat. I assured him that smock and shorts were the most suitable wear. He had tears in his eyes when he said goodbye.

I had convinced myself that running 50 miles was just like running a mile but keeping it up for longer. 'Only the first step is difficult.' I hadn't fully considered the effects of altitude. And since I hadn't considered them I didn't notice them. When I reached the first landslide I discovered that the land was still sliding. Between me and the point where the road continued opposite was what appeared to be a rock waterfall. I realized that it was necessary to run across not directly but upwards at an angle which, combined with the downwards flow of the rocks, would deliver me to my point of disembarkation – otherwise I would be carried over the precipice. Necessity enabled me to perfect this technique quickly, and many landslides later I sensed that I was now on the downhill stretch. By now I was shrouded in thick mist and suddenly I saw ahead of me a Yeti, followed by another, and another. They transpired to be the Indian army in full mountain gear: huge snow boots, padded jackets, helmets, and tall rucksacks that towered above their heads. They were all carrying ice picks and ropes. 'Can we get through?' they enquired as I ran past in my smock and shorts.

When I reached Srinagar all I wanted was a hot bath, but instead I had to report to the various authorities on the conditions in Ladakh as I was the first person to emerge and there had been no communication for several days. I then caught a stand-by flight to Delhi and arrived as my Sunbird group was sitting down to its first meal, having just been informed that 'Mr Bland is lost on the wrong side of the Himalaya'.

The next day we all flew back to Srinagar to spend many delightful days relaxing on a luxury cedar-wood houseboat on Dal Lake and exploring Dachigam reserve and the surrounding mountains. Picnicking on one mountain top we were approached by an Indian family. 'Where are you from?' enquired the father, addressing a lady in our group. 'England,' she replied. 'Where in England?' 'London.' 'Where in London?' 'Enfield.' 'Where in Enfield?' Thinking how meaningless this was to an Indian on a remote mountain top in Kashmir she nevertheless politely named the street, only to be pressed further for the number. 'I thought so,' said the father. 'We live at no 35.' They too were on holiday.

Eventually Ali arrived with my luggage. The road to Ladakh was now repaired and negotiable – wide enough for cars, though not lorries. A

An eye-level Lammergeier was always
a possibility in the mountains.

truck in front of Ali had plunged 300m. 'Were the occupants killed?' I asked. 'Of course. But they were only army,' was the casual reply. Another group also using our ground agent set off for Leh immediately. We decided to spend one more day in this earthly paradise of the Vale of Kashmir – a good move, as it happened. Fighting broke out again in Leh and all tourists were impounded in their hotels. In due course we heard the details from our agent's other group. After several days in their hotel an adjutant arrived to announce that his general was going to lead them all to safety. All the tourist vehicles left in convoy. The road was lined with soldiers like poplar trees in France. Then they turned a corner. No more soldiers. Just Buddhists with rocks. The whole convoy was stoned. The tourists cowered on the floor of their vehicles. Nevertheless most were cut and bruised and some severely injured. The drivers, unable to crouch, were not so lucky. Eight were killed. Apparently the Buddhist aggressors were very polite. They would stop a vehicle, ask the tourists to get out, insist that they check they had all their belongings, and only then set fire to the vehicle and push it over a cliff.

All this happened, unbeknown to us, whilst we were still happily birding in the mountains. We did suspect that something, somewhere, was amiss. The army stopped us at Kargil. They had banned all road traffic, even in the remote mountains, and we would have been stranded in no-man's-land had I not visited the DC (Deputy Commissioner). He received me in his dressing gown. 'Is it true that you are the ultimate authority here, even over the police and the army?' I asked. He confirmed this was so. I explained that we were looking for Tibetan Snowfinch and Mountain Chiffchaff, but were being prevented from travelling in any direction. Apologizing for being unable to provide an armed escort, he tore off a corner of the paper on his desk and wrote on it 'To General Mahmoud. Please let them pass at their own risk and responsibility'. Not even headed notepaper: his signature was sufficient. This ensured unrestricted travel throughout Ladakh and reconfirmed the power of the permit. In India, having the right piece of paper is paramount. All I needed to do was avoid trouble. My Kashmiri Muslim drivers were most loyal and willing, but I assured them I would not lead them into danger. I temporarily exchanged them for Ladakhi Buddhist drivers and when we had seen all our target birds only one goal remained: a visit to Lamayuru Monastery which I thought would be sufficiently distant from Leh to be trouble-free. Fortunately for us, whilst we were breakfasting, the battered and beaten remnants of the Leh convoy arrived at the hotel. Surveying the bandaged and blood-stained passengers and hearing that the violence was heading our way, we opted to return to the Vale of Kashmir. As we did so the Pakistan army was amassing on the border. Taking advantage of the unrest, it seemed that Pakistan was again renewing its claim to the Indian state of Jammu and Kashmir and that there would be further hostilities between Hindu and Muslim.

It's a pity we never reached Leh. I had actually arranged with the military authorities (pending a counter-signature from Delhi) that they would call a temporary ceasefire to their skirmish with China on the plain bordering Tibet long enough for us to find a Black-necked Crane. It is amazing what can be done if only you ask. Why don't governments do this?

Sadly, although the conflict in Ladakh is now resolved, people are still being shot in Srinagar, and Sunbird's Kashmir and Ladakh trip has never run again. There is, however, one curious postscript. Some years later, on my annual Northern India tour, I was checking in to a hotel in Nainital when the clerk enquired if I was the same Mr Bland who was once lost in Ladakh. I explained the circumstances and asked if it was our ground agent who had told him. 'No,' he replied. 'It was on the front page of the newspapers at the time' – a fact of which I had been unaware. The group mused that by now the story had probably been much embroidered in the retelling over the years and there were no doubt local folk songs recounting the exploits of a bearded madman. I've never been back to check: even as I write, this morning's news bulletin announced that 11 people had been shot in Srinagar.

India has also been the setting for several more dramatic 'might-have-beens'. In 1984 David Hunt wrote his autobiographical *Confessions of a Scilly Birdman* and early in 1985 I discussed with him over the phone the caption to the last of over 60 line illustrations I had sketched for the book. Ironically it was 'That's all folks!' David then went off to lead a birding trip to northern India; I departed to lead one to Mexico. On my return I was told that David had been eaten by a Tiger. The following year I was also leading a tour in Corbett National Park with Harak Singh, the local guide who had been with David when he was killed. At High Bank I stopped the coach to look for Brown Dipper

That's all folks

and jumped over the low wall at the top of the cliff for a better view. Unfortunately, I had left on the coach seat the large *Pictorial Guide* that I normally kept wedged tightly in the back of my shorts. Thus unrestricted the shorts took advantage of their new-found freedom and made a break for it, falling to my ankles. This prevented me from opening my legs on landing and, losing my balance, I seemed destined to crash down to the river below. Poor Harak Singh was running towards me in terror, not wanting to lose another guide. Fortunately, I managed to shift my weight and fall backwards onto the wall and into his outstretched arms. On another occasion, on a solo reconnaissance of Dachigam reserve, I was surprised to see two locals approaching me stop in their tracks and view me with alarm. Surely they must have seen a white man before, I thought, and sought to alleviate their fears with a broad smile and a reassuring friendly greeting. It transpired that their consternation was not occasioned by my approach, but by that of the Himalayan Black Bear which was following me.

I was also lucky to enjoy many Tiger sightings at Corbett and live to tell the tale. Occasionally a Tiger would indulge in a false charge, but it would always stop before it reached our elephant. Once, however, a Tiger attacked for real. Even the most obsessional birder is always keen to see a Tiger. When I heard tell-tale monkey alarm calls on this occasion I therefore directed our three elephants through the jungle towards the sound source. Sure enough there was a Tiger. Magnificent views. Then it charged. My elephant accepted the challenge and returned the charge. The mahout lost control. All was fury. Roaring and trumpeting and complete pandemonium as the equally matched adversaries came face to face. The Tiger crouched and braced itself for a leap. As I was positioned left front I reckoned it would probably land on me and maybe tear me from my perch. Fortunately, in that split second the other two elephants joined in the skirmish and came crashing in from both sides. Distracted, the Tiger then bounced between the three elephants not knowing which to engage first. 'Thank you, Bryan. That's good enough. We can leave now,' said one terrified client, seemingly unaware that the situation was beyond my control – and indeed beyond the control of the mahouts. After an eternity of heart-stopping minutes, however, order was resumed and the mahouts persuaded the elephants to back off. And no one had taken a photograph. It transpired that everyone was either rigid with fear or gripping tightly to their seats. The Sunbird newsletter had to make do with my sketch.

Most newsletter reports are less dramatic and summarise the joys of visiting India. Here's a typical example reviewing the birds and history tour of November and December 1999:

> 'Transvestite dancing, a bearded leader in a skirt, drug-dealing, opium drinking... this wasn't listed in the brochure,' commented one participant on this year's trip. But before there is a rush to book for (or cancel) next year's tour, we must explain that – respectively – the dancing girl (who was indeed a young man) was a celebrated professional just back from a tour of France, the skirt was to cover up Bryan's offending knees in a Muslim holy place, the drugs were merely aspirins to ease the pain in a headman's head, and the opium ceremony (optional) was a matter of courtesy in a Bishnoi village. Nor did the brochure mention that the group – and only our group – would be sleeping in the newly restored Royal Monsoon Palace at Jodhpur, including the Maharajah's own bedroom (33 metres across, not counting the various anterooms and en-suite lounges). Other groups were allocated the stable block. Similarly we did not anticipate that our private tour of Deeg Palace would be with a charming and erudite member of (another) Maharajah's family. Such touches – and the personal reminiscences of our wonderful history guide Mahandra – really helped history come alive for us on this fascinating tour of Rajasthan, which ranged from privileged glimpses of life in the villages to the more famous tourist venues of the Taj Mahal, the Red Fort, Fatehpur Sikri, the Amber Fort, the City Palace and Observatory at Jaipur, and the magnificent citadels of Jodhpur and Jaisalmer.
>
> Another surprise awaited us in the Thar Desert. Off-road jeeps are now outlawed (too many over-enthusiastic drivers flushing

the wildlife) in favour of camel carts, which at a more relaxed pace enable a much closer approach to the Indian Bustards and Stoliczka's Bushchats – both of which we saw very well on two days, together with Pallid Harrier, Laggar Falcon, Cream-coloured Courser, Chestnut-bellied Sandgrouse, Asian Desert Warbler, and a selection of larks, plus (completely unexpectedly) superb views of three Sykes's Nightjars which flew up from our feet to settle nearby.

Serendipity ruled supreme even in our traffic jam, which allowed us to stretch our legs in the middle of nowhere and discover the only Yellow-wattled Lapwings and Indian Coursers of the trip. As for the other birding highlights, the thousands of Demoiselle Cranes at Keechan topped most of our lists, but close contenders were the Siberian Cranes, Yellow and Black Bitterns, and myriads of waterbirds at Bharatpur, along with Red-naped Ibis, Greater Painted-snipe, Crested Serpent-eagle, Brown Crake, Dusky Eagle Owl, Large-tailed Nightjar, Verditer Flycatcher, Siberian Rubythroat, Thick-billed Flowerpecker, and – bird of the trip for one participant – Orange-headed Thrush.

Add to this a wealth of experiences from our elephant ride up to the Amber Fort to a sequence of fine meals and musical interludes and this trip provided enough memories to last the whole winter through.

Or this one, reflecting on the 2001 tour:

Indian Bustard is a proper rarity. Not one of your subtle LBJs, but a huge stately bird which when it heaves itself into the air looks like a roof in a slow tornado. What's more, this year – as befits an endangered species – it kept us waiting just long enough to ensure that suitable elation followed the first sighting. Also big and impressive were the six species of vulture we saw in the desert, including the mighty Eurasian Black (aka Cinereous or Monk, the largest in the Old World), and in particular the mixed selection of 70 birds at a camel carcass, a rare sight in India since the catastrophic crash (by 97 per cent) to near-extinction in the late 1990s. Other desert delights (besides the eponymous warbler, lark, and wheatear) included Cream-coloured Courser, Chestnut-bellied Sandgrouse, Laggar Falcon, White-eyed Buzzard, Bimaculated Lark and Black-crowned Sparrow-lark, and Red-tailed and Variable Wheatears.

These top prizes of the Thar Desert became all the more significant in retrospect when the news on our return home was that India was laying mines along the Pakistan border. We were lucky to obtain permits – particularly with a leader who constantly provoked cries of 'Osama bin Laden'.

Our other major area of exploration – Bharatpur, with so much water and shade and a wealth of herons, storks, and waterfowl – could not have been more different or provided a more contrasting selection of species and memorable images. Here too there were rarities to impress even the non-birder. Photographically close views of the only conveniently viewable pair of Siberian Cranes in the world were an obvious highlight. So was the Brown Hawk Owl – the first bird we saw as we entered the park (a good omen), the 100 Great White Pelicans that timed their brief visit to coincide with our arrival, the male and female Black Bitterns, and the Ruddy-breasted Crake. Other popular performers were Siberian Rubythroat, Orange-headed Thrush, Verditer Flycatcher, and Crested Serpent-eagle. Subtle tones of grey and brown and the most delicate of vermiculations were provided by Large-tailed and Indian Nightjars, Collared Scops and Dusky Eagle Owls, and Spotted Creeper. But it was big and gaudy that was voted bird of the trip – the ubiquitous and very visible Painted Stork.

For many years Bharatpur hosted the only conveniently viewable Siberian Cranes in the world, keeping good company with Sarus Cranes and Painted and Black-necked Storks.

Between the Thar Desert and the Bharatpur *jheels*, a variety of locations yielded extra species – from Okhla Dam with our only River Lapwings on day one to our only Brown-headed Gull as we explored the Bishnoi villages towards the end of our tour. An outing to Bund Barata added Brown Crake, Jungle Bush-quail, Plum-headed Parakeet, Ashy-crowned Sparrow-lark, and White-capped and Grey-necked Buntings. Keechan gave us the unique spectacle of 10,000 Demoiselle Cranes. A coffee stop was notable for Yellow-wattled Lapwings. And even the World Heritage Sites provided birds as well as history to satisfy our dual interests, with our only Peregrine Falcons over the Taj Mahal and our only Bonelli's Eagles over the mighty Mehrangargh Fort at Jodphur (most appropriate, for of this place 'the work of angels, fairies, and giants... built by Titans' Rudyard Kipling wrote 'he who walks through it loses sense of being among buildings: it is as though he walked through mountain gorges').

If we had voted for building of the trip, this magnificent mountain of a monument would no doubt have vied for first place with the Taj Mahal itself. But close contenders would have included Fatehpur Sikri, the Red Fort at Agra, the Amber Fort at Jaipur, the Qatab Minar and Humayan's Tomb in Delhi, and the whole of the old city of Jaisalmar. On a more intimate scale, the cenotaphs of the Mandor Gardens and the faded charm of Deeg Palace also had their part to play.

Perhaps I should explain the reference to Osama bin Laden. In October 2001, on a tour of Peru, the group pointed out that everyone was shouting 'Osama bin Laden' at me. I assumed that for non-hirsuit Peruvians I was probably the only bearded man they had seen, apart from television pictures of Osama. I vaguely wondered whether I should have a beard trim before my visit to the India/Pakistan border the following month but decided that, since half the Northern Alliance look like my twin brothers, there would be no danger of the Osama comparison there. Not so. The cries of 'Osama bin Laden' followed me throughout Rajasthan and into the Thar Desert. One sophisticated receptionist at a four-star hotel who was making a botched job of our check-in even threw down her pen and ran off crying, 'It's no good. You look too much like Osama bin Laden.' Maybe it was because in hot countries I do wear Arab gear. Or maybe it was because every evening the television news was reporting that Osama had been seen at the Pakistan border (although when I was back home it occurred to me that these reports could have referred to me). At least no one shot first and asked questions afterwards.

Brown Rock Chat and Dusky Crag Martins at Fatehpur Sikri.

I can't see the resemblance myself. Fidel Castro perhaps (another taunt). Or Omar al Mukhtar. When I first visited Libya I thought the constant cries of 'Omar al Mukhtar' were an alternative Arabic greeting to '*Salaam ali mecum*' – until I saw the 10-dinar note and realized the locals were likening me to their celebrated freedom fighter, as portrayed by Anthony Quinn in the film *Lion of the Desert*. Now that's an honour. And one of the most comforting aspects of the Galápagos Islands was the fact that, on a first walk along San Cristóbal high street, my group recorded only five 'Osama bin Ladens' to 12 'Charles Darwins'. At least towards the end of December some of the calls were amended to 'Osama bin Claus'. There are also a surprising number of obscure saints in eastern European churches for which I have been accused of being the artist's model. Really, any bald old man with a beard will do. In India, I'm usually happy enough to accept various ancient gurus as my twin image. But Osama bin Laden? (See Plate 16, page 248, for a selection of lookalikes.)

It all depends on the time of the year. I give up hair for Lent (originally a gesture to Betty, who was allergic even to one hair left in the bath). So on Shrove Tuesday the beard is little more than stubble. But by the New Year it is admittedly rather John the Baptist. The only non-Lent trim was in January 1984. I was leading a group through Holkham pines and heard a crossbill singing – but a song that included some unfamiliar notes. On locating the bird my suspicions that this was a Parrot Crossbill proved true. What's more, not only was it a male holding territory, but it was accompanied by a female and the pair were building a nest. On the 31st John O'Sullivan (Jos) and Chris Durdin, RSPB officers for East Anglia, were summoned to the scene to arrange protection. We watched the male and female snapping off twigs, stripping bark, and gathering grass and willowherb. Then when the nest seemed complete the male transferred his attention to the barbed-wire fence, apparently searching in vain for horse hair or the like as a lining. Not even a badger had passed that way so, anxious that the bird should not abort his attempt at this final stage, I asked Jos if he had a knife. Unfortunately it was blunt, but it served its purpose. Tufts of my beard were scattered along the wire and these were immediately taken to the nest. More was added every day for one week. Then on 7 February we watched the female lay the first egg and the male, having peered into the nest, sing the jubilant boast of a proud father. Not exactly Edward Lear (no owls, no hens, no larks, no wrens) but the first Parrot Crossbills to breed in Britain really had nested in my beard.

Osama bin Laden, Omar al Mukhtar, and Parrot Crossbills have lured us a long way from India. More typical of the many joyful occasions which that country has provided came one year in Nainital. An American participant mentioned that it was his wedding anniversary and could I organize a cake as a surprise for his wife. I decided to go one better. The hotel was splendidly cooperative. That evening in the banqueting hall all members of the group found themselves guests at a traditional Indian wedding ceremony with lavish floral displays, rose petals everywhere, and even a real fire mounted on a tin tray in the centre of the room as a focal point. With a Brahman priest engaged especially for the occasion the happy couple were able to renew their wedding vows.

An instance of the Indian joie de vivre transforming even the dullest moment came when a broken spring on our coach was being repaired. Instead of kicking our heels around the garage we were all garlanded and taken on a rickshaw convoy around the town, including a visit to the railway station where one of our group, a keen steam enthusiast, was allowed to clamber all over the engines.

So let's enliven this Indian section with another upbeat tour report – the 2005 birds and history trip.

After over a quarter of a century of visiting the country, this year's birds and history tour must rate as the most perfect and trouble-free trip to India imaginable – luxury accommodation throughout, all showers working, excellent meals and no significant tummy troubles, more sites and sights that ever before, every target species seen (and seen well) and no less than 23 write-ins – an indication on a tour that has been running for so long that this year the birds were coming at us thick and fast from all directions, every day: 36 species of raptor, 27 waders, 23 herons and allies, and 18 wildfowl. This was thanks largely to a good monsoon (after several dry years) and the corollary of a sequence of superb desert days.

At Bharatpur the overwhelming feeling of wandering into a Rousseau painting of the creation of the universe was stronger than ever, the thousands of close Painted Storks and assorted egrets, herons, ibises, spoonbills, cranes, ducks, geese, waders, and other waterbirds being complemented by a selection of exciting extras: Yellow and Black Bitterns, Collared Scops Owl, Dusky Eagle Owl, Large-tailed and Grey Nightjars, Greater Painted-snipe, Crested Serpent-eagle, Indian Spotted Eagle, Dalmatian Pelican, Orange-headed Thrush, Verditer Flycatcher, Brooks's Leaf Warbler, and the rare endemic Green Avadavat. Our history sorties outside the national park added Plum-headed Parakeet, Brown Crake, Indian Courser, Yellow-wattled Lapwing, Jungle Prinia, Rosy Pipit, and Red-headed Bunting. Yet this wealth of birdlife (some 42,000 individuals representing 213 species before we left Bharatpur) was probably eclipsed in the Thar Desert near the Pakistan border by the most classic desert day possible, a never-to-be-repeated experience that began at sunrise with Cream-coloured Coursers and a perched Red-necked Falcon, continued non-stop with Asian Desert Warbler, Chestnut-bellied Sandgrouse, Laggar Falcon, Long-legged Buzzard, Common Quail, all the larks and wheatears, and eight species of vulture, and climaxed towards sunset with the endemic Stoliczka's Bushchat and both Macqueen's and Indian Bustards. Adding to our desert experience were Tawny, Steppe, and Eastern Imperial Eagles, Lesser Kestrel, and the thrilling spectacle of 8,000 Demoiselle Cranes at Keechan, almost close enough to touch. The birds kept coming even during our history interludes – Pallas's Gull, Indian Grey Hornbill, and Spotted Owlet at the Taj Mahal, Brown Rock Chat and Booted Eagle at Fatehpur Sikri, Brown-headed and Coppersmith Barbets at Deeg Water Palace, vultures over the Amber Fort at Jaipur and the mighty Mehrangarh Fort at Jodhpur, Bonelli's Eagle over the Jain temples at Osiyan, a Peregrine Falcon perched on the Qutab Minar tower in Delhi...

And even when we were studying the culture and life of the Bishnoi people in their remote villages we had definitive views of Pied Wheatear, Red Collared Dove, and Yellow-crowned Woodpecker, so inextricable were the birds and history elements throughout the tour. Certainly in just 15 days we could not have enjoyed more birds, been more exposed to Indian history, and above all experienced more directly all aspects of Indian life today – from those remote Bishnoi households and Sohan Lal's village to our private lunch in the maharajah's dining room overlooking the oldest man-made lake in Rajasthan and an incredibly over-the-top wedding reception at the former residence of the prime minister of Jaipur.

I also recall that on one occasion, driving down from Nainital, we intercepted a flock of migrating Steppe Eagles. We tried to count them as they wheeled around the coach, but never came up with the same number twice – although it was always around 40. Eventually, rejecting a round number as indicative of merely a rough estimate, we opted for 39 – not only because this suggested an actual count, but also because the John Buchan fans considered Thirty-nine Steppes an appropriately literary entry in their notebooks.

In 1994, when Betty was suffering from terminal cancer, one of the most practical offers of help was from Sunbird leader Paul Holt. 'Tell Bryan not to worry about his tours,' he said. 'I'll clear my schedule so that I can take over at a moment's notice if need be. Equally if he chooses to carry on leading that's okay by me.' Little did I know then that 16 years later I would be able to do the same for him when his brother was dying. In 2010 I had to take over his Gujarat and Rann of Kutch tour at 24 hours' notice and put myself on standby for the next few weeks. Despite the tragic circumstances that occasioned my visit, I was impressed by the wealth of birdlife in this area, which had first

Purple Sunbirds at the Taj Mahal.

been recommended to me by James Hancock when we were discussing herons at Bharatpur 20 years previously. In many ways, the state offered an amalgam of Bharatpur and the Thar Desert.

28 November–12 December 2010

Gujarat means Land of the Tradesmen. But for us it was indisputably Land of the Birds. On our first drive from Ahmadabad to Bhavnagar, one roadside pool after another was filled with a profusion of waterbirds – egrets, storks, ibises, flamingos, pelicans, ducks, waders – and this wealth of wildlife continued throughout the trip. What's more, in addition to sheer numbers, the speciality species count was impressive, so that quantity and quality combined to provide a most satisfying experience. In all, 36 species of wader, 27 raptors, over 20 herons and allies, and 14 ducks and geese. The selection included 23 endemics, plus three near-endemics, with six species either critically endangered or vulnerable. But the accolades for bird of the trip went to none of those. It was a close call between Crab-plover and Hypocolius, with Pallid Scops Owl and Macqueen's Bustard as runners-up. We were indeed spoilt for choice.

Typifying this was the first of many impressive reserves – the Blackbuck sanctuary at Velevadar grassland: not only the largest harrier roost in the world (with a count of 3,000 Pallid, Montagu's, and Western Marsh), but also home to our first Sykes's Warbler, Stoliczka's Bushchat, and Dalmatian Pelican, and our only Sarus Cranes and Indian Eagle Owl. Nearby were Greater and Lesser Flamingos and Black Ibis.

Then came the contrasting habitat of Gir Forest with a succession of star attractions: our only Long-billed Vulture to greet us on our arrival, then Crested Serpent-eagle, Crested

Hawk-eagle, Bonelli's Eagle, Collared Scops Owl, two cuddling Mottled Wood Owls, White-bellied Minivet, Plum-headed Parakeet, Black-naped Monarch, Asian Paradise-flycatcher, Grey-headed Canary-flycatcher, Tickell's Blue Flycatcher, Tricoloured Munia, and Tawny-bellied Babbler. A fruiting Pepol tree provided a lively performance area for a cabaret of class acts: Thick-billed Flowerpecker, Coppersmith Barbet, Indian Pygmy Woodpecker, Common Iora, Common Woodshrike, White-browed Fantail, Small Minivet, Indian Golden Oriole, and Asian Koel. Even so, it was a mammal that stole the show. The only Lions outside Africa delayed our breakfast on our first game drive when we were already an hour overdue. More came on our third drive – plus a Leopard on the second. (Other cats were to feature later in the tour: Jungle Cat, Sand Cat, and Small Indian Civet – well, at least it meows.)

Different again was the Narara marine park. This provided us with one of the most fascinating walks of the tour. Although the target species was Crab-plover (of which we saw 1,500-2,000), there were so many other life forms to intrigue us, from Octopus and Puffer Fish to various anemones, sea slugs, and sea cucumbers – plus Heuglin's, Slender-billed, and Pallas's Gulls, Terek Sandpiper, and an endless carpet of Greater and Lesser Sand Plovers. A short diversion to Phapoda on our return to the hotel at Jamnager added more than 200 Demoiselle Cranes. And yet another impressive reserve (Khiyadiya, with its vast saltwater and freshwater pools) presented a host of new species before sunset: Black-necked Storks, the daddy of them all, Black-necked Grebe, Comb Duck, Black-headed Wagtail, Indian Reed Warbler, Great Thick-Knee, Temminck's Stint, and the most obliging Baillon's Crake ever.

हैपी वरथडे chris

Our stay with Jugal Tiwari at Nakhtrana lived up to expectations and 6th December was an indisputable red-letter day, particularly for birthday girl Chris (whose presents included six lifers), and for Lois and Kirk who on seeing Hypocolius completed their tally of all the bird families in the world. New species were delivered throughout the day (White-naped Tit, Sirkeer Malkoha, Chestnut-bellied Sandgrouse, Asian Desert Warbler, Eastern Orphean Warbler, Desert Lesser Whitethroat, Red-tailed Wheatear, Marshall's Iora, Sykes's Lark), and our night drive yielded not only superb views of a perched Sykes's Nightjar, but also a completely unexpected Pallid Scops Owl (plus Saw-scaled Viper, Red Earth Boa, Golden Jackal, Red Fox, and Bengal Fox). Other specialities during our stay here included Grey-necked Bunting, Brown Rock Chat, Dusky Crag Martin, our first Indian Coursers, and definitive views of Stoliczka's Bushchat.

Our final home was the perfect place to conclude our tour. Rann Riders offered not only comfortable accommodation in an attractive and peaceful setting and the best cuisine on a trip that was notable for good food and a complete absence of tummy trouble, but also a satisfying selection of birds and butterflies to keep us happy during our free time – Black-crowned Night Heron, Pheasant-tailed Jacana, Cotton Pygmy-goose, Purple Sunbird, Southern Coucal, Spotted Owlet, and Sykes's, Booted, and Paddyfield Warblers, plus a much-visited Chequered Keelback snake and a delightful Fulvous Fruit Bat. But our main target species were a little further afield in the Rann of Kutch and gave us the opportunity of several jolly charabanc excursions reminiscent of those post-war Sunday School trips and works outings – though despite the presence of the most beautiful donkeys in the world there was no one to accept our sixpences for a ride on the sand (but at least one of our American clients discovered the importance of a knotted hanky). After so many days in a convoy of three vehicles it was good to be all together in the lodge's sturdy, open-sided safari bus. First came 23 Sociable Lapwings, then eight Macqueen's Bustards, followed by Small, Collared, and Oriental Pratincoles, White-tailed Lapwing, Black-headed Bunting, regular Black-winged Kites, a splendid perched Red-necked Falcon, 29 more Indian Coursers, Pin-tailed Snipe, Jungle Prinia, and a succession of welcome reprises.

Returning to Ahmadabad on our last day, our journey was not without excitement. A short detour took us to a productive area that required neither permits nor camera fees – a local abattoir. Birding tours really do reach those parts that most holiday brochures fail to feature. At last we saw vultures (18 Egyptians) and the best views of several raptors hitherto only glimpsed or seen at a distance, including White-eyed Buzzard, Black Kite, Black-eared Kite, Tawny Eagle, Steppe Eagle, and most importantly Indian Spotted Eagle.

Rounding off our Gujarat experience was a delightful Gujarat evening with typical traditional cuisine and appropriate entertainment of dancing, music, and a puppet show. It would have been difficult in just two weeks to sample more of the state's 200,000 square kilometres of habitat and wildlife.

4. *The magic of Maghreb al Aksa*

In common with most exploratory birding trips in the 1970s, accommodation in Morocco in 1976 was in tents. Although the official campsites were invariably noisy, thanks to barking dogs, traffic, and muezzins, there were (and of course still are) endless miles of open space on beaches, deserts, and mountain plateaux. The open plain near Midelt offered one such opportunity and we pitched there to facilitate a pre-dawn search for Dupont's Lark. As it happened, I had misremembered the map reference. It wasn't the Dupont's Lark spot. But we did discover the first Pallas's Grasshopper Warbler for Morocco. In fact, camping in Morocco can be so pleasurable that even on the three-week spring tour by long-wheel-base Land Rover that I developed with Mike McHugo in the pre-Sunbird days, we still spent one night per week under canvas – in the desert beyond Merzouga, in the mountains beyond the Eagle's Nest at Telouet reached by a road not marked on the maps and which even the locals denied existed, and on various remote beaches. It was all very romantic, but it did seem odd to spend the following night in a luxury hotel. On one occasion, arriving at the Mamounia Marrakech (Winston Churchill's favourite hotel), I must have looked as though I still belonged in a tent, even after a shower. A member of staff, resplendent in *jelabia*, Tommy Cooper *tarbouche*, and curly-toed slippers, barred me from entering the dining room. Assuming that it was not yet open I took out my room card to check the times. Realizing at that point that I was actually a guest at the hotel and not some bearded beggar who had wandered in from the street, the poor man flung himself to the floor and begged my forgiveness.

Needless to say I was more embarrassed than he was. About this time I also discovered that the code NSU on my airline ticket stood for Not Suitable for Upgrading.

At these five-star hotels birdwatchers were routinely regarded as second-class guests. The waiters at the Palais Jamais at Fez once persistently ignored our breakfast order, again and again serving later arrivals. It became obvious that this was deliberate. Preferential treatment was reserved for the better class of person. Naturally we were anxious to be out birding, so eventually I stood up and read out our requests at town-crier pitch. Posh hotels can't cope with such behaviour, of course. The head waiter rushed over and pleaded with me to sit down. I explained that I would sit down as soon as we received 'the following items' and continued to recite our order. The effect was magical. Immediately waiters began to appear from all directions. Not only did we instantly receive all the items we had ordered, but also multiple teas, coffees, milks, butters, toasts, scrambled eggs, etc, continued to arrive. Even when the table was full to overflowing, more waiters tried to balance fresh supplies on the ever-growing pile. Wave after wave of waiters lapped at our table until we received a veritable tsunami of provisions. 'The sorcerer's apprentice' would have been appropriate background music. I had to tour the restaurant distributing all our surplus to the other guests – 'with great largesse' as one participant wrote in his journal.

On those early pre-Sunbird tours in Morocco, in our quest to explore out-of-the-way locations, we used to spend a couple of days pony trekking in the Atlas Mountains. We ate dinner with Omar the muleteer, and his wife would shyly serve the meal and retreat at once into the kitchen. One year some of our feisty American women's libbers took the opportunity to challenge Omar. 'Why is it,' they demanded, 'that everywhere we go the women are doing the work and the men sleeping by the roadside?' In all seriousness Omar explained 'Yes, the women are lucky. All they need to do is the hard labour and they live to a great age. We men have to do all their thinking for them and we die young.' Thereafter, whenever we saw a pile of old rags sleeping by the roadside, the ladies would comment on the spot of hard thinking that was going on.

A similar incident occurred in Mexico. A local passed us riding his donkey with his wife walking behind. 'Why are you riding and your wife walking?' 'Because my wife has no donkey.' Silly question.

On my very first visit to Morocco I was disturbed by the constant hassle and non-stop demands for money. I soon discovered that the trick was to get in first. So, knowing that a picnic stop would inevitably draw a crowd (mostly children) in a matter of minutes, it seemed sensible to make the show official. '*Venez ici. Venez ici. Regardez l'homme qui mange...*' ran the French patter. 'Roll up. Roll up. Come see the famous Eating Man. Will he consume his sandwich in one bite or two? Will he choose sardines or cheese?...' Then, when the crowd was peaking, came the punch line: '*Seulement cinq dirhams pour regardez le spectacle.*'

Western Mourning Wheatear and typical Moroccan kasbah.

('Only five dirhams to see the show'). As if by magic, the crowd would immediately disperse. Much more effective than asking them to leave.

Reciprocal hassle and haggling turns this endless gentle mugging into a game. Always thrust out your own open palm first. This bewilders the opposition. Whilst camping in the dunes near Merzouga in 1981 an American lady in our group was photographing a Desert Skink. Materializing out of nowhere, a young local ran over, grabbed the lizard, and – claiming that it was his pet – demanded five dirhams. His aggressive attitude ensured that the money was handed over, at which point he dropped the lizard, which scampered away across the sand. Still smirking at his con, the youth then asked if we had any bread. I offered him some loaves and demanded five dirhams. 'But that's more than they charge in Erfoud,' he gasped. I then pointed out that this was not Erfoud, this was many miles from the nearest bakery, and after a brief explanation of the laws of supply and demand watched him hand back five dirhams to our American client. A small victory. But making a profit on selling yesterday's bread to an Arab gave me a new perspective on wheeling and dealing which ensured that never again was I troubled by demands for money. In fact it is better to accept that even a simple request for directions comes at a price and cost this into the tour budget. (And always carry a good supply of pens and sweets for the children.)

It was in Morocco that I first discovered the pitfalls of heat haze. On one occasion a client (we'll call him George) was particularly keen to see a Long-legged Buzzard. Eventually, in the desert, we spotted one perched in a shallow gully. But where was George? Suddenly the buzzard stood up and hoisted its trousers. In an instant we discovered the whereabouts of George and the errors in identification that can be occasioned by the distorting effect of heat haze. It reminded me of another incident back in 1976 when Pete Milford and I were wandering in the desert near Goulimime. 'What on earth are those two collie dogs doing fighting out here miles from any habitation?' I asked. The two dogs then began to glide away. 'Idiot,' said Pete, 'it's not two dogs: it's an Arab on a bike.' Arab and bike then took to the air and flew away. It had been a displaying Houbara Bustard. Years later, in the Negev Desert in Israel, I suddenly saw two collie dogs fighting. 'Bustard,' I instinctively yelled to my group. And it was.

Despite 35 years' familiarity with Morocco, the country still seems as exotically foreign as any further-flung country. Its culture is very different from our own, and the atmosphere and scenic splendour of this ancient kingdom is unrivalled. This has nowhere been more dramatically illustrated than in the cinema. Not only has Morocco provided the most obvious locations for the rolling sand dunes of the Middle East in *Lawrence of Arabia*, but from Orson Welles with his *Othello* to the latest Italian version of *Marco Polo* this amazing country has doubled for settings as far apart as Cyprus and China. Most significantly of all in the Sean Connery/Michael Cane epic *The Man Who Would Be King*, Morocco dramatically represented north-west India, Afghanistan, and the western Himalaya. Even so, communication is no problem, as most Moroccans speak French. One exception was a family of Berbers encamped in the Forest of Marmora. I was trying to ascertain whether they had seen a Double-spurred Francolin thereabouts. '*Francolin a double eperon*' met with blank looks – and needless to say so did *Doppelspornfrankolin*, *Francolino bisperonato*, and *Francolin bicspolado*. I then picked up a stick and sketched in the sandy soil what I considered was a very credible likeness of the bird. A flash of comprehension lit up the old lady's face and she ran into her tent and emerged a moment later to offer me a hen's egg.

Incidentally, discovering local names for birds can be a fascinating study. One client on an Alaskan tour, watching Snow Buntings around an Inuit settlement, wondered what the Inuits called them. Approaching the head man she slowly enunciated 'What you call that bird?' In measured tones he replied 'We call that bird Snow Bunting.'

One year on our first-day visit to the Bridal Veil waterfalls at Imouzzer the locals were, as usual, offering to dive from the clifftop into the small pools below for a nominal financial remuneration. Their cries of '*Regardez le plonguer*' reminded the older members of the group of that celebrated catch-phrase from the 40s 'Don't forget the diver, sir'. 'Well, it's the only diver you are likely to see on this trip,' I confidently announced. The very next morning at the Souss Estuary (on 18 November 1986) I was proved wrong. We found a Great Northern Diver, bizarrely swimming through the legs of a Greater Flamingo. It was the first 20th-century record for the country (and even then the one in 1895 had been off Tangiers, not down here south of Agadir).

Our 1986 tour found the first 20th-century record of Great Northern Diver for Morocco on the Souss Estuary and watched it through Greater Flamingo legs.

Another year when the birds showed just how wrong I could be was when American Bob Behrstock was co-leader in 1993. At Heathrow airport he had asked where, in the few hours he had spare on his return, he could see some Scandinavian species – in particular Fieldfare and Redwing. I assured him that a London park was probably his best bet as he certainly wouldn't see any in Morocco. A few days later, at a desert oasis way south of Goulimime, we came across a mixed flock of Fieldfares, Redwings, and Eurasian Siskins – the most southerly records ever, anywhere in the world, of these essentially northern species. Bob must be the sole birder to have seen Redwing *only* south of 29°N. It just goes to show that, in birding, the two words you should never use are 'always' and 'never'. (The irony was reinforced when I returned to Norfolk and saw a Desert Wheatear at Hunstanton.)

On the same trip I recall Bob imitating the call of a Thick-billed Lark flying overhead. He had never heard it before, but reproduced it so accurately that the lark swung around, circled him a few times, landed at his feet, then followed him around like a doting puppy.

I first met Bob at the Audubon shop in Houston, Texas, in 1982, and have since co-led with him not only in Morocco, but also in destinations as far apart as Texas and Costa Rica. He always exhibits a splendidly matter-of-fact attitude to life's little problems. When one participant asked whether the leaders had seen a certain bird well enough for her to count it his sensible observation was 'Lady, it's your list.'

Once when he met me at Houston airport he observed that I was not wearing binoculars as stipulated in the final information. 'They're packed,' I said, 'I'm travelling incognito.' At that point a British birder, there by coincidence, ran across exclaiming 'Bryan, what are you doing here?' – followed by a succession of American birding friends who, by pure chance, also happened to be around. 'Glad to see you are travelling incognito,' said Bob. It really is a small world. I always used to tell

Betty I could never get up to any mischief, even in the remotest jungle, as there was always someone who knew me. I know I must have been spotted by one tour group in Arctic Norway because I discovered I was listed in their 'mammals seen' section, somewhere between Beluga and Reindeer.

The fact that I am easy to recognize – bald, big beard, broken nose, smock, shorts – was well known to Will Russell, so when he asked me on the phone how the incoming Wings group for the 1982 Great British Experience (my annual history and natural history tour of England, Scotland, and Wales) would pick me out I assumed he was joking and offered to wear a bowler hat. 'There might be lots of bald bearded men in smock and shorts wearing bowler hats,' he argued. 'Very well. I'll have a stuffed heron on my shoulder,' I said, assuming that would be the end of the matter. But the morning I was due to leave for the airport I received a copy of the final tour information that Will had circulated to all the participants. 'To assist you in identifying your tour guide at Heathrow airport,' it read 'in case the beard, smock, and shorts are insufficient Bryan will be wearing a bowler hat and will have a stuffed heron on his shoulder. The pink carnation is the clincher.' Fortunately I had a stuffed heron in the house, so I wired it to my shoulder and found a pink carnation in a friend's garden. Unfortunately the incoming flights were delayed. I had to spend all morning at the meeting point. Various polite policemen kept asking if they could help. And numerous ladies kept asking me if the heron was alive. As I shook my head and explained that it was stuffed the heron nodded. I could hear them returning to their husbands with the invariable conclusion 'He says it's stuffed but I could see it moving.' As it happened no other bearded tour representatives were wearing smock, shorts, bowler hat, and herons. They were merely holding up signs declaring 'Cosmos', 'Thomas Cook', etc. So the pink carnation was superfluous.

On a recent Sunbird tour to Morocco the group included a high percentage of caffeine addicts. And every day around about mid-morning there was an increasingly insistent call for elevenses. One morning on the wide open sands of the Souss Estuary, far away from any cafés and the possibility of the wonder drug, the distant hazy figure of an Arab riding a camel began to approach – just like the famous scene in *Lawrence of Arabia*. When the rider eventually reached us someone enquired, 'What do you call your camel?' 'Cappuccino,' was the reply. This was seen as a sign from God and yet again we had to abandon the birding.

But intervention is not always divine. In 2001 we introduced a new feature into this popular tour: a pioneering pelagic to the Atlantic shelf to add a few seabirds. We chartered a luxuriously appointed French-owned catamaran with a plentiful supply of coffee and croissants, sandwiches, wine, beer, and Coke, and set off from Agadir on a remarkably calm sea. Soon after leaving the harbour we were intercepted by a gunboat of the Moroccan Navy. Our boatman had been conducting shark-fishing trips for 15 years and had never known this before. But the captain of the gunboat was obviously keen for promotion. He sent a boarding party to investigate. Finding nothing suspicious (we were obviously not drug smuggling or people smuggling), they returned to the gunboat. But no sooner had we set off again than they were sent back to examine our paperwork. This was in the Agadir office, but a phone call brought a speedboat bearing all our necessary authorization. Again the boarding party left satisfied that all was well. But the captain of the gunboat was determined not to lose face and intercepted us yet again. 'Your papers are incorrect,' he proclaimed. 'They state that you are tourists. But if you are birdwatching you are scientists.' By now our boatman was losing patience. He phoned first the King then the General who was in charge of military activities in southern Morocco (both, apparently, personal friends), but neither was available. Not wanting to spend any more time bobbing up and down in the Atlantic, I suggested we try again the next day. That evening we received profuse apologies from the General with the explanation, 'Please forgive the captain – he's from Casablanca.' Shades of Manuel and *Fawlty Towers*. The following morning the gunboat was impounded in the harbour and we no sooner reached the continental shelf and started chumming than the birds came thick and fast: storm-petrels (European, Madeiran, Wilson's, and Leach's), shearwaters (Cory's, Manx, Balearic, and Sooty), and skuas (Great, Pomarine, Arctic, and Long-tailed). Sabine's Gull, Bulwer's Petrel, a feeding frenzy of Common Dolphins, and a pod of Risso's Dolphins were welcome bonuses.

After many years of conducting a spring great-circle tour of Morocco encompassing Lac de Sidi-Bour-Harba (Marsh Owl, Red-knobbed Coot), the cedar forests of the Middle Atlas (Levaillant's Green Woodpecker), the classic Saharan landscape around Merzouga (Desert Sparrow, African Desert Warbler, Egyptian Nightjar), the Gorge du Todra (Egyptian Vulture, Bonelli's Eagle), the Tagdilt track

*The islets at Essaouira hosted many
Eleonora's Falcons.*

(Houbara Bustard, wheatears, larks, sandgrouse), the Draa Valley (Pale Crag Martin), Taroudannt (Dark Chanting-goshawk, Tawny Eagle), Essaouira (Eleonora's Falcon), and Oukaimeden (African Crimson-winged Finch), I delegated this to other leaders in favour of developing April/May tours to many other locations. Moreover there was a growing demand to create a shorter winter tour in Morocco so that clients could experience the wonders in a nutshell and also set themselves up for the winter in Britain. This entailed exploring new areas in the south to discover speciality stake-outs within easy drives from Agadir – in many cases species beyond their hitherto known range. It was invariably a case of 'find the habitat and find the bird' as the old adage has it. These shorter breaks have provided many happy experiences for 20 years now, as recorded in these extracts from recent trip reports.

5–12 November 1999

So many gems in such perfect settings – the jewels in the Western Palearctic's crown. Morocco is such a varied country that it is difficult to do it justice in just a week. Nevertheless we do our best. And every year clients are amazed at the experience.

So what was best? Surely seeing so well half of the world's

population of a species near to extinction – a large flock of Northern Bald Ibis on the stony fields near Tamri. Or maybe the close views of other north-west African endemics, such as the delightful Tristram's Warbler and Moussier's Redstart. But in reality it was no one species or experience but the accumulation of target birds in impressive contexts that made each day so memorable and the whole week so richly rewarding.

There were the magnificent deserts of course, with Black-bellied Sandgrouse, Trumpeter Finch, Fulvous Babbler, Long-legged Buzzard, Lanner Falcon, Red-rumped, Desert and White-crowned Wheatears, Melodious and Spectacled Warblers and a variety of larks – Greater and Lesser Short-toed, Greater Hoopoe, Thick-billed, Temminck's and Bar-tailed all gave themselves up in well-paced sequence. Then eventually a much sought-after species – this year two Cream-coloured Coursers alongside the vehicle, so perfectly matched in colour to their sandy background that at times only four white legs and a couple of head patterns were visible.

Lots of sand, too, on the vast beaches backed by the Atlantic rollers and offering comparisons of Royal and Lesser Crested Terns, Audouin's and Slender-billed Gulls, and Northern Gannet, Cory's Shearwater, and Arctic Skua offshore.

Then there were the river mouths – the Souss spectacle of thousands of Greater Flamingos plus Eurasian Spoonbill, White Stork, and assorted waders, or the even more photogenic Massa with its Marbled Duck, Glossy Ibis, Booted and Short-toed Eagles, Black-crowned Tchagra, Little Swift and Brown-throated Martin.

The agricultural areas added Eurasian Hoopoe, Laughing Dove, Black-winged Kite, Common Quail, and Spanish Sparrow, and the dramatic mountain circuits Red-billed Chough, Bonelli's and Golden Eagles, Desert Lark, Blue Rock Thrush, and Eurasian Crag Martin.

Above all, there was constantly an awareness of a lifestyle unchanged for centuries – a veiled woman ploughing the arid ground with a donkey, an old lady leading her donkey laden with water bottles to a fortified hilltop village, a camel cart, the piles of brightly coloured spices in a labyrinthine medina. And once more we enjoyed the contrast between the overwhelming night sky in the desert – so many stars and the rings of Saturn 'just like the book' – and our lunch breaks in the heat of the day to sample yet another tagine (beef with almonds and prawns, chicken with lemon, lamb with olives) or couscous or brochette and relax in a lively local restaurant, the cool elegance of the Palais Salaam at Tarouddant, or a spacious Berber tent.

Little wonder that we couldn't spare the time for a pelagic. But maybe an extra day next year will solve that one.

12–19 November 2000

111 lifers was the tally for one participant on this year's Morocco trip. Not bad for just one week in the Western Palearctic, particularly with nearly half as many again as (very impressive) padders. But the abiding memories are of quality not quantity – breathtakingly close views of north-west African endemics and 'difficult' desert species. The top six (in order of their scores in the bird of the trip contest) were: the Northern Bald Ibis feeding close enough to reveal every detail of their poor bruised red and purple heads, orange irises, and the subtle sheen of their bronze-green, copper, and violet plumage; the Tristram's Warbler with its toiletry tones of boudouir-blue and peachy pink offsetting

that chestnut wing panel; the ubiquitous and always-arresting Moussier's Redstarts; the Black-bellied Sandgrouse so cryptically camouflaged that despite their proximity only movement betrayed their presence; the charismatic happy band of Fulvous Babblers; and the striking streamline elegance of Greater Hoopoe Larks. And as ever with Morocco the settings were as memorable as the birds.

An earlier-than-usual direct flight to Agadir gave us lunch at the hotel and a leisurely extra afternoon in the attractive Souss Estuary, easing us into the ornithological riches of the country with a varied selection of birds – Great White Egret, White Stork, Eurasian Spoonbill, Glossy Ibis, Greater Flamingo, Black-winged Stilt, Pied Avocet, Mediterranean Gull, Gull-billed Tern, Pallid Swift, Zitting Cisticola. A midday flight a week later afforded us a return visit en route to the airport.

It is significant that we saw 13 species on our first reconnaissance that we did not see on our return, and even more significant that we saw 19 different birds on that last morning, including 10 new for the trip (Slender-billed Gull and Bluethroat being the most popular). These were particularly appreciated as the King was staying in the adjacent palace and the guards could easily have forbidden us access.

Our first full day took us up the mountain road to Imouzzer through a series of climatic belts from bananas and palms, olives and grenadines shading plots of winter barley, past gnarled trunks of almonds and apples, and finally the conifer belt. The birds were similarly varied: Cirl Bunting, Barbary Partridge, Black Wheatear, Blue Rock Thrush, Eurasian Crag Martin, Western Olivaceous Warbler, Coal Tit, Eurasian Jay, the Atlas race of Common Crossbill (known as Atlas Crossbill), and ultimately two Bonelli's Eagles from our lunchtime terrace at the Hotel des Cascades at 1,170m. A return to the coast and the sweeping Atlantic beaches added Black-crowned Tchagra, Barbary Falcon, Long-legged Buzzard, Lesser Crested Tern, Audouin's Gull, 150 Cory's Shearwaters, and finally our last target bird of the day – a considerable percentage of the world's population of Northern Bald Ibis. Our second day took us south to the Massa – the photogenic estuary that in the 17th century was a thriving port for Genoese and Portuguese traders, but now shelters only coots, ducks, and waders against a backdrop of sand dunes and palms, and forms the perfect setting for the many myths of Massa, which claims to be the beach where Jonah was disgorged by the whale, where the Arab conqueror Uqba Ben Nafi, having spread Islam across Africa, rode his horse into the Atlantic to show Allah that there was no land further west for him to conquer for the true faith ('O God, I take you to witness that there is no ford here. If there was I would cross it'), and from where the Antichrist will first be recognized, rising naked and sublimely beautiful from the sea. For us, Massa provided not the Antichrist but Laughing Dove, Northern Lapwing, Little Owl, House Bunting, Brown-throated Martin, Whiskered Tern, Common Crane, Squacco Heron, 200 Marbled Ducks, and a single Ferruginous Duck.

Morocco is the final stronghold of the Northern Bald Ibis.

Our afternoon in the nearby desert brought the day to another wonderful close with Desert Wheatear, Lesser Short-toed Lark, and Black-bellied Sandgrouse.

Subsequent days east along the Souss Valley to Taroudannt and beyond, and south to Goulimime and beyond, added Red-rumped and White-crowned Wheatears, Bar-tailed and Temminck's Larks, Trumpeter Finch, Eurasian Hoopoe, and Stone-curlew. And our night at the oasis of Ait-Boukha provided us with our annual night-sky spectacular: shooting stars, the rings of Saturn, the four moons of Jupiter, and a million more stars than usual. But scenically our most impressive circuit was left to our final full day. Indeed, Morocco travel expert Barnaby Rogerson believes that 'the round trip to Tafraoute is one of the most classically beautiful journeys that you can make in Morocco'. Across the Tiznit Desert, through the valley that was once the long-impregnable sanctuary of El Hiba the Blue Sultan, winding up past Col-du-Kerdous (once a kasbah, then an Islamic school, now a hotel and convenient coffee stop), through the territory of the Ammeln (a tribal sub-division of the Chleuh Berbers and the best known of the six tribes of the Anti-Atlas Mountains), to the amphitheatre of Tafraoute itself, where the bizarre and massive red rock formations have been compared to meteorite showers on Mars. Here we enjoyed the best meal of the trip – thick harira soup, couscous or tagines of chicken and lemon or lamb with olives and prunes, fresh oranges laced with honey and cinnamon, and mint tea – eaten Moroccan style in the elegance of a Berber ceremonial tent. Then over the passes of Tizi-Mlil (1,662m) and Tizi-n'Tarakatine with Adrar-Mqorn towering above at 2,344m and down to the fortress village of Tioulit, a spectacular example of the homeland of the Illalen, a confederation of 18 tribes that occupy the mountain plateau between Tafraoute and Ait-Baha.

The *agadirs* of the Illalen are known to have contained as many as 300 compartments, in several storeys on either side of a central aisle. New birds ranged from Golden Eagle to Desert Lark, but the most unexpected was Hawfinch, which here in the Anti-Atlas must surely be the world's most southerly record.

Morocco was long known in the Muslim world as *Maghreb al Aksa*, the land of the furthest west, literally the edge of the world and a place notorious for its powerful magicians and demon-like jinn. It is still intensely foreign and fascinating, and despite 30 years of familiarity (for two of the group) it can still produce the unexpected. The magicians are still there.

3–11 November 2001

Despite the 10 or 12 new species that were added to Sunbird's cumulative trip list this year by the inclusion of a pelagic to the Atlantic shelf, it was the familiar faces, the traditional Moroccan specialities, which won the bird of the trip contest: overwhelmingly the 18 Northern Bald Ibises that wandered amongst us, then the regional endemic but ubiquitous Moussier's Redstart, the charismatic Black-crowned Tchagra and Greater Hoopoe Lark (both obligingly close), the nine Cream-coloured Coursers that ran towards us, the Lanner Falcon which performed so aerodynamically just above our heads at a desert oasis, and the happy band of Fulvous Babblers that posed on the bushes. Madeiran Storm-petrel was only voted number 8.

The desert certainly did us proud – not only with the specialities itemized above, but also with the quick succession of larks (Bar-tailed to compare with the Desert we had just enjoyed on a mountain pass, Thick-billed, Temminck's, and Greater and Lesser Short-toed) and wheatears (Desert, Red-rumped, White-crowned to compare with Black just up the road). Lilac-and-pink Trumpeter Finches were everywhere. Spectacled Warblers dodged from bush to bush. Black-bellied Sandgrouse and Stone-curlew eventually obliged.

In the agricultural areas Black-winged Kite, Laughing Dove, Eurasian Hoopoe, and Zitting Cisticola perched for the telescopes. In the estuaries White Stork, Glossy Ibis, Eurasian Spoonbill, Greater Flamingo, Marbled Duck, Northern Goshawk, gulls (Audouin's, Slender-billed, Mediterranean), and a range of waders provided variety. And in the mountains Golden Eagle, Barbary Partridge, and a perched Barbary Falcon captured our attention. We thought that last year 111 lifers was a good tally for one participant for a week in the Western Palearctic. This year that record was broken by another American client with 'about 170'. Where else but Morocco?

2–9 November 2002

Once more our annual winter week in Morocco provided a little lifetime in seven days – a club sandwich of layered variety enclosed by two very different sessions at the Souss Estuary. En route to our hotel room from Agadir airport our introductory visit gave us a fine selection of waders (including our only Eurasian Whimbrel and Spotted Redshank of the trip), and a range of specialities from White Stork, Glossy Ibis, and Greater Flamingo to Gull-billed Tern, Mediterranean Gull, Zitting Cisticola, and Southern Grey Shrike, plus a charismatic Wryneck that posed long enough for everyone to appreciate its amazing cryptic plumage. On our final morning before our afternoon flight home, our Souss selection of 20-plus waders – despite the intervening action-packed and bird-filled week – still included seven new ones for the trip, most excitingly Collared Pratincole. New also were Slender-billed Gull and Bluethroat. But even the repeats – a superbly close Black-crowned Tchagra, a perched Common Kingfisher, Glossy Ibis, Barbary Partridge, and Bonelli's Eagle – ensured that for some participants this relaxed morning of non-stop birdwatching and endless species variety in a photogenic setting was a highlight of the trip rather than merely a convenient reprise on the local patch.

Between these two Souss visits each day offered a different experience. Our first morning winding up the mountains to Imouzzer gave us instant views of our target birds, Tristram's Warbler and Atlas Crossbill, plus a satisfying sequence of extras – Black Wheatear, Blue Rock Thrush, Barbary Partridge, Cirl, House and Rock Buntings, and of course the ever-present Moussier's Redstarts and Sardinian Warblers. In the afternoon our drive past the sweeping beaches and Atlantic rollers took us to Tamri where three Northern Bald Ibis were waiting for us by the roadside with Audouin's Gulls, Ruddy Shelduck, and Royal and Lesser Crested Terns side-by-side on the sands below.

The action on our 11-hour pelagic the following day began as soon as we left Agadir harbour – with instant skuas (Arctic, Great, and Pomarine – some with spoons) and shearwaters (Cory's, Great, Sooty, Manx, and Balearic – at times all together in great rafts around our catamaran). This was in contrast to last year when the journey to the Atlantic Shelf was fairly uneventful, but the destination yielded a frenzy of Wilson's, Leach's, European, and Madeiran Storm-petrels (which this year were in very short supply – though two Grey Phalaropes were new for all our Moroccan lists).

Our day at the Massa was memorable for Marbled and

Ferruginous Ducks, Squacco Heron, Laughing Dove, Brown-throated Martin, our first Black-crowned Tchagra, and particularly close and sustained views of the newly split Western Olivaceous Warbler with its long, strong, swollen bill. Again, a range of species from Osprey and Little Owl to Eurasian Spoonbill and Curlew Sandpiper provided constant interest – until the heat of the day reminded us of the chicken and lemon tagine and other culinary delights awaiting us in the cool of the old kasbah. A happy day was rounded off by our first views of Black-bellied Sandgrouse and Desert Wheatear in the nearby desert. But the real desert experience came the next two days beyond Goulimime, with Cream-coloured Courser, Stone-curlew, Fulvous Babbler, Long-legged Buzzard, White-crowned and Red-rumped Wheatears, Trumpeter Finch, Spectacled Warbler, and all those larks (Thick-billed, Greater Hoopoe, Bar-tailed, Temminck's, and Greater Short-toed), plus unexpected European Bee-eater and Woodchat Shrike, and satisfyingly close views of several Bonelli's Eagles, both perched and in flight. Our newly refurbished oasis auberge offered a truly silent night, an amazing array of scattered stars like spilt salt, and mouth-wateringly tender meat and delicious vegetables.

A high success rate on these first six days meant we could devote our last day to driving the round trip through the Anti-Atlas Mountains to Tafroute. Our birding started shortly after sunrise with a perched Barbary Falcon and a flock of Lesser Short-toed Larks, and finished just before sunset with our target Rock Sparrows. But the abiding memories of the day were of endlessly dramatic mountain views, fortified hill-top Berber villages, the red-rock Mars-scape of Tafroute itself, and lunch in a ceremonial Berber tent.

A week in Morocco is certainly full of birds (over 170 species) and new experiences. Yet some participants found time to relax on the beach and shop in the souks (the advantage of returning to the same hotel on every night but one). It is without doubt a wonderful way to prepare for the winter back home.

1–8 November 2003

This must be the first time ever that the star bird on a pelagic was Northern Bald Ibis – eclipsing the five species of shearwater, three skuas (including close Pomarine with spoons), and even the Killer Whales alongside our catamaran. An equally surprising feature of this year's tour was the number of opportunities for photographing Black-crowned Tchagra, which is normally such an elusive skulker.

Other memorable moments included the Stone-curlew on the runway as our plane touched down, the displaying Greater Hoopoe Larks, a Lanner Falcon's 300-metre power-drive above Le Chapeau de Napoleon rock formation, a pristine juvenile Tawny Eagle low overhead, two Barbary Falcons demonstrating sparring and formation flying, an all-too brief Red-necked Nightjar, and standing in the morning stillness of the desert surrounded by a flock of 16 Cream-coloured Coursers. Just as rewarding were the views of the endemic Tristram's Warbler, several Spectacled Warblers, the newly split Ultramarine Tit, and the surely soon-to-follow Moroccan Wagtail (race *subpersonata*). So many other images still vie for attention – estuaries with Marbled Duck, Ruddy Shelduck, and Glossy Ibis; rocky slopes with Barbary Partridge, Rock Bunting, and Moussier's Redstart; Audouin's Gulls and Lesser Crested Tern against a backdrop of Atlantic rollers; Fulvous Babblers and Wryneck in the bushes; Desert and

Bar-tailed Larks, and Desert and Red-rumped Wheatears hardly distinguishable from their sandy surroundings; Laughing Dove and Brown-throated Martin; and a satisfying selection of raptors – Black-winged Kite, Long-legged Buzzard, and Golden and Bonelli's Eagles. But for many participants a particular highlight – despite the fact that no new birds were involved – was a desert pool with one species after another coming down to drink: Black-bellied Sandgrouse, Trumpeter Finch, Temminck's Lark, and Lesser Short-toed Lark. And all this in one week.

The current issue of *Birding World* includes an appraisal of the recently published *Birds of Morocco* by Thévenot, Vernon, and Bergier. In it the reviewer observes 'Morocco is an amazing and exciting country, as beautiful and diverse in its habitats, and therefore in its avifauna, as any area in the Western Palearctic'. I couldn't have put it better myself (particularly since I was the reviewer).

30 October–6 November 2004

Thanks to an unbroken sequence of first-time-lucky stops right from day one, our winter week in Morocco this year managed to visit more locations then ever before and presented as complete a picture as possible in just seven days of the varied habitats of this magnificent country. On the very first morning our instant success with Black-crowned Tchagra, Tristram's Warbler, Rock Bunting, Barbary Partridge, and Atlas Crossbill on the scenic mountain road to Imouzzer freed us to devote the afternoon to driving the beautiful coastal route to Aghrod (for hundreds of Audouin's Gulls) and Tamri (for Northern Bald Ibis alongside our vehicle and Ruddy Shelduck, Black-necked Grebe, Barbary Falcon, and assorted ducks in the estuary below).

Similarly only one visit to the photogenic Massa Estuary was required for splendid views of Marbled Duck, Glossy Ibis, Squacco Heron, Brown-throated Martin, Laughing Dove, Little Owl, Common Kingfisher, and Cetti's Warbler – plus our first close Bonelli's Eagle and Black-bellied Sandgrouse, species that we enjoyed again in the atmospheric deserts south of Goulimime, where the specialities included Red-rumped, Desert, and White-crowned Wheatears; Long-legged Buzzard; Lanner Falcon; Fulvous Babbler; and an array of larks (Thick-billed, Greater Hoopoe, Greater and Lesser Short-toed, and Desert and Bar-tailed). Extras ranged from Ring Ouzel to Black-winged Kite.

Moussier's Redstart must surely be one of the world's most attractive regional endemics.

Desert species, including Desert Lark, White-crowned Wheatear, sandgrouse, and Trumpeter Finch, also presented themselves on the high plateaux of the Anti-Atlas on the impressive mountain circuit to Tafroute.

By contrast, down at sea level our catamaran was surrounded by at least 50 storm-petrels (representing four species) and by three species of both shearwater and skua, plus Grey Phalarope, Risso's Dolphin, and Sunfish. And in the delightful estuary of the Souss 20 species of wader vied for our attention with Greater Flamingo, Eurasian Spoonbill, Slender-billed and Mediterranean Gulls, Osprey,

Western Marsh Harrier, and Zitting Cisticola. Even our non-birding interval in Taroudannt, where we explored the Arab medina and the Berber souk, gave us 74 White Storks overhead as we lunched in the elegant gardens of the old palace. So it was no surprise that a couple of Stone-curlews came to see us off as we walked across the tarmac in our final minutes at Agadir.

As we waited for that plane no less that 41 species of the 160-plus seen were short-listed for our bird of the trip contest. The winner was one of the most attractive and colourful regional endemics in the Western Palearctic, Moussier's Redstart. But the most significant bird of the trip was the most nondescript, washed-out, and tatty of all – a first-winter Isabelline Shrike. Not a prepossessing sight, but you can't do better than finding a first for the country.

29 October–6 November 2005

Morocco is an amazing country – sweeping Atlantic beaches, bird-filled estuaries, dramatic mountainscapes, beguiling deserts, and a fascinating culture. An important aspect of sampling this culture was our sequence of authentic lunches in varied settings – chicken and lemon tagine in an old kasbah and caravanserie, couscous or lamb with prunes and almonds in a Berber tent, and fresh fish kebabs or tender shoulder of lamb overlooking the beach where Jonah was washed up by the whale.

This year each day of our trip seemed perfectly paced – opening with a star turn, followed by a series of fine supporting acts, then finishing with a climactic show-stopper – just like *Sunday Night at the London Palladium.*

Our very first day began with definitive views of the normally elusive Black-crowned Tchagra, continued with such delightful north-west African endemics as Moussier's Redstart, Tristram's Warbler, and Atlas Crossbill, plus flight views of Bonelli's, Booted, and Golden Eagles, and closed with unexpected cliff-top sightings of Long-legged Buzzard, Barbary Falcon, and Moroccan Shag (European Shag of the race *riggenbachi*, which is endemic to Morocco and with only 20 pairs in the world considered 'Endangered'), plus Marbled Duck and Moroccan Wagtail in the nearby estuary.

A pelagic the following morning started with Lesser Crested Tern, three skua species, and hundreds of close Cory's Shearwaters, plus smaller numbers of Manx and Balearic Shearwaters, and the day closed in the Souss Estuary with Eurasian Spoonbill, Greater Flamingo, and an assortment of waders.

The Massa then gave us Ferruginous Duck, Red-crested Pochard, and Greater Scaup (all scarce birds in Morocco), Squacco Heron, Glossy Ibis, Pallid and Little Swifts, Woodchat Shrike, and Laughing Dove, followed by Western Olivaceous and Melodious Warblers at lunch, Black-winged Kite and Brown-throated Martin in the agricultural area, and a breathtakingly close pair of Black-bellied Sandgrouse at sunset.

Our first desert day began with 29 Stone-curlews posing by the roadside, continued with Desert Lark, Desert and White-crowned Wheatears and a pair of Red-rumped Wheatears facing Mecca and genuflecting for the midday muezzin, and closed with superb views of Greater Hoopoe Lark perched in the setting sun. Our second day started with Fulvous Babblers and a Lanner Falcon catching and eating prey, a 'Larksville' set of Thick-billed, Temminck's, Bar-tailed, and Greater and Lesser Short-toed Larks, plus Trumpeter Finches, and climaxed with a pair of the endemic race of Scrub Warbler (surely soon to be a full species).

Even this was topped the next day by the instant Northern Bald Ibis on our arrival at suitable habitat north of Tamri – and not just one but a flock of 250-300. Pager messages from Britain meanwhile informed us that no less that three Franklin's Gulls had arrived there from America. So why not Morocco? On a whim, we went to the Souss to find one – and did, within three minutes (accompanied by Slender-billed and Audouin's Gulls), the second record for Morocco. To close, a speculative trawl for Red-necked Nightjar brought one immediately flying towards and around us.

Our Anti-Atlas circuit to Tafroute provided the photographers with close views of Cirl and House Buntings, Barbary Partridge, Golden Eagle, and a flock of 120 Red-billed Choughs at 1,660m.

Virtually all our target birds. Except one. Cream-coloured Courser. This gave us a clear quest for our extra day (necessitated by a change in BA's flight schedule). Yet a day of walking and driving over the deserts to the north and south of the Massa failed to add the missing species. Admittedly there were new

Cream-coloured Courser –
as sandy as its setting.

birds – Short-eared Owl and European Golden Plover in the desert, White-winged Tern on the river, Common Scoter on the seawatch. But finally at 5.30pm we had to leave to reach the airport for our 6.30pm check-in. Then, just a kilometre from the main road, 22 C³s provided the cherry on the top. The fat lady sang and we reached the airport in time.

26 November–3 December 2006

Once more our winter week in Morocco was a delightful sequence of varied experiences that even with hindsight couldn't have been better planned or paced. Our first exposure to a cross-section of Moroccan birds was at the Souss Estuary with Greater Flamingo, Eurasian Spoonbill, Black-winged Stilt, Pied Avocet, Kentish Plover, Little Stint, Mediterranean, Slender-billed, and Audouin's Gulls, Zitting Cisticola, and Sardinian Warbler. Then followed the Massa Estuary with Glossy Ibis, Marbled Duck, Laughing Dove, Little Owl, Common Kingfisher, Brown-throated Martin, Moussier's Redstart, and Black-crowned Tchagra. And, after a delicious chicken and lemon tagine at an amazing secret and secluded kasbah and caravanserie and an exploration of the agricultural areas, the day closed with our first Black-bellied Sandgrouse and Desert Wheatears.

The following day we opted for a dramatic mountain circuit via Paradise Valley and Imouzzer that brought us Cirl Bunting, Tristram's Warbler, Black Wheatear, Barbary Partridge, Bonelli's Eagle, Northern Goshawk, Atlas Crossbill, and Ultramarine Tit, another relaxing lunch break on the terrace of the Hotel des Cascades, and a grand finale north of Tamri with 200 Northern Bald Ibis, magnificent Atlantic breakers, and the most photogenic sunset over the sea (and yes there was a green flash).

Then came an even more breathtaking mountain circuit to Tafroute, which gave us our first looks at more desert birds – Trumpeter Finch, Thick-billed and Greater Hoopoe Larks, White-crowned Wheatear, and Desert Lark – and also Red-billed Chough and Barbary Falcon at 1,660m, plus bizarre rock formations, fascinating Berber citadels and fortified hilltop villages, and another taste of authentic Moroccan cuisine (the meat this time complemented by almonds and prunes).

More desert birds followed the next day south of Goulimime: Red-rumped Wheatears, Fulvous Babblers, and Greater Hoopoe Larks for a thrilling finale at sunset. En route we added migrating White Storks, Black-winged Kite, Long-legged Buzzard, Great Spotted Cuckoo, and Eurasian Hoopoe. And for our evening meal at our delightful oasis auberge what else but camel tagine?

The following morning got off to a good start with a pair of Scrub Warblers (soon to be split as the rare endemic Streaked Scrub Warbler), another Great Spotted Cuckoo, many more Red-rumped and Desert Wheatears, Trumpeter Finches, and Black-bellied Sandgrouse, but most significantly all the larks: Bar-tailed, Temminck's, Greater and Lesser Short-toed, Thekla and Crested, and Thick-billed. This freed us to return to the Souss for a reprise of waders, wildfowl, gulls, terns (including Gull-billed), and dusk glimpses of Red-necked Nightjar and Short-eared Owl.

After such an action-packed week Saturday was decreed an Options Day: relaxing in Agadir (the beach, the shops, and the bird gardens); a land-based return to Paradise Valley and the Atlantic coast for some much-desired repeats for those who missed Tuesday's success story (Tristram's Warbler, Barbary Partridge, Cirl Bunting, Northern Bald Ibis – plus Moroccan Wagtail, which was new for all); or a laid-back pelagic out to the

Atlantic shelf for shearwaters (Cory's, Manx, and Balearic), skuas (Arctic and Great), Grey Phalarope, and Green and Hawksbill Turtles alongside our catamaran.

With only one significant target bird still missing, the choice for our final day was now obvious: the deserts around Massa to search for the elusive Cream-coloured Courser. But first the river provided us with yet more new birds (Ferruginous Duck, Red-crested Pochard, Ruddy Shelduck, Squacco Heron, Little Swift). The superb lunch at the Ksar Massa (*pastilla*, the ultimate Moroccan speciality – layers of flaky pastry, pigeon breast, eggs, almonds, raisins, spices, and honey – followed by melt-in-the-mouth shoulder of lamb, and fresh fruit) was probably the best of the trip, made all the more enjoyable as we ate overlooking the impressive Sidi Rabat beach and the mighty rollers. (Though James's seawatching commentary was not entirely to be believed: 'gannet ... gannet ... Arctic Skua ... Yellow-legged Gull ... Antichrist ... two more gannets ... cormorant ...') The coursers, however, continued to elude us as we drove over many kilometres of hamada desert knowing that we had to set off for the airport at 5pm. Then, in an uncanny action-replay of last year's scenario, at the eleventh hour (4.30pm), there they were: seven Cream-coloured Coursers being entertained by a cabaret act from a displaying Greater Hoopoe Lark. Perfect timing – which earned for them the accolade of bird of the trip (with 124 votes, beating Northern Bald Ibis by 10 votes).

A wonderful week with perfect weather, a classic selection of birds, as much scenery as it was possible to pack into seven days, some memorable meals, and the most congenial group of travelling companions possible.

2–9 November 2007

Once more our annual winter week in Morocco packed a fortnight's experiences into seven very different, lively days. Our amazing quality-and-quantity trip list was launched the moment we arrived at Agadir airport by a splendid Lesser Kestrel performing above us as we loaded our minibus. After lunch by our hotel pool (the only time we saw it in daylight), the action continued at the Souss Estuary with over 100 Greater Flamingos and as many Black-winged Stilts, 20 thermalling White Storks, and educational comparisons of Common Ringed and Kentish Plovers, Temminck's and Little Stints, Black-tailed and Bar-tailed Godwits, and Curlew Sandpiper and Dunlin. Tamri Estuary then provided Eurasian Spoonbill and Ruddy Shelduck (and a green flash as the sun set over the sea), and the beaches in between hundreds of Audouin's Gulls. A satisfying cross-section of species for our first afternoon.

A raptor also launched us on our second day – a Barbary Falcon perched on our hotel – but the highlights on our first mountain circuit (to Imouzzer) were the delightful Tristram's Warbler, Atlas Crossbill, Black Wheatear, Blue Rock Thrush, Moussier's and Common Redstarts, Barbary Partridge, and all three stripe-headed buntings together (Rock, Cirl, and House). Again, sunset at Tamri – and a perched Common Kingfisher – brought the day to a close.

Our planned pelagic was aborted through engine trouble before we even left the harbour, but our visit to the port did provide the only two Western Olivaceous Warblers of the trip and still left the whole day to explore the wonderful Massa Estuary with its Glossy Ibis, Marbled and Ferruginous Ducks, Lanner Falcon, and Little Owl. We relaxed over a fine lunch overlooking the sweeping beach of Sidi Rabat where for us the hoped-for Northern Bald Ibis flew by on cue. Our day concluded with a desert spectacular of B³C³ (Bob's birthday bird: Cream-coloured Courser), plus Greater Hoopoe Lark and a Eurasian Dotterel (a rare sighting in this part of the country and our first write-in). Appropriately, the hotel had scattered rose petals all over our dining table, together with a large floral display and a calorie-cake.

The next day began with another spectacular – Trumpeter Finch, Desert Wheatear, Thick-billed and Temminck's Larks, followed by White-crowned Wheatear and Desert Lark – as we climbed to Tafroute on the great Anti-Atlas circuit with Red-billed Choughs, increasingly close views of nine Bonelli's Eagles, Golden Eagles, another Barbary Falcon, and most excitingly a Griffon Vulture. But the star of the show was the scenery, the dramatic hilltop kasbahs, the Berber villages seemingly sculpted out of the red rock, and an absolutely splendid Moroccan lunch.

Then came our overnight stay in the deep south beyond Goulimime 'gateway to the Sahara' – more desert birds (Long-legged Buzzard, Black-bellied Sandgrouse, Red-rumped Wheatear, Bar-tailed Lark, and more Cream-coloured Coursers, Desert and White-crowned Wheatears, Thick-billed, Desert, and Greater Hoopoe Larks, and even another Golden Eagle), which kept coming right up to sunset and even beyond, as two Red-necked Nightjars flew around us in our oasis hotel courtyard as we arrived back for a shower (well, a dribble – but welcome), a tasty camel tagine, and the final surprise of the day as we were stargazing on the roof: Comet Holmes looking like a ghostly jellyfish amongst the pin-sharp planets and shooting stars.

Our desert opener the following morning was equally exciting: two Streaked Scrub Warblers (of the taxon *theresae*, endemic to

Black-winged Kites seem particularly common in the Souss Valley.

south-western Morocco) and yet more Cream-coloured Coursers, Lanner Falcons, Long-legged Buzzards, Black-bellied Sandgrouse, Trumpeter Finches, Bar-tailed, Thick-billed, and Temminck's Larks, plus both Greater and Lesser Short-toed Larks. This desert clean-sweep left us time to return to the Massa to explore the agricultural area and add Black-winged Kite, Laughing Dove, Yellow Wagtail, Brown-throated Martin, 200 Glossy Ibis, another Bonelli's Eagle, and a couple of Stone-curlews as darkness fell. Grand finales were certainly a daily feature of this trip as much as the exciting openers.

A complete change of pace the next day was provided by our nine-hour pelagic – the ultimate relaxing experience on a calm (at times almost glassy) sea with hundreds of well-spaced seabirds to hold our interest in the bright sunshine (Cory's, Sooty, Manx, and Balearic Shearwaters; Arctic, Great, and Pomarine Skuas; Common Scoter; Grey Phalarope; and 70 Mediterranean Gulls) – plus a requested Sunfish on demand – but a mysterious absence of life whenever we entered a fog bank. Back on land an end-of-day return visit to the Souss yielded close White Storks and Slender-billed Gull, which brought our trip list to one short of last year's total.

The final morning, on the sea cliffs north of Tamri, a Peregrine Falcon over a sand dune was the equalizer, quickly followed by two Moroccan Shags, and a Subalpine Warbler (the latest date ever – by one day – for this migrant). In the estuary our main remaining target bird obliged – a Black-crowned Tchagra – and then on Tarhazout beach the final one: Royal Tern (a scarce bird as most migrate south from their Mauritanian breeding grounds). A right royal finale to our trip list total. We then had our final picnic by the Souss Estuary before arriving at the airport at the specified check-in time only to find that (despite our phone call that morning) this had been brought forward and the plane was already boarding. Full marks to Agadir airport for opening up all the check-in desks and whisking us all across the tarmac for immediate departure with none of that tiresome waiting around that is the usual anticlimax to an action-packed week. Not a minute was wasted and even with hindsight we couldn't have enjoyed a more satisfactory sequence of experiences in this magnificent and magical country.

The reference to Comet Holmes in the 2007 trip report that ends this section is worthy of more comment. For our one night away from

Agadir we discovered, some years ago, a delightful auberge at an oasis in the desert beyond Goulimime – with Laughing Doves and Red-necked Nightjar around the palms, and Greater Hoopoe Lark and Red-rumped Wheatear in the hamada, and so beautifully quiet compared with the busy, bustling town. A bonus is the night sky, so we always persuade the staff to turn off all the lights during our star-gazing session on the flat roof. On 6 November, having scoped several planets, co-leader Dan Brown and I were both having difficulty in focusing on one particular bright object that remained obstinately fuzzy. We both agreed that it must therefore be a comet. 'But comets have long streaming tails,' argued one lady. 'Not if they're heading straight towards you,' we reasoned. She then transferred from my telescope, which happened to be set at 30x magnification, to Dan's, which was on 60x. 'Goodness, it's got bigger already,' she cried. 'It must be coming at a tremendous lick,' we said. In fact, we discovered later that a tail was developing, but was difficult to observe as cometary tails always point away from the sun – we were aligned perfectly between the sun and the comet and were therefore looking straight down the tail (know as opposition). We texted Dan's father in Wales, an amateur astronomer, and received the confirmation that it was indeed a comet: Comet 17p/Holmes. Towards the end of October the comet had increased its magnitude 832,320 times, becoming clearly visible to the naked eye. Other comets have brightened in the past, but not on this scale. It was first reported from Tenerife and Barcelona. To us our unexpected discovery was as exciting as finding a new bird. Yet the only mention we could subsequently find in the media was this small paragraph tucked away in the middle pages of *The Times* on 16 November:

A violent comet has knocked the sun off its perch to become the biggest object in the solar system. Comet Holmes has swelled into a monster puffball after a huge explosion. It can be seen with the naked eye and with a diameter of 1,450,000km (900,000 miles) it is big enough to swallow up 1,400,000 Earths.

Another strange object made a temporary appearance in the desert one year. The tracks leading to Merzouga and the great dunes were often obliterated by sandstorms, but after many years of driving them the thought of getting lost never occurred to me. One year, however, I saw in the distance a giant pyramid – more Mayan than Egyptian – which I had never noticed before. Obviously I was lost. Inevitably the group began quizzing me as to its origin. 'I don't know; it wasn't here last year,' seemed an inadequate answer. As we drew nearer we saw that it was surrounded by giant white and/or transparent balloons like huge bubbles, and that it was further festooned by a dozen or more scantily clad young women, the very ones we had noticed in the hotel swimming pool the previous evening. (We had noticed them only because there were no males in attendance.) To my relief the structure was not 2,000 years old. It had been there only two weeks. And it was not stone: it was wooden and mostly two-dimensional, propped up at the rear by struts. I hadn't taken a wrong turn. I had stumbled on the filming of a French TV commercial for washing machines.

5. *The Western Palearctic's ultimate birds and history*

Egypt is another favourite destination. I've been leading birds and history tours there for more than 20 years now. In any other country that would have ensured the evolution of a standard itinerary, perfected over the years. But the details for Egypt have to be reconsidered and revised for every tour. The reasons for this are manifold. Where once a single hotel along a remote stretch of Red Sea coast used to offer the only opportunity for migrants to rest and refuel, there are now miles of continuous development and consequently no concentration of birds in just one garden oasis. At Hurghada there used to be a couple of hotels. Now there are 164. Similarly, 30 years ago Sharm el Sheikh was a remote fishing village: there are now five million visitors a year and 190 hotels – and still counting. Muddy estuaries have been 'improved' by concrete revetments. Traditional sewage farms have become polluted oil dumps and have been replaced by less bird-friendly modern structures. Marshes have been drained. Wasteland has been fenced off. But most of all, ever-changing security measures deny access to an increasing number of desert roads and out-of-the-way locations, and impose convoy travel even on the tourist routes. This was occasioned by the terrorist actions of a fundamentalist Muslim minority anxious to destroy Egypt's lucrative tourist trade. In particular, after the 'incident' at Luxor in 1997 a considerable percentage of the male population was recruited as armed tourist police – a bold and most commendable move by the authorities and very effective in protecting the average tourist visiting the usual tourist sites (which, however, do not include sewage farms and remote wadis).

Even before the Luxor massacre, our group often seemed to be the only tourists in the country, including at such star attractions as the Valley of the Kings and Abu Simbel temples. Yet only once during all our annual visits had terrorists even tried to bomb us. At the end of the 1993 tour we had seen all the target species except Greater Painted-snipe. So, having heard that one had been seen at El Fayoum oasis, we opted to visit the area on our last day. What we did not know was that on that day the CIA were extraditing from Cairo a suspect wanted in connection with the (first) bombing of the World Trade Centre, a

follower of a blind ayatollah from El Fayoum. His sympathizers were seeking a reciprocal gesture. En route a rather smart black Mercedes tried to force our coach off the road. Only our driver, co-leader Sherif Baha El Din, and I noticed the guns pointing at us. The group, not realizing the significance of the apparent contest, merely commented on the foolishness of 'those young tearaways'.

Our driver skilfully out-manoeuvred the Mercedes (we heard later that the occupants had bombed a coach-load of German tourists instead), but when we reached the El Fayoum turn-off the authorities insisted on providing us with an armed

Amongst the many highlights on the 1993 birds and history tour were (from top to bottom): Long-tailed Cormorant, Greater Painted-snipe, Buff-bellied Pipit (which was a first for Egypt) and Three-banded Plover (another first).

escort. Eventually, however, even under their protection they would not allow us to proceed further, stopping a kilometre short of the ayatollah's village (which by a frustrating coincidence was the stake-out for our Greater Painted-snipe). Discussing the health and safety implications with our guards I noticed that amongst the Little Stints alongside us in a roadside pool was a Temminck's – a lifer for the Americans in our group. As I focused the Questar on it I also noticed a Buff-bellied Pipit. 'That's a first for Egypt,' announced Sherif. It seemed that this arbitrary spot was not such a non-birding location after all. We walked across the field to a phragmites-fringed ditch and flushed a Greater Painted-snipe. At the airport we were interviewed by a reporter from the *Daily Telegraph*. An article appeared under the heading 'British birdwatchers unfazed'.

Protective measures peaked on our April 2009 trip. On our first day in the delta – despite the fact that there had never been any terrorist action in the vicinity of Abessa fish farm – the authorities insisted on providing us with a personal escort of no less than 21 armed guards: one inside our coach, two motorcycle outriders, an officer and six men in each of the two escort vehicles fore and aft, and four fellows in a fire engine in case we burst into flames. Rather over the top, we thought, though our convoy did ensure the seemingly impenetrable streets crowded with vehicles and pedestrians parted like the Red Sea in front of Moses, and we did have sustained and uninterrupted views of Greater Painted-snipe in the open, plus a profusion of White-throated Kingfishers, Senegal Thick-knees, Spotted Crake, Glossy Ibis, and Marsh Sandpipers. Similarly, at the end of our grand tour our excursion one or two kilometres into the desert beyond the Abu Simbel checkpoint necessitated two armed guards and two weeks of prior pleading – but we did see Spotted and Crowned Sandgrouse. These precautions seemed particularly curious in view of the fact that the usual armed convoys along the Nile Valley and across the eastern desert were replaced this year by pieces of paper festooned with official stamps. (Presumably in the event of a terrorist attack these were to be waved at any would-be aggressor to establish that we were exempt from harm. Shades of Lady Addle*) However, not only did they work, but they also enabled us to negotiate the back streets of Kom Ombo to the camel market (which added the delightful little Namaqua Dove to our cumulative list), and to explore further than ever before down to the administrative border with the Sudan at Shalatein.

Not that the changes to the itinerary were always down to security or disappearing habitat. On the 2008 tour a telephone call from our agent as we were approaching Sharm el Sheik informed us that the scheduled catamaran ferry to Hurghada was cancelled. Retracing our steps for 500km across Sinai and then driving a further 500km along the Red Sea coast was not an appealing option. Nor was a sleepless period including late-night and early-morning flights via Cairo. So Sunbird chartered a luxury 35m boat to transport the group in comfort from Asia back to Africa. This seemed a little extravagant at US$3,500, but when I saw the boat I wondered how we managed to charter it for so little. A huge ocean-going vessel with a crew of 18 (our group numbered only ten clients), it towered above us at the quayside, deck upon deck. The top deck even had an open-air jacuzzi. It was an excellent vantage point for viewing White-cheeked and Lesser Crested Terns (see Plate 6, page 118).

When I first started leading tours to Egypt the trip was run back-to-

---

* From *The Memoirs of Mipsie*, the fourth volume of the reminiscences of the Lady Addle of Eigg edited by Mary Dunn: 'Mipsie faced the angry crowd, holding in her hand an empty envelope. 'I have here' she said in clarion tones 'a letter to our foreign secretary Sir Edward Grey. Beside me' she pointed with a firm hand 'is a pillar box. Unless you go quietly to your homes I shall post this letter and in less than two months the entire British Army will come to my aid, and you and your wives and children will be annihilated'.

The Moon Valley Mountains above Eilat in Israel provided
Hooded Wheatears and spectacular raptor migration.

back with an Israel tour. When one tour finished I used to take a bus across the Sinai from one country to the other. This essentially Egyptian territory was occupied by Israel from 1967 to 1982, and on this flimsy pretext all Sinai bird records are cheekily included in Hadoram Shirahai's *Birds of Israel,* a fact that still rankles with Egyptian ornithologists. After the Battle of Sinai in 1973 (one of the longest tank battles in history), Israel began a gradual withdrawal from the area and eventually restored the whole of the Sinai to Egyptian control by April 1982. But relations between the two countries remained tense – and not only because of the disputed bird records. The situation was a tad more serious than Suffolk claiming the Norfolk sightings along the south side of the River Yare. It was a little disconcerting, therefore, when on my first evening in Egypt (checking wheatears on an escarpment on the outskirts of Cairo) I became aware that I had wandered into a military zone and was being encircled by soldiers from the adjacent camp. The military mind all over the world is suspicious of strangers with binoculars. What's more my pockets were still full of Israeli currency. I wondered what secret installations had been out of focus beyond the wheatears, and what was the penalty for being an Israeli spy. Even being taken away for interrogation would disrupt plans to meet the incoming group. So I played the show-them-the-field-guide card (see plate 16, page 248). Happily, it worked.

I have employed this technique in many countries when being questioned by men in uniforms. Firstly, it is essential not to understand a word. Even if you know the Spanish for 'You are in a restricted area. You must come with me,' the correct English response is 'Really? Where did you see it?' This must be accompanied by much delighted smiling and enthusiastic pointing to an appropriate bird in the field guide. Bonhomie is essential. After several minutes of this there are only two scenarios, it seems. Either the man in charge will become so frustrated that he will wave you on your way, or he will excitedly take the field guide and begin pointing to species he has seen. A frequent happy development is the joint enjoyment of a distant species frame-filling the scope view. On one occasion it seemed that a whole regiment stood in line to share its officer's enthusiastic response. Birding can be bonding.

Sometimes the bond already exists. On one occasion in Israel David Fisher was leading a group up a gully at En Gedi, which was at that time the only known stake-out for Hume's Owl. Suddenly night became day when powerful searchlights were shone on the group and a military voice demanded to know their intentions. 'Birdwatching,' said David. His answer was relayed to the officer in charge, who presumably spoke no English. 'Birdwatching at night?' 'Yes, owls,' replied David, who was then taken aback when the next question came from the officer: '*Strix aluco?*' 'No, *Strix butleri*,' explained David. At this the officer – apparently a birder – emerged from the darkness and asked if he could join the group.

On another occasion in Israel David and I were driving two minibuses and leap-frogging each other as we made a series of roadside stops en route for Eilat and lunch. Distracted by yet more raptor watching, I suddenly realized that David's minibus was out of sight, so I accelerated until it came into view. I was surprised when it turned off the main road. I couldn't think of a restaurant that way. The minibus was then admitted through some large gates, and as they began to close I hurried to follow. At once alarms sounded and soldiers with cocked guns converged on us from all directions. The penny dropped. I was following the wrong minibus. This was a military base.

Accessing Masada to view Tristram's Starlings, Fan-tailed Ravens, and assorted vultures is not as difficult for the modern tourist as it was for the Romans, but entering 20th-century Israeli military encampments proved more problematical.

I guess I have been lucky not to have been incarcerated over the years. In 1970 I was holidaying with Betty in Montenegro. I decided to take a day off to look for Pygmy Cormorants in Albania. I caught the overnight bus to Titograd and asked the driver to drop me off halfway along the causeway crossing Lake Scutari. (I had been told it was necessary to find a boatman and ask to be rowed across the border to a breeding colony.) First light revealed that the causeway consisted of a road and a railway, with nothing except water stretching out on either side (see photo on

Plate 1, page 113). But as the early-morning mist lifted a magnificent backdrop of mountains was revealed. When trucks were thundering by it was necessary to walk along the rails. When a train came along the road was the safer bet. When trucks and train coincided it was more sensible to negotiate the slope of the stone embankment. The old steam engines were delightfully quaint, with their insides on the outside, so when one approached at walking pace I took the opportunity of photographing it. I was amazed when an armed guard jumped down and demanded I hand over the film. It never occurred to me to consider the possibility of a rocket base or military installation in the background. But after I returned home I was glad that a Pygmy Cormorant had flown over me before I had found a boatman to row me into Albania. A party of plane spotters was imprisoned in Albania for spying.

Binoculars are not always bonding. And certainly (to return to Egypt) not as bonding as the photograph (see Plate 6, page 118) would suggest. This shot of me with a bellydancer (wearing little else but netting) on a Nile boat was sent to the Sunbird office by an American client. I can't quite remember the circumstances, but I think I was discussing with her the finer points of primary projections in *Acrocephalus* warblers and tertial edgings in juvenile waders. The picture was sneaked into a company newsletter for a caption competition and provoked a very healthy response. Needless to say, there were numerous variations on 'a bird in the hand' theme, as well as more than a few references to a certain member of the gannet family found in those parts ('If you come to the Red Sea with me I could show you a couple of Brown Boobies.' 'It's OK: I can see them quite well from here.' What on earth does that mean?) But the ones that caused the most office mirth were:

'It's OK everyone! I've found a pulse'

'Yes, I know I usually say start at the head of the bird!'

'Bearded Vulture takes Blue-banded Belly-bird'

'Is that a Questar in your pocket or are you just pleased to see me?'
'I love *Parus* in the springtime'

There were also some allusions to various ringing practices, of which the winner (receiving a copy of the new large-format *Collins Bird Guide*) was 'Excuse me, Madam, can I have my mist net back?'

Egypt really is the ideal country for a birds and history tour and has provided us with many happy moments. These extracts from tour reports highlight a few.

> 23 March–7 April 2002
> On the Egypt birds and history tour these two interests are always directly intertwined (this year, Palestine Sunbird, Blackstart, Yellow-vented Bulbul, and Bonelli's Eagle at the Nun's Monastery; Sinai Rosefinch, Tristram's Starling, and Chukar Partridge at St Catherine's; Trumpeter Finch at Amen Khopshef's tomb in the Valley of the Queens; 200 White Storks from Philae temple). But never before has the Barn Owl at the Karnak sound and light show appeared so exactly on cue – as the commentary intoned 'and a winged shape, perhaps the soul, left the body…'

Would that the other owls (Pharaoh Eagle and Hume's) had performed so theatrically at their appointed hours. Unprompted, the other specialities timed their appearances to perfection – from the Greater Painted-snipe on the first day (plus the other Delta target birds: Senegal Coucal, Senegal Thick-knee, and White-throated Kingfisher) to the eleventh-hour Pink-backed Pelican on the last (together with Yellow-billed Stork, African Pied Wagtail, and Kittlitz's Plover). The desert species obliged throughout: Greater Hoopoe Lark, Cream-coloured Courser, Scrub Warbler, and Desert, Isabelline, and Eastern Mourning Wheatears in Wadi Hegul; Sand Partridge and Hooded Wheatear in Wadi Kid; Crowned and Spotted Sandgrouse at the Abu Simbel camel stop. The banks of the Nile yielded African Swamphen, Black-winged Kite, and eight species of heron. The Red Sea added Sooty and White-eyed Gulls, Greater Crested and White-cheeked Terns, Western Reef Egret, Greater Sand Plover, and an impressive passage of raptors, including Steppe, Greater Spotted, and Eastern Imperial Eagles, and Sooty Falcon. And the hotel gardens held an assortment of passage migrants and breeding birds: Rufous-tailed Rock Thrush, Common and Thrush Nightingales, Rüppell's Warbler, Wryneck, Red-throated Pipit, Rufous Scrub Robin, and everyone's favourite bird – the dazzlingly metallic and strikingly long-tailed Nile Valley Sunbird.

Over the years the continual upgrading of the hotels has meant that they have changed from being just somewhere to stay to a sequence of highlight memories in themselves, offering wonderful opportunities not just for convenient birding but also for swimming and relaxing. Sitting on our balconies at the Cataract Hotel, Aswan, gazing out over Elephantine and Kitchener Islands with the sun setting behind the sand dunes of the west bank, as the white-sailed feluccas continuously flushed the Striated Herons and Little Bitterns below, remains an abiding image of the trip to set beside the splendours of ruined temples and still-bright wall paintings, the instant profusion of vividly coloured tropical fish at Ras Mohammed, and the daily variety of exciting birds. Everyone should experience these pleasures at least once in a lifetime. Egypt has so much to offer.

18 March–2 April 2004

So much of Egypt has remained the same for millennia that the rapid changes now taking place every year are difficult to accept. Yet the essential magic is still there. The wonders of the pyramids, the Sphinx, St Catherine's monastery, Karnak and Luxor temples, the tombs in the Valley of the Kings, Edfu, Kom Ombo, Philae, and perhaps above all Abu Simbel cannot fail to arouse a sense of wonder and awe. Similarly, despite all the development and the increasing number of no-go areas, the selection of birds still amazes and delights even the most jaded ornithological palate. Sometimes sheer numbers astound – this year newly sprinkled hotel lawns virtually flowering with Yellow Wagtails, hundreds of White Storks and thousands of Common Cranes spiralling into a blue infinity, or even an unprecedented 43 Trumpeter Finches in the seemingly parched and lifeless Valley of the Kings, or no less that 30 White-throated Kingfishers in the one little corner of Africa where this Asian species occurs. Sometimes it is those edge-of-the-range specialities that thrill – this year Senegal Coucal and the first Senegal Thick-knees at Abessa fish farm; Brown Booby, Greater Crested Tern, and White-eyed and Sooty Gulls on the Red Sea; Chukar Partridge, Sinai Rosefinch, and Tristram's Starling at St Catherine's.

Sinai Rosefinches frequent the hills around St Catherine's monastery.

In addition, the hotel grounds held a succession of migrants: Bluethroats, Masked and Woodchat Shrikes, Rufous-tailed and Blue Rock Thrushes, and a variety of warblers (Eastern Olivaceous, Rüppell's, Subalpine, Sardinian); the deserts yielded Spotted and Crowned Sandgrouse, Isabelline and Desert Wheatears, and Desert and Greater Hoopoe Larks; Blackstarts and Yellow-vented Bulbuls showed well in Wadi Feran and Citrine Wagtail and Bimaculated Larks at Sharm el Sheikh; and a succession of raptors showed briefly but clearly – Black-winged and Yellow-billed Kites, Egyptian Vulture, Short-toed Eagle, Pallid Harrier, Levant Sparrowhawk, and several *Aquila* eagles. Other cameos linger in the mind's eye: the Little Owl in the whispering crack of one of the Colossi of Memnon, a Western Reef Egret dancing amongst the mangroves at the very tip of the Sinai Peninsula, a glittering galaxy of iridescent male Nile Valley Sunbirds amongst the red blossoms, an African Swamphen picking its way through the Water Hyacinths, a Striated Heron alongside our felucca, and an assortment of waders from Marsh Sandpiper to Temminck's Stint. But most of all, surely, was our last-day grand climax of a private boat trip on Lake Nasser – such a struggle to arrange with the authorities in these days of increased security, but rewarding enough to justify all the effort – with six pairs of African Pied

Wagtails (some flying around and landing on our boat), more Senegal Thick-knees, Great White Pelicans, Eurasian Spoonbills, Blue-cheeked Bee-eater, White-winged Terns, Egyptian Geese, a new island breeding location for Kittlitz's Plover (with superb views and even half an eggshell to prove it), and finally the last bird of the trip – a majestic Yellow-billed Stork in the very location that in the past had given us (in rationed sequence) Egyptian Nightjar, Greater Painted-snipe, White-tailed Lapwing, Pink-backed Pelican, African Skimmer, and Rufous Scrub Robin (see Plate 6, page 118).

4–19 April 2008

After resting this popular once-annual tour to ensure a smooth-running holiday adapted to the many changes in the country, the 2008 relaunch was as successful, happy, and hassle-free as any trip to date.

Beginning with Sakkara (the oldest pyramid and the exquisite carvings in the mastabas of Mereruka and Ti), El Fayoum oasis (our only Marsh Sandpiper and our first Little Bitterns), the Egyptian Museum, and the Delta (15 Greater Painted-snipe, 20 White-throated Kingfishers, Kittlitz's Plover, Streaked Weaver, Senegal Thick-knee, Blue-cheeked Bee-eater, and Woodchat Shrike), we crossed the eastern desert to Suez, encountering a remarkable number of desert specialities – Greater Hoopoe, Desert, and Lesser Short-toed Larks, and not only Eastern Mourning, Isabelline, Hooded, and Eastern Black-eared Wheatears, but also a Cyprus on passage. The missing target bird (Cream-coloured Courser) appeared unexpectedly alongside our coach the following morning en route to St Paul's monastery, where (despite a praying and fasting day that denied us the monastery itself) several migrants awaited us at the entrance – Thrush Nightingale, Marsh Warbler, Eastern Bonelli's Warbler, Wryneck – plus an all-too-brief pair of Sand Partridges. St Catherine's monastery the following day was even more productive, with Sinai Rosefinch, Tristram's Starling, Scrub Warbler, and a concentration of migrants in the gardens – Ortolan Bunting, Common Redstart, and Collared, Semicollared, and Pied Flycatchers. Nearby Wadi Feran yielded the rest of the Sinai set – Palestine Sunbird, Blackstart, and Yellow-vented Bulbul – plus our first Masked Shrike. Deeper into the spectacular Sinai wilderness, Wadi Kid produced a second Blackstart (wing and tail flicking like a nervous Wallcreeper), a Persian Wheatear, and our only Common Cuckoo – though equally fascinating were a Nubian Ibex and a large green-and-blue agama lizard. The mangoes then gave us our first Western Reef Egrets (both light and dark morphs) and White-eyed and Sooty Gulls. But for some the most remarkable image from the southern tip of the Sinai was the instant kaleidoscope of tropical fish as we snorkelled from the beach at Ras Mohammed.

More snorkelling (and Red Sea endemics) came the next day at Hurghada with a relaxing time on our private boat (not quite as big as our charter from Sharm, but impressive nevertheless). Also impressive was the raptor passage at El Gouna – 10,000 Steppe Buzzards in one hour plus Eastern Imperial, Steppe, Booted, Greater Spotted, Tawny, and Short-toed Eagles, Black Stork, and Egyptian Vulture.

After our convoy back across the eastern desert to the lush pastures of the Nile, it was wonderful to spend two nights on Crocodile Island at Luxor surrounded by Nile Valley Sunbirds, African Swamphens, and Red Avadavats, and to enjoy more classic Egyptian history with visits to Karnak temple (by night and day),

Red Sea endemics: White-eyed and Sooty Gulls.

Luxor temple, the Valley of the Kings, the Valley of the Queens (with close views of Trumpeter Finches), the mortuary temple of Ramses III, and the Colossi of Memnon. More birds and history followed with whistle-stop visits to the temples of Edfu and Kom Ombo – a route lined with Black-winged Kites and European Bee-eaters. Then another wonderfully relaxing afternoon on yet another private boat cruising around the islands and the first cataract at Aswan. We saw no less than eight species of heron (a Striated on a nest with young just metres from our cameras was particularly appealing – especially as these are the only ones in the Western Palearctic and *BWP* observes 'local breeding along the Nile highly probable though nests not found'), plus a pair of Ferruginous Ducks and even-better views of Nile Valley Sunbird, Senegal Thick-knee, and Pied Kingfishers. Our private-boat tradition continued the next day with a visit to Agilika island to view Philae temple (White-winged and Whiskered Terns en route). This was followed by a welcome break at Tut Amun village abandoned hotel for mid-morning drinks and casual birding before yet another convoy drive took us almost to the Sudan border at Abu Simbel and another sound-and-light spectacular at the awesome temples.

Here we scored our greatest victory – in receiving permission to charter a private boat on Lake Nasser (the first time any tourists have been granted this privilege since we were on our last trip), ensuring that this furthest point in our Egyptian odyssey provided us with an appropriately grand finale. On a day that began with Crowned and Spotted Sandgrouse and finished with Egyptian Nightjar we had amazing views of the sub-Saharan specialities for which this corner of the Western Palaearctic is famous – African Pied Wagtail, Yellow-billed Stork, and Pink-backed Pelican (only five records elsewhere in the Western Palearctic) – with a supporting cast of Great White Pelican, Greater Flamingo, Eurasian Spoonbill, Glossy Ibis, Egyptian Goose, a curious Egyptian Goose x Common Shelduck hybrid, and most excitingly two Nile Crocodiles. All this and the temples by daylight.

Our flight back to Cairo was in time for us to lunch at the traditional Egyptian restaurant in Khan el-Khalili (a fascinating maze of retail therapy opportunities) and another afternoon with our charming and lucid history guide at the Great Pyramids, the Sphinx, and the Solar Boat. Yet even after this our final half day was no anticlimax as our hotel grounds provided new birds (Rufous Scrub Robin, Common Nightingale, and Common Whitethroat) and our stroll around the Gezira Sports Club grounds gave us not only Ring-necked but also Alexandrine Parakeet, the latest eastern species to establish a feral breeding population in the Western Palearctic, leaving time for our sixth and final boat experience – lunch on the Nile.

17 March–1 April 2009

New this year was an extension down to the administrative border with the Sudan. On the first of these days we saw two

Two black-and-white attractions at the two Abu Simbel temples: White-crowned Wheatear (above) ...

species from the vagrants section of the *Collins Bird Guide* (Greater Crested Tern and African Collared Dove). On the second we enjoyed best-ever views of Lappet-faced Vulture and Hume's Owl – plus Cretzschmar's Bunting, Siberian Stonechat, and Masked and Isabelline Shrikes in the hotel gardens.

It must be said that the authorities everywhere were as helpful and obliging as their bureaucracy would permit and, thanks to the efficiency and hard work of Abdullah and the rest of our excellent ground agent's team, we did manage to travel everywhere we wanted with a minimum of hassle and inconvenience. We were even given permission for a boat trip on Lake Nasser that gave us close views of African Pied Wagtail, Senegal Thick-knee, and Egyptian Goose, plus Great White Pelicans and Yellow-billed and White Storks, and Blue-cheeked Bee-eaters and Kittlitz's Plovers from the shore.

The birds too were, in general, obliging and courteous – with a meet-and-greet and goodbye-have-a-nice-day policy that was very noticeable at Zaafarana, where Cream-coloured Courser, Woodchat Shrike, Eurasian Hoopoe, Eastern Black-eared and Isabelline Wheatears, and

... and African Pied Wagtail (below).

THE PROFIT IN PICTURES (PART I)

I realize that some readers will consider many of these images to be 'too small'. But I have deliberately opted for a lively kaleidoscope of colour with as many visual references as possible. The text remains the most important element. The 300-plus photographs are here merely to illustrate various points in the narrative and to arouse interest. I grow weary of coffee-table books with overblown images. I have also limited the number of bird portraits (they abound in so many journals these days), and chosen instead a predominately people-and-places selection so that the reader can experience some armchair travelling. Most of the images are mine but I am indebted for the good ones to Sunbird co-leaders Patty Briggs, Dan Brown, Stuart Elsom, Martin Hrouzek, and James Lidster, and Sunbird/Wings clients and friends Bruce Bennett, Bill and Charlotte Byers, Phil and Ann Farrer, Steve Gantlett, John and Christine Hamilton, Barrie Hanson, Terry Lee, Jan Morgan, Richard Porter, Laurens Steijn, and Phil Yates (full credits appear on page 4). Thank you for sharing your images as well as so many happy memories.

Plate 1 (page 113): *Birding around the world: the surgical stocking years (in the Golan heights, Israel, and on the road to Timbuktu; at the Kaieteur Falls, Guyana (two views); Sanetti plateau, Ethiopia; Martial glacier, Argentina; Antarctica (two views); Shennong stream, China; Palenque, Mexico; Crater Lake, Oregon, USA; Abu Simbel, Egypt; Gough Island, South Atlantic; Lake Scutari, Yugoslavia/Albania; Atlantic rollers in Morocco; Tahiti; Moorea, French Polynesia; and the dunes on the Libya/Tunisia/Algeria border.*

Plate 2 (page 114): *Leh, capital of Ladakh: the roof of the world, reached by the highest roads in the world including the Zojila pass (see page 39); Mount Everest; Ladakh headgear; the author disguised as a local in Bhutan (by wearing the distinctive short socks); Bhutanese village life; cedarwood houseboat in Kashmir.*

Plate 3 (page 115): *The Thar Desert on the India/Pakistan border: a Sunbird group aboard camel carts searching for Indian Bustard and Stoliczka's Bushchat; a taxi rank at Sam sand dunes; Sunbird clients taking advantage of a ride; and the sunset dance session there. (Rajasthan is the leading state for music and dancing. It seems only polite to join in.)*

Plate 4 (page 116): *Some of the birds of India: Chestnut-bellied Sandgrouse, Changeable Hawk-eagle, Indian Grey Hornbill, House Crow making an emergency landing on a White-rumped Vulture, Eastern Imperial Eagle, Crested Honey-buzzard, Indian Bustard, Demoiselle Crane, Crested Serpent-eagle, Black-rumped Flameback, more Demoiselle Cranes, White-throated Kingfisher, Sykes's Nightjar, Large-tailed Nightjar, White-naped Tit, Yellow-footed Green Pigeons, Indian Courser, Great Thick-knee, Crab-plover, Coppersmith Barbet, Black-necked Stork, Sarus Crane (the male is demonstrating to his mate the size of the eel that got away but she's heard it all before), Hypocolius, Painted Stork, and Collared Scops Owl.*

(continued on page 121)

PLATE I

PLATE 2

PLATE 3

PLATE 4

PLATE 5

PLATE 6

PLATE 7

PLATE 8

(continued from page 112)

Plate 5 (page 117): *Despite its proximity to Europe, Morocco remains one of the most 'foreign' countries imaginable – which is why it has provided so many diverse film locations. Moussier's Redstart is surely one of the most attractive regional endemics in the world. Even out in the desert this Bedouin family has spotted a nice little earner. The Mayan pyramid that wasn't there last time (see page 94). Betty mule-trekking in the Atlas mountains 30 years ago. Sunbird groups at the Oued Massa and in Paradise Valley near Agadir. The fortified hilltop villages of the Illalen at Tioulit. On the pelagic it is always a challenge to pick out Scopoli's Shearwaters amongst the hundreds of Cory's. Other species featured are Greater Hoopoe Lark, Tristram's Warbler, Franklin's Gull (see page 85), Red-rumped Wheatear, Scrub Warbler, Cream-coloured Courser, and Northern Bald Ibis.*

Plate 6 (page 118): *A bonus on Sunbird's post-revolution Egypt tour in 2011 was the absence of tourists. Sunbird groups aboard our private charter to cross from Asia to Africa (see page 98), at the two Abu Simbel temples, looking at sandgrouse near the Sudan border, disembarking on 'Sunbird island' (Lake Nasser), and birding in the Sinai. The original Burning Bush at St Catherine's monastery (note the fire extinguisher). And some birds: Yellow-billed Stork and Nile Crocodile, Lappet-faced Vulture at Shalatein, the Western Palearctic's first African Mourning Dove, Pink-backed Pelican, African Pied Wagtail, Greater Painted-snipe, and the unprepossessing but equally rare (in Egypt) Pale Rock Sparrow. For details of the erudite ornithological discussion under way bottom left see page 102.*

Plate 7 (page 119): *The warm glow of the Haydn Festival in Austria: world-famous conductor Adam Fischer at a concert in the Haydnsaal, rehearsing with the Austro-Hungarian Haydn Philharmonic, and exchanging baton for wooden spoon to cook our goulash; and Prince Anton Esterházy welcoming our group, presenting the phiton award (see page 154), and sitting with the group in the Empiresaal of Eisenstadt Palace, venue for chamber music – as opposed to the highly-painted Haydnsaal (main picture) and (below) the Leopoldinen temple and the music room of the summer palace at Esterhaza. Also shown is yet another TV interview, a client meeting her most favourite tenor in the world (Thomas Quasthof), Betty on her very last tour, conductor Richard Hickox, and vice-mayor (now mayor) Andrea Fraunscheil presenting the Joseph Haydn silver medal. Main courses in Austria tend to be substantial – and so are the desserts. The typical statue on the Road of Remembrance at Andau is a poignant reminder of Iron Curtain days. Target birds are White Stork and Great Bustard. The terrain around Lake Neusiedl is much beloved by cyclists, but the landscape looking from the Hohe Wand to Schneeberg and from Schneeberg (from the Emperor's bedroom) to the Hohe Wand demands more than pedal power – and there have been occasions when the Schneeberg has lived up to its name and surprised us with the depth of snow.*

Plate 8 (page 120): *The Czech Republic birds and music tours are a delight for the eye and the ear: attractive architecture in fairytale Cesky Krumlov, Prague, and Telc (typical shield houses), and even our hotels, ranging from the rustic Arnika in the Sumava mountains, with its convenient birding balconies, to the elegant Hranicni Zamacek in Moravia, a 200-year-old border castle surrounded by Golden Orioles and Common Nightingales. Pruhonice park on the outskirts of Prague is another excellent location for pre-breakfast birding. The Ride of the King Festival offers many cymbalo groups in the streets of Vlcnov, in contrast to Prague's three sumptuous opera houses. Also pictured are Vlastimil and Vera Leysek, our front-row view of A Night with Mozart at the Villa Bertramka, our private cymbalo trio in the wine cellars, our private recital by the Janácek Quartet in the very room where Janácek composed his distinctive music, the opening concert of the 2011 Concentus Moravia festival, and the Pipers of Trebon.*

Greater Short-toed Larks were all gathered right outside the reception of our hotel, and Egyptian Vulture and Sand Partridge welcomed us to St Paul's monastery down the road. Similarly Scrub Warbler, Desert Lark, and Tristram's Starling awaited us at St Catherine's; Yellow-vented Bulbul and the spectacular violet, blue, and green Palestine Sunbird at Wadi Feran; Nile Valley Sunbird and Black-winged Kite on Crocodile Island; African Swamphen and seven species of heron at Aswan; Eastern Mourning and White-crowned Wheatears, Blue Rock Thrush, Red-rumped Swallow, and Trumpeter Finch in a magic wadi en route to Suez; and White-eyed and Sooty Gulls on the Red Sea islands.

And notwithstanding this wealth of special birds, as on previous tours we experienced even more of Egypt's history than the average tourist.

Sooty Falcons in the Sinai.

After so many years of combining the birds and history of Egypt, a plan was eventually formed to alternate this with a birds and history tour of the neighbouring Great Socialist People's Libyan Arab Jamahiriya. This was launched in 2006 to coincide with a total eclipse of the sun (which we watched beyond Jalo oasis in the Great Sand Sea, in the company of Bill Clinton, Oprah Winfrey, and two of Colonel Gaddafi's sons – identified by our escort when they overtook us en route in the only Hummer in the country).

The history far exceeded our expectations, beginning with the extensive Roman and Greek ruins at Leptis Magna and Cyrene (the dividing line between the western – Latin – part of the Roman Empire and the eastern – Greek – part was halfway between these two cities), plus Ptolemais, Apollonia, Sabratha, Castle Libya, and the Temple of Zeus. There were also the ancient fortified granaries of the Jabal Nefusa resembling something out of a *Star Wars* film (probably because this was indeed one of the actual locations), the mosque of Abdullah bin Abi Alsarah in Awjilah (one of the very first mosques in North Africa), and the fascinating border town of Ghadamis on the old Saharan trade route to Taoudenni and Timbuktu. Incidentally, we took four-wheel-drive vehicles into the desert from here to a point where the sand-dunes of Libya, Tunisia, and Algeria converged (see Plate 1, page 113) – as remote a spot as possible, yet even here I was greeted by the inevitable 'Hello Bryan' from two ladies who had attended one of my residential courses in Norfolk. Is there nowhere I can misbehave?

The birds, however, were neither as numerous nor as obliging as those in Egypt to the east or Morocco to the west. In this instance the middle was not the best. And our US clients were not too keen on sending many holiday postcards bearing the 'American Aggression' stamps still on sale (see plate 15, page 247). Five years later the accusation seemed ironic in the light of Gaddafi's airforce and tanks bombarding his own people.

Even in 2006 we were surprised at the number of Libyans who openly expressed their hatred of their leader and his corrupt clique (despite the very real possibility of annihilation if overheard) and asked us why we couldn't do for them what we had done for Iraq. We noted whole hillsides napalmed into charred wastelands because they had been sheltering pockets of resistance. Everywhere there were huge posters of Gaddafi gazing heavenwards, often with a giant falcon peering over his shoulder (see Plate 15 again). Was he a closet birder? And, as Libya has no pantomime tradition, was there no one to shout 'It's behind you'? We assumed the falcon represented Horus and recalled the famous statue of the Egyptian pharaoh Khafre. Here, The Leader of the Revolution, God's Caliph, The Thinker, The Challenger, was also The Lone Hawk. The Colonel obviously saw himself as a god. This view was not shared by all his people, as subsequent events proved.

So I was happy that 2011 saw me still visiting post-revolution Egypt rather than strife-torn Libya – especially as Sunbird serendipity ensured that, even in the aftermath of the revolution there, we were always in the right place at the right time. If we had planned our visit to the Egyptian Museum in Cairo the previous weekend, for instance, we would have been thwarted by the fact that people were still being shot dead in the square. As it was, only one man tried to kill me – and that was nothing to do with the revolution. At Shalatein (formally part of the Sudan) I spotted a Lappet-faced Vulture sitting out in the desert and immediately set up my telescope. Suddenly there was a great roaring and bellowing behind me and I turned to see a white-robed figure with purple face and protruding eyes bursting out of his cardboard and corrugated iron hut and rushing towards me with a mighty weapon raised high above his head. It was like a close-up from some movie and as the gap between us narrowed, I tried to recall whether it was *Beau Geste,* or *The Four Feathers,* or *Lawrence of Arabia,* or *Khartoum.* Happily our two drivers and the mad Mahdi's three sons managed to grapple him to a standstill before my skull was split. Apparently he thought I was spying on the ladies of Shalatein at their ablutions. I didn't think our escort appeased his fury by explaining that we did not want to look at his women as we thought his women were ugly.

The most amazing aspect of visiting Egypt after a major incident was, yet again, the absence of tourists. The Valley of the Kings usually welcomes 10,000 visitors a day. In 2011 we arrived to find the car park completely empty. We were the only tourists there. Similarly we were the only guests at our Abu Simbel hotel.

Our history guides have always been both charming and erudite – with one exception. 'Henry' was the most egotistical and arrogant control freak imaginable. On our first day, whilst he was pontificating on the building of Egypt's first pyramid – the stepped pyramid at Sakkara – I spotted a Pharaoh Eagle Owl perched amongst the stones and courteously waited for him to finish before I invited the group to look at it in the telescope. Henry was furious that we were excited at something to which he had not drawn our attention, and on subsequent days any interest we showed in a bird was taken as a personal affront. Despite his shaky grasp of history and physics (he claimed that the library at Alexandria was destroyed by the Christians, not the caliph Omar, and assured us that a razor blade stored within a pyramid-shaped box would never lose its sharp edge), he constantly claimed to be 'the best guide in the country, as used by Abercrombie and Kent and Page and Moy'. My team that year also included Mindy Baha el Din and Ahmed Rhiad, a young Egyptian ornithologist, but whenever a participant addressed a question to either of them Henry would immediately interrupt, shouting, 'Silence. I will answer that. I am the only person qualified to answer questions. I am the only person here authorized by the government to be a guide.' Finally, as we arrived at Aswan, I announced to the group that there were three options: visiting the Nubian Museum with Henry, shopping in the market with Mindy, or birding with me in the gardens of the Old Cataract Hotel where Agatha Christie wrote *Murder on the Nile*. Henry was outraged. 'Nobody has discussed these options with me,' he proclaimed. 'Only I can tell you what to do. I am the boss here.' I pointed out that in fact I was the boss and that he was merely one of my team. He was indignant and waved his guide ID card in the air, screaming that he was the only person with any authority. 'What's more,' he added, 'the likes of you will not be allowed in the gardens of the Old Cataract Hotel; that is only for better-class tourists.' The time had come for a dénouement. I told him I could prove who was the boss. He was fired. He had to leave us immediately and go to the airport to arrange his flight back to Cairo. We did not want to see him again. I then led the birding party into the gardens of the Old Cataract Hotel, where I was welcomed by the guards who knew me well from previous years. A chambermaid gathering flowers asked if we would like to look inside the hotel. Once inside we were asked if we would like to see the VIP floor. We were then invited into the President's suite. At that point there was a telephone call for me. It was Henry phoning from the airport to confirm he was booked on the next flight to Cairo. He had phoned the Old Cataract Hotel not really expecting us to have received permission to enter the grounds and had been told that Mr Bland and party were in the President's suite. The likes of me found that very satisfying.

6. *Great Bustards, greater music, greatest diva*

When I first mooted the idea of a holiday combining birds and music I was vaguely thinking of Salzburg, but by a happy coincidence the Haydn Festival at Eisenstadt had just been launched. Eastern Austria has been a favourite Sunbird destination since 1979 and I already knew the area from leading tours to Lake Neusiedl. The festival was the brainchild of world-famous conductor Adam Fischer, entrepreneur Rudi Morovitch, and culture-tour king Robert Avery – all of whom quickly became good friends – and by combining with Robert's Habsburg Heritage groups we have been able to enjoy many extra musical offerings. Moreover Eisenstadt was known to be 'tranquil, uncrowded, the sensible music lover's alternative to Salzburg: a gracious place to hear music without the snobbery or the inflated prices'. And so it has proved every year for 20 years: the friendliest of festivals. As I wrote in an article for the *Haydn Society Journal* in 2000:

Arriving at the Esterházy Palace at Eisenstadt for the opening concert of the Haydn Festival 2000 was reminiscent of attending a family wedding, with a succession of old friends greeting us happily and enthusiastically: an off-duty Adam Fischer in jeans and denim jacket together with his daughter Golda (now studying at Edinburgh University), Director Walter Reicher and a radiantly pregnant Mrs Reicher (which no doubt accounted for the unexpectedly late presence of a White Stork on a Rust rooftop), Prince Anton Esterházy and his gracious Princess (who always charms our group with her poise and elegance), and in fact a very large percentage of the Austrian audience who have for so many years welcomed 'The Birdwatchers' into their extended family.

A Viennese journalist handed us a copy of her preview of the festival ending with the paragraph 'Since Haydn's stay in London in 1790-92 and 1794-95 he has had a large community of fans there. A group of British birdwatchers travels here annually to watch birds in the morning armed with their binoculars in the reedbeds of Neusiedlersee and then adore their idol Haydn in the evenings. A special kind of festival package!' And after the concert Dr Reicher invited us to a private champagne reception to meet Paul Goodwin, who had so splendidly conducted the Academy of Ancient Music. No wonder that Eisenstadt is a second home.

From the beginning The Birdwatchers have been accepted as an integral part of the festival. An early convert was Nicolai Neu, cellist with the Haydn Quartet of Burgenland. Noticing us sitting there with our binoculars he established why and asked if he could join us on our next visit. Our next visit happened to be the following spring, and although this was a birds-only tour (the festival takes place in September), some of the group had asked if we could include a Haydn concert in the palace. Steve Rooke, co-leading, was not keen on the idea as he predicted that only one or two participants would be interested, leaving him to cope alone with the other 14. As it happened, almost everyone opted for the concert, leaving Steve with a group of one. We decided to attend the next morning's quartet recital. By coincidence, Nicolai rang that evening to remind us of our promise to take him birding (he had obviously made a note in his diary last September), and I mentioned we would be attending his recital. After a productive session of birding in the palace park we arrived with only minutes to spare. 'We will begin by playing Haydn's quartet The Birds,' announced Nicolai. And then '… we now continue our ornithological theme by playing Haydn's quartet The Lark.' 'What a happy coincidence,' I remarked after the concert. 'That wasn't a coincidence,' replied Nicolai. 'That was in your honour.' We then took Nicolai to the Seewinkel pools and focused the telescope on a flock of assorted waders. 'Wow, it's just like a zoo,' was his astonished reaction.

Over the years we have hosted many others on our birding jaunts, not only indigenous musicians but also visiting celebrities such as Trevor Pinnock. Even the director of the festival, Dr Walter Reicher, joined us on a dawn walk in the palace park and was astounded by the selection of woodpeckers, the range of passerines from Hawfinches to Long-tailed Tits, and the spectacular blood-red sunrise. He wrote afterwards: 'The opportunity you gave to me last September to be with you birdwatching was a wonderful experience for me. Since then I look at birds in a different way and I am more aware of them. The Schloss park also has a new quality for me and together with my children we spend hours in it now. I hope I can be again on a pre-breakfast excursion with you next year.'

The following year a television crew accompanied us on our pre-breakfast walk in the park. They were surprisingly courteous and discreet and never once interrupted our birding. When we broke for breakfast the producer politely asked if she could ask me a few questions on camera. Later, as we walked up the main street to the morning concert, the crew were hiding in a doorway to film us. Once we were seated the producer explained that when the musicians entered the crew would not be allowed to intrude – so they asked if they could film us now, pretending to listen to the music. I asked whether they would prefer us to pretend to listen to the Haydn or the Schubert. After a brief discussion they opted for Haydn. I suggested to the group that we fool them and pretend to listen to the Schubert. That evening a masterly mini-documentary entitled *Natur und Kultur* was broadcast on Austrian television after the news. We were attending another concert, of course, but the producer thoughtfully left a videotape for us at the hotel. It is amazing what ten minutes on the telly can do. The next day we were greeted like old friends by the entire population of Eisenstadt, from waiters to curators. Many other interviews with Austrian television and radio have followed. Birdwatching is not a common occupation in Austria and the concept of combining birdwatching and listening to music is even more baffling to them. Interviewers always assume an inextricable link. 'Is it because you appreciate birdsong that you love

The sketch presented to festival director Dr Walter Reicher to commemorate his first birding experience in Eisenstadt Palace Park.

music? Or does your love of music lead you to appreciate birdsong?' Curiously, these regular media moments helped to promote the Haydn Festival within Austria, and maybe this was a factor in prompting the capital of Burgenland to present me with the prestigious Joseph Haydn silver medal in 2002 'in appreciation of his special contribution to the success of Haydn Festival in Eisenstadt'.

In 1993 Dr Reicher forwarded various photocopies from the Haydn archives of letters from Haydn to a Bland family, suggesting it may be worth me looking in the attic for some lost Haydn letters. A published commentary on these states: 'Perhaps the most interesting part of the letter from the biographical standpoint is the mention of the (British) razors, which of course confirms the story of Bland coming upon Haydn while the latter was shaving badly. "I would give my latest quartet for a pair of good razors". Bland promised to supply the razors and Haydn gave him the Razor Quartet (op 55, no 2) as well as the autograph of the Cantata Arianna a Naxos.'

In view of this obsession with shaving, I think it unlikely that this particular James Bland was an ancestor of mine. (In fact my great-grandfather, James Bland, was the captain-owner of a fishing yawl that sank off Great Yarmouth over 100 years ago.) But maybe he was an ancestor of my identical twin brother.

It seems amazing now to reflect that the festival promoted détente before the momentous developments in Eastern Europe that were about to take place in its infancy. Despite the Iron Curtain restrictions then in place, permission was granted for concerts to be held in the Esterházy summer palace at Fertod in Hungary. This was appropriate not only because Haydn spent 30 years as court composer commuting between the two palaces, but also because the principal orchestra especially formed for the festival by conductor Adam Fischer (himself holding dual Austrian and Hungarian nationality) was created from members of both the Vienna Philharmonic and the Hungarian State Orchestra. Strange, too, to recall that when our groups first visited the area our birding along the border was overlooked by machine-gun-wielding guards in high watch-towers, and that the border was mined. Suddenly everything changed. In no time at all not only were visas unnecessary, but also it became possible to pass from Austria into Hungary without even showing a passport.

Eisenstadt changed too. The pedestrianization of the high street was a significant development. Attending the first festival after this was completed it was initially difficult to pinpoint exactly what was so wonderful. Then it dawned. Gone was all the traffic noise. The only sounds were people laughing and Black Redstarts singing. The area in front of the palace was also remodelled, with flower beds instead of vehicles. And then the park was relandscaped to restore it to the English 18th-century style that Haydn knew – a project dear to the heart of Dr Prost, Eisenstadt's general practitioner.

That year when I was arriving in Eisenstadt and parking my minibus near the palace, Dr Prost ran across the road to inform me in excited tones that at last the project was complete and that the group was invited to the opening of the restored Leopoldinen Temple on Thursday. I assumed the couple accompanying him were his parents and subsequently met his father many times that week in our hotel – a most friendly and jovial character always anxious to exchange pleasantries. At the ceremony on Thursday came the announcement that the restored temple was to be opened by the new Prince Esterházy. Up popped Dr Prost's dad (as I had thought). After the ceremony I apologized for my misconception and the fact that all week I had been treating him like one of the lads. 'But I am one of the lads,' he assured me. 'It's just that my ancestors had a little more money than the rest of the lads.' Apparently he had enjoyed having normal conversations as the Austrians were too respectful. A typical example of his gracious bonhomie came a few years later. One participant had been particularly helpful in very efficiently changing a tyre in a situation where a too-many-cooks scenario was rapidly developing. For such service beyond the call of duty I decided to present him with a medal at lunch on our last day. I sketched his portrait on one side of a cardboard disc and his favourite bird, a Great Bustard, on the other. Not having any ribbon I had to use dental floss. At the Haydn Mass on the Sunday morning, however, I spotted Prince Anton in the front pew and asked him whether it was beneath his dignity to present a cardboard medal with a dental-floss ribbon. 'One should never pass up the opportunity for a good laugh,' he replied. So on the steps of the cathedral, with a bewildered Austrian congregation passing respectfully by, the Prince hung the medal around Roy's neck, made an appropriate speech, and shook him warmly by the hand. I'm sure that wouldn't have happened in Salzburg.

Further proof of the friendly face of this intimate festival came with a diva's bouquet. One year an elderly client tripped on the steps leading from a central courtyard in Forchtenstein castle and, although she was a stoical Quaker and eager to dismiss her fall nonchalantly, I was conscious of the possible damage to old bones (particularly those of an octogenarian on steroids) and insisted she should not attempt to get up. Amazingly, I was granted permission to drive our minibus into the heart of the castle, through passageways and up stairs (fortunately not too steep), to a point where we could lift our casualty into the vehicle and drive her directly to Eisenstadt hospital. This proved fortunate as she had indeed broken her leg in two places. She received instant attention and excellent treatment – and a bouquet of flowers taken to her bedside by the celebrated soprano Jennifer Smith, who had just been presented with them on stage after her superb performance in the Haydn opera *Philemon and Baucis*.

Nor is this kindly concern confined to Eisenstadt itself. On our annual visits to the Hohe Wand (or 'High Wall'), the 100m-high tree-covered plateau offering a panoramic view of the Vienna basin, Lake Neusiedl, the Schneeberg, and the foothills of the alps, we always called at our favourite restaurant on our ascent and ordered our lunch to enjoy after our walk around the summit. Slow spit-roasted duck was a popular choice. Indeed, one year a client added this entry to the voting forms for our bird of the trip contest and Spit-roasted Duck scored maximum points. After many years of weekend visits we switched to a Monday. As usual we called at the restaurant on our way up the mountain and received an effusive welcome. When we returned for lunch we commented on the absence of other customers. Only then were we told that the restaurant was closed on Mondays but, not wishing to disappoint us, they had opened especially for us. Eating alfresco here often provided the bonus of a Spotted Nutcracker overhead or a Crested Tit on the feeders. But one year the group opted to eat inside. Suddenly, I sensed the cheery bonhomie giving way to alarmed silence as a whisper circulated. One of the participants had noticed the photographs on the wall showing our host in the uniform of a Waffen SS officer. I had to draw the group's attention to other familiar faces in the line-up – including Telly Savalas as an American Lieutenant. Our host was a famous Austrian film actor. The party atmosphere was restored.

Little wonder that I regard the Haydntage as the friendliest of festivals, as outlined in extracts from 20 years of trip reports. A recurrent theme is the joy of listening to wonderful music each evening whilst reliving the birding highlights of the day. But perhaps the most extraordinary integration of birds and music came on the very bicentenary of Haydn's death when, after two decades of attending the festival in September, we took the opportunity of a May visit.

This was the true climax of a joyful week and proved the most satisfying experience imaginable – the Haydn Todestag was a celebration not of death but of life. The music and locations were perfect: a thrilling and inspiring Creation Mass in the Bergkirche (for which it was written and where Haydn is buried), a breathtakingly wonderful performance of The Creation in the Haydnsaal of the palace at Eisenstadt (where Haydn conducted for 30 years), and the Farewell Symphony in the summer palace at Fertod (Esterháza) in the very room where Haydn first surprised his prince with this most diplomatic of hints (and on this occasion in the presence of the current Prince Esterházy), culminating with champagne and fireworks in the garden. Even more wonderful for music-loving birdwatchers, before and between the concerts we were able to experience God's Creation at first hand – and specifically as Haydn outlined it: 'On mighty pens uplifted soars the eagle aloft and cleaves the air in swiftest flight to the blazing sun' (we watched a White-tailed Eagle near Fertod); 'His welcome bids to morn the merry lark' (Skylarks in the Seewinkel area); 'And cooing calls the tender dove his mate' (Collared and Turtle Doves plus Woodpigeons in the palace grounds); 'From ev'ry bush and grove resound the nightingale's delightful notes' (a particularly fine songster at Illmitz); 'In lofty circles play and hover in the air the cheerful host of birds, and as they flying whirl their glittering plumes are dy'd as rainbows by the sun' (European Bee-eaters at Oslip, the ultimate rainbow bird, Golden Orioles and Eurasian Hoopoe in Eisenstadt park); even 'by heavy beasts the ground is trod' was evoked by the mighty Hungarian grey-horned cattle – and all in the context of 'the gently sloping hills' of Burgenland and beyond. The only creature not encountered, despite a complete circumnavigation of Lake Neusiedl, was a Leviathan. 'And God said, Let the waters bring forth abundantly the moving creatures that hath life, and fowl that may fly above the earth in the open firmament of heaven.'

All in all, the most miraculous day of double-whammies, which lasted from 6am until midnight and epitomised the very essence of Haydn, of his strong religious faith and infectious humour, of the Esterházy legacy, of the delightful Burgenland countryside, and of all the glories of God's Creation. Truly, the heavens were telling the glory of God, and the wonder of his work displayed the firmament.

> *Sing to the Lord, ye voices all,*
> *Magnify his name thro' all creation,*
> *Celebrate his power and glory,*
> *Let his name resound on high.*
> *Praise the Lord. Utter thanks.*
> *Jehovah's praise for ever shall endure. Amen.*

Haydn was one of the most positive and life-affirming composers of all time. How appropriate that exactly 200 years after his death we were able to capture a little of his joie de vivre to call our own.

It might be assumed that visiting the same festival and the same birding locations on the same dates every year would be merely repeating the same experience. It is true that there is a sense of continuity and reassuring familiarity, but each year brings very different experiences. Plus ça change, yes, but also vice versa. The similarities and the differences are conveyed in the trip reports. This chapter is therefore rounded off with an unbroken sequence of a whole decade of these (written without reference to each other). Readers not interested in playing this compare-and-contrast game – and particularly readers who are not music enthusiasts – are advised to speed-read or skip the remainder of this chapter.

8–19 September 1999

Although we have attended the Haydn Festival every year throughout this last decade of the 20th century, these happy Haydn days – even for the leaders and those clients repeating the experience – are as fresh and exciting as ever. And this year's trip could not have been bettered. Marvellous music, superbly performed. Lots of speciality bird species, closely observed. Warm and sunny weather with those blood-red suns morning and evening for which Burgenland is famous. Excellent meals in a variety of fine restaurants, with a chance to sample celebrated Burgenland wines. Visits to more bird habitats than ever before, from the Schneeberg, Hohe Wand, and the Leitha Hills to the Seewinkel pools, the Tadten Plain, and Marchegg forest, plus the castles of Forchtenstein, Eisenstadt, Fertod, Nagycenk, Harrach, and Kitsee, and the city splendours of Vienna and Bratislava. And above all a very happy and congenial (and for the first time ever all-American) group that quickly became a little family and was soon identified by the entire populace (even without their binoculars as chains of office) as The Birdwatchers.

From the first evening, when a Red-footed Falcon welcomed us to the Parndorfer Plain with Eurasian Hobby and Common Kestrel as comparisons, everything seemed to go well. Our first day got our bird lists off to a good start with a Syrian Woodpecker perched on the other side of the glass from our breakfast table and 20 species of wader on the Seewinkel pools, including Red-necked Phalarope, Temminck's and Little Stints, Marsh and Curlew Sandpipers, Ruff, and Spotted Redshank. Little Gull and White-winged Tern gave close views. A range of species from Red-backed Shrike and European Goldfinch to Eurasian Bittern and Water Rail put in significant appearances. And four Great Bustards provided the climax.

Our second day started with Common Kingfisher and Little and Spotted Crakes, and continued with exciting views of Black Stork, Northern Goshawk, Collared Flycatcher, Short-toed Treecreeper, and Middle Spotted Woodpeckers in Marchegg forest. But before the evening roll-call the Zurich Chamber Orchestra had provided us with some non-ornithological highlights with two Haydn symphonies (numbers 30 Alleluja and 60 Il distratto) and Beethoven's second piano concerto.

Twenty-four hours later the Hohe Wand had yielded close views of Rock Bunting, Firecrest, Crested Tit, and Spotted Nutcracker, and the highly painted Haydnsaal in the Esterházy Palace had been the setting for a rare production of Haydn's opera *Armida* (which both leaders saw in the Buxton opera house in 1988, the only other professional production in the last two centuries).

Sunday began with Moustached Warblers at Morbisch marina and Haydn's Theresien Mass in full liturgical setting at the

Bergkirche, where it was first performed almost exactly 200 years ago for Prince Nicholas Esterházy. It seemed appropriate that the current head of the family, Prince Anton, personally welcomed our little group to Eisenstadt after the service, apologizing that the hunting season and the mood of the Wild Boars prevented him from inviting us to bird in the hunting park. Even so the palace park began to yield the first of its ornithological treasures both before and after the open-air concert at the Leopoldinen Temple. But the day's highlight had to be the evening recital by Sumi Jo (stepping in at short notice for Bo Skovhus, who was indisposed).

Alpine Chough was our target bird on Monday when we took the rack-and-pinion railway to the summit of Schneeberg, travelling up on the brand new diesel and returning on a centenarian steam engine. We not only saw our quarry instantly. We were within three inches of touching it. The supporting cast of Common Ravens, Water Pipits, and Dunnocks was also obliging. But the highlight was undoubtedly the view from this 'King of the Nordic Alps'. Our spirits were still soaring with the choughs and ravens as we sat in the classical elegance of the small Empiresaal that evening to enjoy a concert of chamber music by the Haydn brothers performed by the Vienna Piccolo Concert.

This rich mix of birds and music continued throughout our stay. On some mornings the palace park provided six species of woodpecker – Black and European Green being particularly fine performers, and on one occasion Great and Middle Spotted and Syrian appearing together in the same tree top. For our American clients Hawfinch, European Greenfinch, Eurasian Nuthatch, Long-tailed, Coal, and Marsh Tits, Firecrest, and Black Redstart were nearly as exciting. Musical highlights by the

*In the early days we used to see our first
Middle Spotted Woodpecker in the
Schonbrunn palace grounds in Vienna*

Austro-Hungarian Haydn Philharmonic included a magnificent
Creation (conducted by Richard Hickox); Haydn's symphony
102 and Mozart's Prague symphony (conducted by Trevor
Pinnock); and Haydn's symphonies 68 and 101 plus the violin
concerto (conducted by Adam Fischer).

By contrast, our private concerts included the Budapest
Baryton* Trio playing for us in the very room in the Esterháza
summer palace in Hungary for which Haydn wrote the Farewell
symphony, and Professor Ingomar Rainer playing and talking
about the Haydn organs in the Bergkirche and the Kirche der
Barmherzigen Brüder.

Despite all this, we still managed to have an hour or two of free
time each day plus an official free afternoon during which the
group indulged in a variety of activities – swimming, sleeping,
shopping, sauna, cycling, museum crawling, and watching on

---

* The baryton is a fascinating 18th-century cross between a cello and a guitar, consisting of six melody
strings played with a bow and with from 16 to 40 'resonant' strings that could be plucked
in acccompaniment or simply left to vibrate in sympathy with the melody strings.

the big screen a video of Haydn's opera *Orlando Paladino* in the house where he lived.

Typical of the warm welcome we now receive at this most friendly of festivals were such social extras as a private wine reception at the town hall by the mayor of Eisenstadt, and a private champagne reception by the festival director, our good friend Dr Walter Reicher, to meet the British Ambassador and the conductor of the Hanover Band (Anthony Halstead) and their soloist (Jeremy Ward), who had delighted us with Haydn's symphonies 39 and 72 and Mozart's symphony 39 and bassoon concerto. But most appropriate was Adam Fischer's farewell to us at our final lunch when we were still relishing his conducting of Haydn's Farewell symphony an hour before – a very fitting finale to 12 days of sheer delight.

6–17 September 2000

What a magnificent sequence of concerts (and birds) this year. 'Eine besondere Art von Festpiel-Paket' indeed. For not only did we feast our eyes and ears on the beautifully painted Haydnsaal every evening, relishing along with capacity audiences some of the most wonderful music ever composed. We could also reflect on the birds of the day. The double-joy of Haydn's March for the Royal Suite of Musicians and his symphony 103 (Drumroll) and the Mozart march and his Posthorn Serenade, plus images of both Black and White Storks and Collared Flycatcher at Marchegg forest that morning and close views of four Long-legged Buzzards hunting European Sousliks at Bad Deutsch Altenburg (a new bird even for Bryan's Austria list). Or on the following evening to be bowled over by a stunning production of Haydn's opera *L'incontro improvviso* whilst reliving our day up the Hohe Wand and our views of Spotted Nutcracker, Northern Goshawk, Eurasian Bullfinch, and Crested, Marsh, and Willow Tits. Or the next day which started with Haydn's Nelson Mass in full liturgical setting in the church for which it was written exactly 200 years ago, and finished in the Haydnsaal with a fine lieder recital (Haydn, Mozart, Beethoven) by the celebrated tenor Peter Schreier, and also included Middle Spotted and Syrian Woodpeckers in the palace park both before and after an afternoon concert at the Leopoldinen Temple (Scheidt, Bach, Moret, Haydn, Lehar, Dvorak, Strobel, Debussy, Joplin, Farkas, Strauss, Myrow). Or the next when, whilst enjoying the Oxford Orchestra das Camera playing Handel's Water Music, Hummel's trumpet concerto, Haydn's symphony 92 (Oxford) and divertimento no 9, and Balfour's Millennium Surprise, we could dream of our day on top of Schneeberg and the Alpine Choughs, Water Pipits, Peregrine Falcon, Northern Wheatear, and Firecrests.

The mix continued throughout our ten days at Eisenstadt. Favourite concerts included the Lithuanian Chamber Orchestra (conductor Saulius Sondeckis) playing Beethoven's symphony 3 (Eroica) and Haydn's symphony 100 (Military) and trumpet concerto; the Jess Trio playing the trio version of Haydn's symphony 100 and Trio All'ongarese, and works by Mozart and Hummel; the Wiener Concert-Verein with Johannes and Eduard Kutrowatz playing Haydn's piano concertos in G and F and concerto for two pianos by Bach and Mozart; Anima Eterna (conductor Jos van Immerseel) playing Haydn's symphonies 44 (Trauer) and 57 and piano concerto in D, plus Mozart's piano concerto no 14 K449; and the Austro-Hungarian Haydn Orchestra (conductor Adam Fischer) bringing the festival to a magnificent close with Haydn's concerto for violin and piano in F and symphonies 35 (Echo), 94 (Surprise), and 45 (Farewell). We also enjoyed a private recital and talk by Haydn's direct musical descendant: the current Kapelmeister at the Bergkirche.

Sightseeing included the Bridge of Andau and the Road of Remembrance, Forchtenstein Castle, Liszt's birthplace at Raiding, Haydn's birthplace at Rohrau and the Harrach Castle, and Haydn's house in Vienna and the Esterházy city palace (opened especially for us). And even this non-birding day featured an unprecedented gathering of 100 Great White Egrets in a field beside the motorway.

Despite this busy schedule, we found time on most days to relax in the afternoon and enjoy swimming, shopping, and wandering at leisure through this delightfully intimate capital of Burgenland. As usual, we ate at a variety of fine restaurants and had plenty of opportunity to taste the famous wines of the area.

Most of our days began on the orangery terrace before breakfast with flocks of Hawfinches and six species of woodpecker, which contrasted perfectly with the selection we had seen around the reedbeds and pools on our first two days at Neusiedl before the festival began – Eurasian Bittern, Purple Heron, Eurasian Spoonbill, Little and Spotted Crakes, Water Rail, Great Bustard, 20 species of wader, Red-backed Shrike, Golden Oriole, a flock of 1,000 Tree Sparrows, and above all a Squacco Heron posing alongside our vehicle at Illmitz (a rarity in these parts and another new bird for Bryan's Austria list, although he has been visiting the country for 50 years).

All in all, the 12 days could hardly be bettered. Or could they? We have just heard that next year Cecilia Bartoli has agreed to return (two years ago she gave the concert of a lifetime in the

Haydnsaal), and there will be an opera double-bill; Haydn's *La canterina* (*The Songstress*) and *Lo speziale* (*The Apothecary*). Eisenstadt's Haydn festival has just been voted among the world's top ten music festivals (along with Salzburg, Bayreuth, Ravenna, and Savonlinna). It looks as though it will certainly hold this position in 2001.

5–16 September 2001
Haydn was writing some of his greatest works exactly 200 years ago. On Sunday 9 September, therefore, we were able to experience his Creation Mass performed in full liturgical setting in the very space for which it was conceived and first performed on the second Sunday in September 1801 – the Bergkirche at Eisenstadt.

It was a deeply satisfying and inspiring start to a day of wonderful music, which continued in the Landesmuseum with the Joseph Haydn Brass Ensemble playing Haydn, Boccherini, Mozart, Rossini, Weber, Katchaturian, Brahms, and Kahn, and concluded with Cecilia Bartoli's amazing concert of Caccini, Vivaldi, Mozart, Haydn, and Schubert in the Haydnsaal of the palace – again including music that has survived not only for 200 years, but for 300 and even 400.

Before and between these musical offerings we enjoyed a range of local birdlife that has remained unchanged throughout these centuries – Great White Egret, Purple Heron, Eurasian Spoonbill, Osprey, Eurasian Hobby, Ruff, Wood and Green Sandpipers, various woodpeckers and warblers, and the everpresent song of Black Redstart. It was a wonderful day for music and birds. But it was probably this awareness of continuity – the fact that life goes on, that a thing of beauty is indeed a joy for ever – which

*Syrian Woodpeckers – such as this one near the Bergkirche –
can be seen in the centre of Eisenstadt.*

enabled us to cope with the dreadful events in New York and
Washington on 11 September and, in the positive and joyful
spirit that pervades the Haydn Festival, enjoy the present and
look forward to a future. The day after the terrorist attacks we
were again gathered in the beautiful Haydnsaal for an uplifting
bi-centennial performance of The Seasons by Adam Fischer and
the New Austro-Hungarian Haydn-Philharmonic – another
joyous affirmation of life – which complemented our birds of the
day: 80 Hawfinches and great looks at a variety of woodpeckers.

This sense of continuity – the unchanging rhythm of both
the day and the year – was in fact the theme of the festival this
year. Vivaldi's Four Seasons was an inevitable choice (performed
by Tatjana Grindenko and the Moscow Academy, together
with Galuppi's suite from his opera *Il re pastore* and Haydn's

violin concerto and Russian quartet). So was the trio of Haydn symphonies Morning, Noon, and Evening (by Richard Hickox and Collegium Musicum 90). The Vienna Instrumental Soloists also took us through the day with Haydn's Sunrise quartet, Schmelzer's Baletto di mattina, Gastoldi's Ah hellen Tagen, Vivaldi's sonata no 3 from Il pastor fido, and Mozart's Eine kliene Nachtmusik – orchestral colours that appropriately evoked the Common Kingfisher seen en route to this morning's concert (rosy dawn breast, blue noon-sky back, and shimmering evening-gown wings).

Our day in Hungary, including a private concert by the Budapest Baryton Trio in the Esterházy summer palace at Fertod and finishing with the Great Bustards just over the border, gave broadcaster Margaret Howard the opening sentence of an article she was writing for *Classic Music* magazine ('Where in the world can you see a baryton and a bustard in the same afternoon?'). Incidentally, seeing a Great Bustard was the culmination of a several-year quest for Margaret. When she interviewed our group for *Howard's Week* on Classic FM in 1996 she asked one member, George, if it looked like a turkey. 'Looks more like a tree to me,' was his reply. Now Margaret has at last seen one she compared it to an Emu. A fair compromise.

As usual, our evenings listening to superb music in the Haydnsaal also provided the opportunity to reflect on the birds of the day. Thus the dual-bill of Haydn operas *La canterina* and *Lo speziale* will forever evoke Spotted Nutcracker, Black Woodpecker, Firecrest, and Crested Tit. And La Stagione Frankfurt with Michael Schneider conducting Haydn's symphonies 24, 13, and 31 are now twinned with Black Stork, Saker Falcon, Red Kite, White-tailed Eagle, European Honey-buzzard, and Collared and Pied Flycatchers, which perched together for comparison.

Curiously, our evening cruise on Lake Neusiedl, with gypsy band and barbecue, did not ensure that waterbirds stole the show: our abiding memories of that day were the Schneeberg mountain-top species – Water Pipit, Dunnock, Lesser Redpoll, Common Crossbill, and Black Grouse. But our 'birds-only' first day was as usual an impressive selection of waders on the Seewinkel pools, and our 'music-only' final day culminated in Adam Fischer conducting the New Austro-Hungarian Haydn-Philharmonic with Haydn's symphonies 78, 95, and 45, and Ingeborg Baldaszti playing Mozart's piano concerto no 4.

In short, then, although the atypically cold, wet, and windy weather this year may have deprived us of numbers, we still saw the specialities. In fact for the second year running the leader even had two Austrian lifers. Not quantity, then, but quality. Rather like the population of Eisenstadt itself. When one client observed 'That was the first time I have shaken hands with a prince,' we realized that our tally for that day also included two princesses and the queen of mezzos. That is the unique quality of this festival – it is so intimate and friendly, truly a family affair with the ever-affable Prince Anton and equally avuncular Dr Reicher presiding as our communal paterfamilias. Our annual home from home.

11–22 September 2002

On Wednesday 18 September a special reception was held in the City Hall at Eisenstadt, at which the capital of Burgenland and Freetown of Eisenstadt presented Bryan with the Joseph Haydn silver medal 'in appreciation of his special contribution to the success of the Haydn Festival in Eisenstadt' – an honour granted to only a few people since its creation. It was a significant accolade for Sunbird's unique birds and music concept, which started as a modest paragraph in the newsletter and has now introduced over 200 enthusiasts to the joys of this very special festival.

The vice-mayor Andrea Fraunscheil, in a charming speech in fluent English, spoke of the Englishman who went up a hill and came down a mountain and alluded not only to Bryan's enthusiasm for Haydn and the festival but also to his success in opening the eyes of Burgenlanders to the birds of their area. Festival director Dr Walter Reicher recalled a newsletter report in which Bryan wrote of attending a concert in the Haydnsaal as being 'the nearest you get to heaven without actually dying'.

This still holds true. The gloriously painted Haydnsaal – exactly as Haydn left it – is the most exquisitely beautiful environment in which to listen to fine music and the acoustics are quite superb. Moreover, the Haydn Festival gathers from all over the world the finest interpreters of Haydn (and other composers – this year the theme was Haydn and Schubert, but also represented were Mozart, Rossini, Caccini, Carissimi, Scarlatti, Strauss, Rimsky-Korsakov, and even Sousa, Lloyd-Webber, and Lennon/McCartney). As if this wasn't enough, the experience for the group is heightened as images of the day's birding highlights float into the mind's eye. Thus, at the opening concert, as the French Limoges Baroque Ensemble (conductor Christopher Coin) played Haydn's symphony 80 and cello concerto in C and Schubert's symphony 5, we could dream of the Black Stork, Northern Goshawk, Middle Spotted Woodpecker, Collared Flycatcher, Blackcap, and Garden Warbler at Marchegg forest and Neusiedl earlier that day. And on the following evening the gala concert by the celebrated Mexican tenor Ramon Vargas (widely hailed as one of the new

Three Tenors) was the climax of a day up the Hohe Wand, which included impressive views of Spotted Nutcrackers and Northern Goshawk, plus a variety of higher-altitude woodland birds. An evening of Haydn choral works (Te Deum in C, Salve regina, Ave regina, The Storm, and other masterpieces) in an inspired performance by the Vienna Chamber Choir and the Austro-Hungarian Haydn Orchestra (conductor Adam Fischer) rounded off a warm and windless day. This had started with Spotted Redshanks and Green Sandpipers, and continued in the Morbisch reedbeds, where huge flocks of Bearded and Eurasian Penduline Tits performed their acrobatics at photographically close range, and at picturesque Rust where one lingering White Stork clattered on its nest while we lunched below it in the town square. On the evening of another day the Belgium ensemble Prima La Musica (conductor Dick Vermeulen) played Haydn's symphonies 9 and 99 and Schubert's symphony 3 and overture 'in the Italian style' as the soundtrack to our action replays of Great Grey Shrike and the subadult male Montagu's Harrier hunting alongside our vehicle at Tadten – though our memories of that day also included our very special tour of the palace and chapel, the Bergkirche Calvary, the Church of the Barmherzigen Brüder, and Haydn's house. Twenty-four hours later the Alpine Choughs, Common Ravens, Dunnocks, and Water Pipits (including a flock of 39) on the top of the snow-capped Schneeberg were still vivid in our memory as we listened to the delicate and dancing interpretations of Haydn's symphony 44 and piano concerto in D, Schubert's rondo in A, and Sammartini's flute concerto in F by the Italian Il Giardino Armonico (conductor Giovanni Antonio). Even our private concert by the Budapest Baryton Trio in the elegant music room at the Esterházy summer palace at

Fertod (the Hungarian Versailles) was preceded by scope views of perched Hawfinch at Nagycenk Palace and a productive session on the orangery terrace in the Eisenstadt castle park with two Black Woodpeckers, delightful white-headed Long-tailed Tits, and Short-toed Treecreepers.

Obviously there were some days when the birds took priority and the music was limited to the tapes on our minibuses. Before the festival started, our two days based at Neusiedl, concentrating on the Seewinkel pools and over the border in Hungary at Zsilip and Nyirkai-Kishaz, gave us an impressive selection to launch our lists: a Syrian Woodpecker right outside the window at breakfast, then Red-necked Grebe, Little and Great White Egrets, Purple Heron, Eurasian Spoonbill, Common Shelduck, Red-crested Pochard, Ferruginous Duck, Western Marsh and Hen Harriers, Eurasian Hobby, Common Crane, Little Crake, Pied Avocet, various plovers, Little Stint, Curlew Sandpiper, Ruff, Common Snipe, Eurasian Curlew, Wood Sandpiper, Ruddy Turnstone, Black and Whiskered Terns, Yellow Wagtail, Whinchat, Red-backed Shrike, Yellowhammer, and Reed Bunting – giving our American participants in particular a wealth of lifers. Yet our return the following week yielded still more new species: Temminck's Stint, Little Gull, Marsh Sandpiper, Little Grebe from the Bridge of Andau and Grey Partridge on the Parndorfer Plain. Similarly, our other non-concert day (when the opera was being repeated) started on the orangery terrace with our usual six woodpeckers, adding a seventh (Lesser Spotted) at the Rosalia Chapel, plus our only Eurasian Wren and Mistle Thrushes, and gave us another Spotted Nutcracker flying across the fairytale façade of Forchtenstein Castle, which we then enjoyed to the full in our own private tour.

The woods around Forchtenstein Castle hold good numbers of tits and crests.

Equally there were days when the music dominated. Only the odd woodpecker and palace park passerine squeezed into our first Sunday, which began with Haydn's Harmonie Mass in full liturgical setting in the Bergkirche, the church for which it was written exactly 200 years ago, continued with the spirited Brassissimo Vienna wind quintet, and concluded (after an enlightened private introductory talk by the celebrated British music critic Richard Wigmore) with a hugely enjoyable and imaginative performance of Haydn's 1778 Esterháza opera *La Vera Costanza*, conducted at such a spirited pace by Adam Fischer that all three acts were performed as one. A week later Schubert's German Mass in full liturgical setting in the Franciscan church was followed by more fireworks from the Austro-Hungarian Haydn Orchestra playing Schubert's great symphony 9 and Haydn's symphony 93, with his Farewell symphony as the traditional encore to conclude the festival. But two Common Cranes beside the road as we approached the airport ensured that this unique mix of birds and music continued to the end.

As for mammals, Austria is no Kenya but we were delighted to see 19 Alpine Chamois on the Schneeberg, European Sousliks in the Roman amphitheatre at Carnuntum, Water Vole at Marchegg, Weasel on the Road of Remembrance at Andau,

Noctule Bat at Nagycenk Castle, and Roe Deer, Red Squirrel, and Brown Hare in many locations. But without doubt the most delightful non-avian lifeforms were our many Austrian friends and the inhabitants of Burgenland themselves, who form one of the most friendly and welcoming communities imaginable. No wonder we are still glowing like the Haydnsaal. As Rellstab said in his Abschied, so memorably set to music by Schubert in Schwanengesand: *Ade! Du muntre, du fröhliche Stadt, ade!*

10–21 September 2003

'Haydntage'. Literally it just means Haydndays. But since the creation of this happiest of festivals 14 years ago the name for Sunbird groups has acquired multiple meanings beyond a literal translation – with connotations of joy and contentment, excitement and laughter, clear blue skies and blood-red sunsets, gourmet meals and fine wines, bird-filled mornings in the reedbeds and mountains, and music-filled evenings in the exquisitely decorated Haydnsaal: the perfect setting to thrill to the very best performances and allow images of the day's ornithological highlights to surface from the subconscious. Each richly satisfying day seems to outdo the previous one.

This year our trip got off to the best possible start on the first evening with a flock of ten Red-footed Falcons on the Parndorfer Plain. The following day added pre-breakfast Bluethroat and Common Kingfisher, followed by close views of Syrian Woodpecker and Red-backed Shrike and a range of nonpasserines from Eurasian Spoonbill and Purple Heron to Curlew Sandpiper and Whiskered Tern. Then came the daily double-whammies: Richard Hickox conducting Collegium Musicum 90 and the Vienna Chamber Choir in an inspiring performance of Haydn's Nelson Mass, plus his symphony 32 and Salve Regina, whilst White-tailed Eagle, overhead Black Storks, Middle Spotted Woodpecker, and Collared Flycatcher were still vivid memories. Adam Fischer and the Austro Hungarian Haydn Philharmonic with Haydn's Military symphony and Beethoven's 7th, plus mental pictures of the day's assorted woodpeckers and Hawfinches in the palace park – cameos that were reinforced the next day between Beethoven's Mass in C at the Bergkirche, Nova Brass with a windband recital at the Leopoldinen Temple, and Haydn's opera *Philemon and Baucis* in the palace.

Joji Hattori conducting the Vienna Symphony Orchestra in Mozart's violin concerto in B flat, Beethoven's 1st, and Haydn's 60th – with images of the day's Rock Buntings and Crested Tits, the Black Woodpecker that flew across during our alfresco lunch, and the Peregrine Falcon that performed a barrel-roll above our heads up the Hohe Wand. Andras Schiff, Yuuko Shiokawa, and Miklos Perenyi giving the definitive performance of Schubert's lovely trio in E flat minor, plus trios by Haydn and Beethoven, in the music room of Esterháza Palace in Hungary – just a few kilometres from where we had been watching a roadside Black Stork, Crested Larks, and our only male Common Redstart of the trip.

Adam Fischer and the 'house' orchestra again (with the Vienna Singverein) thrilling us with Haydn's Harmonie Mass and symphony 86 as we recalled the Alpine Choughs and Water Pipits on the Schneeberg. Sir Neville Marriner and the Vienna Chamber Orchestra with Haydn's trumpet concerto and Miracle symphony plus Beethoven's 2nd – and Bearded and Eurasian Penduline Tits at Morbisch, a Eurasian Hobby right above us, and the last White Stork at Rust. An unforgettable gala recital by the remarkable mezzo-soprano Vessalina Kasarova on the same day as perched Spotted Nutcrackers and Common Crossbills, an overhead Saker Falcon, and (for some) Black Grouse and European Honey-buzzard. It was ironic, therefore – but fitting in a compensatory way – that our one day without music (except for those who chose to see the opera a second time) produced the bird of the trip (with 77 votes): three Great Bustards on the Tadten Plain majestically strutting, flapping, and flying.

The festival finished with Haydn's Mariazell Mass in the cathedral and Adam Fischer and the Austro-Hungarian Haydn Philharmonic giving us the most rousing rendition possible of Beethoven's 5th and Haydn's 104th, with the Farewell symphony as the now traditional encore.

As usual in recent years we were honoured to be welcomed to Eisenstadt by the charming Princess Ursula Esterházy and to be sent off by Prince Anton, who was also sporting enough to present the Sunbird phiton (practical help in time of need) award in a ceremony outside the cathedral on our final day – possibly the first time he has been asked to present a cardboard medal with a ribbon of dental floss. This warm-hearted and magnanimous gesture really sums up the spirit of this unique festival, which despite its adherence to the very highest standards remains a relaxed and friendly affair. Little wonder that a good proportion of our clients (and this year was no exception) come back for more.

8–19 September 2004

Sheer joy. Even days after arriving back home from dear old Eisenstadt the happiness and contentment remain. This all-pervading red-and-golden glow stems from many sources: ten

Spring is obviously the best time for White Storks at Rust, but in recent years an increasing number have still lingered in September.

days of sitting beneath the colourful ceiling of the Haydnsaal, the flaxen phragmites and sanguine sunsets around Lake Neusiedl, the amber Trockenbeerenauslese and rich sauces of the fine meals. But above all this ultimate feel-good factor derives from the warm welcome of the entire population. There really is no experience to compare with relaxing in the highly painted concert hall every evening listening to magnificent music exquisitely rendered and letting the day's ornithological highlights drift up from the subconscious mind. This year we heard not only 16 works by the Bach family and eight Haydn symphonies, his cello and violin concertos, and the Paukenmesse, but also music ranging from Boccherini and Charpentier to Verdi and Lloyd-Webber.

In the game of birdwatching, we definitely threw a six to start when, on our first evening on the Parndorfer Plain, we saw not only 12 Red-footed Falcons, several Eurasian Hobbies and a distant Saker Falcon, but also an Eastern Imperial Eagle (possibly the world's most westerly individual). The following day brought Moustached Warbler and Bearded Tits before breakfast; Common

Cuckoo, Eurasian Spoonbill, Ferruginous Duck, Pied Avocets, Ruffs, and assorted waders during the day; and 13 Great Bustards as a finale. Then came pre-breakfast Bluethroat and Common Nightingale, a flock of 40 Black Storks – plus a singleton that obligingly perched in a nearby dead tree – and various warblers in the hand at the Hohenau ringing station; Spotted Nutcracker, Firecrest, Eurasian Treecreeper, Crested and Willow Tits, and both Northern Goshawk and Eurasian Sparrowhawk up the Hohe Wand; a regular six species of woodpecker, plus Hawfinch, Short-toed Treecreeper, and Collared Flycatcher in the palace park; two White Storks still on nests in photogenic Rust; and Alpine Chough, Water Pipit, and Lesser Redpoll up the Schneeberg. But perhaps the most amazing sequence of lucky sightings came on our day in Hungary when Common Kingfisher, Crested Lark, Purple Heron, Curlew Sandpiper, Little Stint, Black-winged Stilt, and Black-necked Grebe were trumped first by Little Bittern and then by a majestic Steppe Eagle that flew low towards us and perched in a close tree – both new birds for this tour despite the fact that it had run every year for 15 years. And how satisfying that we could retrospectively savour this excitement whilst sitting in the music room of the Esterházy summer place, the Hungarian Versailles, enjoying a private performance of Haydn's string quartet in G minor op 74 no 3 The Rider before returning to Eisenstadt for an unexpectedly dramatic performance of Haydn's opera L'infedelta delusa. As to quantity, suffice to say that one participant (admittedly an American) notched up over 140 lifers.

7–18 September 2005

Life doesn't come more perfect than a birds and music tour centred on the Haydn Festival: two luxurious hotels, compatible company with a like-minded group and surrounded by so many friends from Eisenstadt and beyond, wonderful music, exciting birds, attractive countryside, gourmet food, and a perpetual relaxed and hassle-free environment. The only frustrating aspect of these 12 endlessly happy and satisfying days is thinking of all the thousands of people in the world who are not sharing these delights yet would love to if only they knew. There really is no better place to be in mid-September.

Every year there is a mix of the reassuringly familiar and unexpected novelty, in both the birds and the music. Typical was standing on the viewing tower at Nyrikai-Kishas reserve in Hungary (surrounded by 500 Great White Egrets and with a Saker Falcon and a single late White Stork overhead) and thinking of the Steppe Eagle that a year ago flew towards us and perched in a nearby tree, then realizing that this year there was a majestic juvenile Eastern Imperial Eagle perched in the same area – then, two hours later, touring the Esterházy summer palace at nearby Fertod and attending a private recital by the Haydn Quartet in the very room where Haydn first played his Farewell symphony (and a few hundred other works). Or the sudden realization that standing next to a solitary Dunlin amongst the Ruffs, Pied Avocets, Eurasian Curlews, and Black-tailed Godwits at Wirten Lacke was a Pectoral Sandpiper (with a Ruddy Shelduck in the background – both new birds for Sunbird's Austria list). Every day brought new birding treats – European Honey-buzzard, Northern Goshawk, Montagu's Harrier, Eurasian Spoonbills, Purple Heron, Red-crested Pochards, Ferruginous Ducks, Little Gull, Common Cuckoo, Crested Larks, European Serin, Hawfinch, three Black Storks circling over us as we stood at the confluence of the Danube and the March, and three rooftop

White Storks looking down on us as we ate our alfresco lunch at Rust. Uncanny too was our accurate count of 172 Turtle Doves on the wires on our first evening, followed by exactly the same number of Pied Avocets on Warmsee the next day.

Even more satisfying than the succession of avian experiences was the sequence of brilliant concerts, each one surpassing the last and culminating in two outstanding performances: Christopher Hogwood and the Basel Chamber Orchestra playing Mozart's Jupiter symphony, Prokofiev's Classical symphony, and Haydn's sinfonia concertante in B flat; and Adam Fischer and the Austro-Hungarian Haydn Philharmonic playing Mozart's 40th symphony and Adagio and Rondo for violin and orchestra, and Haydn's 101st and 45th symphonies.

Even the rain on our penultimate day (after ten days of sunshine and blood-red sunrises and sunsets), which frustrated our plans to bird in the higher-elevation pine forests, was a blessing in disguise as it gave us the opportunity not only to tour the state rooms of the Esterházy Palace and the Jewish Museum at Eisenstadt but also to take advantage of Adam Fischer's invitation to attend his afternoon rehearsal of the festival's final concert – a unique privilege to watch this world-renowned conductor at work (see Plate 7, page 119).

The only consolation when the traditional encore of the Farewell symphony brought this wonderful festival to a close was the realization that, God willing, in one year's time this perfect experience can be savoured yet again.

6–17 September 2006

The more one learns about Haydn, and the more one listens to his music, the more he emerges as a genial and above all warm personality. And it is warmth that is the common denominator of the Haydn Festival – not just the grape-ripening high temperature of these mid-September days in sunny Burgenland, but also the welcoming friendliness of the audiences, townsfolk, and musicians, and the glowing colours of the Haydnsaal and the blood-red sunrises and sunsets that are so much a feature of these Haydntage.

What a joy it is to relax every evening in the best concert hall in Europe listening to glorious music and reliving the ornithological highlights of the day. The opening concert of Adam Fischer conducting the Austro-Hungarian Haydn Philharmonic and Vienna Chamber Choir in a thrilling performance of The Creation could hardly be bettered, but running it a close second was their rendition of Mozart's orchestration of Handel's *Messiah*, Trevor Pinnock conducting the Haydn Academy and Chorus Sine Nomine in Haydn's Theresienmesse and the Oxford symphony, and (an unexpected delight) Michael Schneider and La Stagione Frankfurt with Acis e Galatea. Other concerts included Harry Christophers and the Handel and Haydn Society Boston, Brassissimo Vienna at the Leopoldinen Temple in the palace park, the Prague Chamber Orchestra and Gabor Boldoczki with a trumpet marathon, a gala evening of Schubert songs by Ian Bostridge with Julius Drake at the piano, Ton Koopman and the Amsterdam Baroque Orchestra, and our private concert by the Haydn Quartet in the music room of the Esterházy summer palace.

As with the music, so with the birds. Our first day could hardly be bettered – starting with pre-breakfast Great Reed and Moustached Warblers and ending with Great Bustards, we also enjoyed Purple Herons, Eurasian Spoonbills, Black-necked Grebe, Red-crested Pochard, Black Tern, Black Woodpeckers,

Whinchats, Red-backed and Great Grey Shrikes, and hundreds of European Bee-eaters (the first for years), plus a wealth of wildfowl and waders including Pied Avocet, Little Ringed Plover, Ruff, Spotted Redshank, Common Greenshank, and Wood Sandpiper. But more daily delights were to follow: an instructive comparison of Eurasian Reed and Marsh Warblers in the hand at Hohenau ringing station; Black Storks over the confluence of the Danube and the March opposite Bratislava; more Crested Tits than ever before (plus Marsh and Coal Tits, Firecrests and Goldcrests) up the Hohe Wand, above Forchtenstein Castle, and around Molz; regular Black Woodpeckers (and Syrian and Middle Spotted) in the palace park; four White Storks still lingering at Rust; distantly brief Eastern Imperial Eagle and Saker Falcon; Little Tern and Little Gull; yet more waders (Temminck's and Little Stints, Curlew Sandpipers, Red-necked Phalarope, even Bar-tailed Godwit, which rarely occurs inland during migration or when wintering – two dozen species in all); Alpine Choughs, Common Ravens, Water Pipits, Lesser Redpolls, and Dunnocks up the Schneeberg at 2,000 metres (and an unusual second flowering of all the spring alpine plants – Eidelweiss, gentians, primulas, pinks, catchflies); comparisons of Pied and Collared

Flycatchers; Bearded Tits and Bluethroat in the phragmites; Hawfinches perched in the beeches; and above all White-tailed Eagles spectacularly making duck kills in both Hungary and Austria, to be voted bird of the trip.

So much music (from Schubert to Handel), so many birds, so many fine meals, so many imposing historical settings, such beautiful scenery, so many relaxing moments swimming and shopping, and wonderful weather throughout – yet again, there really was no better place in the world to spend mid- September.

5–16 September 2007

Traditionally, September in Burgenland is hot, sunny, and windless. This year we arrived to cold, wet, and blustery weather. Initially a little dispiriting, this proved to be a blessing. Our first day driving around the Seewinkel pools yielded an endless succession of waders. Yet none of these had been present a few days earlier at the end of an unprecedented dry summer. A return visit a week later proved equally rewarding. Opportunities for instructive comparisons abounded – Temminck's and Little Stints, Ringed and Little Ringed Plovers, Common and Spotted Redshanks, Wood and Green Sandpipers, Dunlin and Curlew Sandpiper, Common Greenshank, Red Knot, Sanderling, Ruff, Pied Avocet, Eurasian Curlew – plus Collared and Pied Flycatchers, Baltic Gull, and such alliterative extras as Eurasian Spoonbill, Common Shelduck, and Eurasian Skylark, with close Red-crested Pochards from the Bridge of Andau. Similarly, gambling on the clouds clearing (which they did), we took the rack-and-pinion railway up the Schneeberg and for the first time ever were the only people wandering on the mountain top – with consequent record numbers of Water Pipits (50), Lesser Redpolls

(40), and Common Crossbills (90), plus Dunnocks, Northern Wheatear, Coal Tits, Eurasian Bullfinches, and Common Ravens. With all but one of the target species so well seen, the timing of the star of the show couldn't be faulted: an Alpine Chough appeared after lunch just before our return train.

With sunshine and higher temperatures now the norm once more, our first walk on the Hohe Wand was the most productive possible, with close Firecrest and Goldcrest, Crested and Willow Tits, Eurasian Sparrowhawk, Spotted Nutcracker, Eurasian Jay, and Black Woodpecker. Black Woodpecker also put on impressive performances in the palace park and at the gloriette (and was voted bird of the trip with three more votes than Black Stork and White Stork, which were joint runners-up). The park also provided us with a constant supply of the other woodpecker species, but perhaps the favourite park regular this year was an obliging Common Kingfisher, with a similarly obliging Short-toed Treecreeper a close second. And curiously the same tree-top twig above the orangery that on our first pre-breakfast visit hosted our only Hawfinch of the trip was the perch for our only Mistle Thrush on our last day.

Our visit to Hohenau ringing station paid dividends not for the passerines in the nets (just Tree Sparrow and Blackcap), but for the thermalling Black Storks and the sequence of raptors whilst we were waiting there – Eastern Imperial and Lesser Spotted Eagles, Red Kites, Saker Falcon, and Northern Goshawk. White Storks still lingered at Rust, Purple Herons at Morbisch, Moustached and Savi's Warblers and Bearded Tits at Breitenbrunn, and Red-backed Shrikes at several locations, whilst our day in Hungary added White-tailed Eagle, Eurasian Penduline Tit, and Crested Lark.

There were a few DBs (distantly briefs) – Pygmy Cormorant (breeding for the first time in Austria), male Golden Oriole (flying ahead of the lead vehicle), Golden Eagle (both presumably on passage), and European Bee-eaters (more distant that brief) – and the occasional disallowed leader-only bird (female Black Grouse and Fieldfare from the Schneeberg train). But in general most of the 140 or so species recorded were seen very well, as indicated by the many excellent photographs obtained.

As to the music, our only disappointment was the Grace Bumbry gala evening. Otherwise the concerts were quite superb: a spectacular opening performance of The Seasons by Adam Fischer and the Austro-Hungarian Haydn Philharmonic, who also thrilled us on three subsequent occasions with Haydn's symphonies 103, 15, and 97 and his Heligmesse Sancti Bernardo von Offida, Mendelssohn's 4th symphony and Dvorák's 9th, Weber's clarinet concerto 2, and Tchaikovsky's variations on a rococo theme for cello and orchestra. The Mahler Chamber Orchestra played Beethoven's overture The Consecration of the House, Haydn's symphony 99, and Schumann's 3rd, the Vienna Academy Bruckner's 1st and Haydn's 95th; the Vienna Chamber Orchestra with Rudolf Buchbinder – a piano marathon of Schumann, Haydn, and Chopin; the Vienna Concert-Verein Haydn's 88th and Gulda's cello concerto; and the Freiburg Baroque Chamber Orchestra Mendelssohn's violin concerto and Haydn symphonies 2, 27, and 80. All so different. But all so joyful.

Our 12 days of birds and music highlights were augmented by private tours of the palaces at Eisenstadt and Fertod, Forchtenstein Castle, Haydn's house in Eisenstadt and his birthplace at Rohrau, and by a series of fine meals culminating in gourmet dining at the Hotel Ohr and the Esterházy restaurant. But the finishing touches to a very happy holiday were without doubt the many encounters with dear friends – festival director Dr Walter Reicher (who invited us on our arrival to a rehearsal of The Seasons), mayor Andrea Fraunscheil (whose re-election posters smiled at us from every street corner; surely the most attractive chief official of any state capital), delightful Doris Fischer and her husband Adam (the brilliant driving force behind the festival), Richard Wigmore (whose comments on the music are always so enlightening), Robert Avery and Rudi Morovitch (who both helped to create this remarkable festival), Anthony von Hoboken (son of the cataloguer of Haydn's works who, maybe surprisingly, died only 24 years ago, aged 95), the affable Prince Anton Esterházy, and the gracious Princess Ursula (who also brought a 21st-century reality to the pages of history), and the countless other regulars who make this happiest of festivals such an intimate family affair.

Once again Eisenstadt proved to be the best place in the world to spend mid-September. And as Adam Fischer said after his performance of the Farewell symphony brought the festival to a close, 'After the Festival is Before the Festival.'

3–14 September 2008

In contrast to the unprecedentedly cold and wet weather in 2007, we were greeted this year by unprecedented heat (32°C). Appropriately there was a Mediterranean bias to our first walk on the Hohe Wand, where our first birds were Eurasian Crag Martins (a write-in for this trip and apparently the most northerly record for Austria) and Rock Buntings ('Rare and very local' in Austria, according to *BWP*). Amazingly these were accompanied by species more usually associated with these higher altitude coniferous woods and indeed our target birds for this walk: Spotted Nutcracker and Crested Tit.

Higher still – later during our stay – the Schneeberg delivered the archetypal alpine bird (Alpine Chough) and the archetypal alpine flower (Edelweiss). But down at lake level one small patch of mud provided us with an equally memorable sighting: a Spotted Crake and a Water Rail walking together with Wood and

Spotted Nutcrackers usually oblige up the Hohe Wand.

Green Sandpipers and a Bluethroat as supporting cast. Around Lake Neusiedl we also saw 20 species of wader, including Red-necked Phalarope, Pectoral Sandpiper, Black-winged Stilt, Pied Avocet, Kentish Plover, Curlew Sandpiper, and Spotted Redshank – plus Purple Heron, Eurasian Spoonbill, Red-crested Pochard, Little Gull, Yellow-legged and Caspian Gulls, and Black Tern. The woodlands provided Hawfinches, Short-toed Treecreepers, and lovely white-headed Long-tailed Tits; the fields Great Grey and Red-backed Shrikes; Common Kingfishers seemed to be in evidence everywhere; and we were lucky to see the last European Bee-eaters of the summer and the first Greater White-fronted Goose of the winter. At Rust at least four White Storks still lingered. And at Hohenau Black Storks and Black Kite performed for us whilst Black Woodpeckers also obliged on a regular basis in the palace park, proving that black was as popular in the field as in the concert hall.

As for the concert hall, the sequence of music was as satisfying as the selection of birds: magnificent performances by Adam Fischer and the Austro-Hungarian Haydn Philharmonic of Haydn's oratorio *Il ritorno di Tobia*, his symphonies 94, 100, and 96, his violin concerto, march for the Royal Society of Musicians, and overture La fedelta premiata, and Schubert's overture in the Italian style and rondo for violin and string orchestra. Equally inspiring was the English Concert (conductor Harry Bicket) playing Haydn symphonies 49 and 64, and Handel arias from Alcina and Ariodante sung by Vessalina Kasarova. The Basel Chamber Orchestra performed on two evenings: Haydn's symphony 37 and Beethoven's Pastoral plus his violin concerto played by Viktoria Mullova, followed by two Haydn cello concertos played by Pieter Wispelwey and music by Rossini and Grieg. L'Orfeo Baroque Orchestra opted for Haydn's symphonies 81 and 91, and Nuria Rial sang arias Haydn composed for Luigia Polzelli. Anima Eterna (conducted by Jos van Immerseel) overwhelmed us with a Haydn Te Deum and his Cecilia Mass and the Vienna Radio Symphony Orchestra played Haydn's first and last symphonies and Mozart's posthorn serenade no 9. And the evening of songs by Hahn, Copland, Rosenthal, Tanguy, Poulenc, Haydn, Bacri, Satie, and Bernstein delivered by the French soprano Patricia

Petibon was – well – extraordinary. Adding considerably to our understanding and enjoyment of the music were talks by Richard Wigmore and Adam Fischer.

History interludes during the heat of the day included tours of the Hungarian Versailles (the summer palace at Fertod), Forchtenstein Castle, Haydn's birthplace, and his house at Eisenstadt. But above all was the perpetual happy ambience and the constant interaction with so many friends that creates a 'family wedding' feel around this most joyful of festivals.

25 May–1 June 2009

Thanks to the special Haydn bicentenary celebrations this year, our birds and music group – after 20 years of attending the Haydn Festival in September – was able to visit Burgenland in May.

Our first evening in Rust highlighted the differences. Not only were there White Storks bill-clattering on every other roof, but also down by the lakeside were Garganey, Ferruginous Duck, and Red-crested Pochards galore. A scarce sighting in September, we counted 29 of the last species that evening. The following day around Seewinkel the tally was 129. Also on that first full day were Eurasian Spoonbills, Montagu's Harrier, Great Bustard, Whiskered Tern, Eurasian Hoopoe, Syrian Woodpecker, Common Nightingale, Fieldfare, Golden Oriole, and various waders and warblers – and all in a temperature of 34°C.

Wednesday, in Hungary, was considerably cooler and windy, but highlights included a close White-tailed Eagle scattering the Black-headed and Mediterranean Gulls, a very distant Eastern Imperial Eagle, Purple Heron, Black-crowned Night Heron, and again five photographable Great Bustards from the Road of Remembrance – plus a tour of the Hungarian Versailles, Prince

Nicholas's palace at Fertod. A complete contrast came next with a trip up the Schneeburg on the rack-and-pinion railway to see Alpine Chough, Ring Ouzel (a fine specimen of the alpine race), Water Pipit (including a nest with eggs), Peregrine Falcon, Dunnock, and glimpses of Alpine Accentor.

The strong wind frustrated us at Brietenbrunn marina the following day, but our walk along the geotrail at the Hohe Wand yielded the target bird, Spotted Nutcracker, and a close overhead European Honey-buzzard, before the temperature again dropped from 26°C to 3°C and we returned to the comforts of our hotel and an insightful talk by Professor Denis McCaldin, director of the Haydn Society of Great Britain, on the evening's music in the Haydnsaal. On Saturday we awoke to persistent rain. But conveniently Adam Fischer invited us to attend a private performance of The Creation (for Austrian television) and Professor McCaldin agreed to give us a double lecture on the weekend's concerts.

Our penultimate day, the actual bicentenary, was appropriately the true climax of a joyful week and proved the most satisfying experience imaginable. On our final day Marchegg forest delivered with the White Stork colony for which it is famous, plus Black Kite, Collared Flycatchers, Middle Spotted Woodpecker, and River Warblers, before our little family began to disperse.

7. *Wherefore have these gifts a curtain before 'em?*

The first birds and music tour (to Austria) was a great success. 'Wonderful,' said one participant. 'But where shall we go next year?'

On 9 November 1989 the East German government had opened its borders, the Berlin Wall had come down, and suddenly there was no Iron Curtain. Also in 1989 there had been prodemocracy demonstrations in Prague, new political parties had been created, the communist party had been stripped of its powers, a grand coalition government had been formed, and there had been calls for the USSR to withdraw its troops. It was obvious, therefore, that Sunbird's second birds and music tour should be centred on the Prague Spring festival in Czechoslovakia.

At the end of the May (birds-only) trip to Austria I boarded a train in Vienna and entered that country for the first time to undertake a reconnaissance. Despite the fact that this was now legal and above-board it was impossible, having seen so many Cold War spy films, not to experience the tiniest frisson of unease as the Czech police in their long greatcoats came along the train to check passports and papers at the border. I had already made contact with Jiri Mikulec, director of E-tours and the only ground agent who had had the entrepreneurial foresight to look west when the Iron Curtain was drawn back. He was also a birdwatcher. He met me in the 12th-century lake town of Trebon where we joined Jiri Jena, director of the Trebon National Park (who was tragically killed in a car accident in 1993), who conducted us around his bird-rich Unesco biosphere reserve, an internationally important wetland.

Trebon is an enchanting place. It is so quiet that every day seems like a Sunday afternoon. Here the familiar songs of Wood Warbler and Golden Oriole blend with those of Fieldfare and Collared Flycatcher in what is for the British birdwatcher an unfamiliar juxtaposition of west, south, north, and east. The Trebon Basin was originally covered by various kinds of wet forest, but was modified between the 14th and 16th centuries by the creation of 500 fishponds and an interconnecting network of canals (to provide carp for the medieval monasteries). Avenues of old oaks along the fishpond dams provide excellent birding, as the various passerines move along with the walker rather than escape into the forest. No problem with the birding then. And the award-winning Pipers of Trebon agreed to give us a private concert. As for music in Prague, we were spoilt for choice: three magnificent opera houses, a renowned concert hall, the Villa Bertramka, and innumerable churches and other venues offering music programmes to suit all tastes. A hotel at Pruhonice, alongside the delightful 'English landscape' park there, solved the birding problem.

The Sumava Mountains also offered good birding: Black Grouse, Corn Crake, Lesser Spotted Eagle, White-backed and Eurasian Three-toed Woodpeckers, Spotted Nutcracker, Common Rosefinch, Red-breasted Flycatcher... But where was the music? Agent Jiri explained that this area had been an Iron Curtain buffer zone that had been closed for 40 years to all but wildlife. I recalled Dvořák's From Sumava suite (op 68, also known as From the Bohemian Forest): pieces for two pianos that he composed while walking in this area. Surely it would be possible to find two pianists, I argued. It was typical of Jiri's 'think big' attitude that when he contacted me later he explained that he had discovered which pianists had performed the suite on the recommended CD, and had commissioned them to drive across the country to give us a private recital on the fine Bechstein piano in Ceský Krumlov Museum. Vlastimil and Vera Lejsek were a celebrated husband-and-wife duo who had been performing together for half a century. '*Lejsek*' in the Czech language means flycatcher. It seemed entirely appropriate, therefore, that on our first tour – after we had spent time earlier in the day comparing black-and-white male Pied and Collared Flycatchers – the Lejseks entered the recital room dressed in black and white. We were very happy to add Lejsek Vera and Lejsek Vlastimil to our Czech list of Lejsek Sedý, Lejsek Malý, Lejsek Belokrký, and Lejsek Cernohlavý. They continued to honour us with a private performance on all our Czech birds and music trips until Vlastimil's death in 2010. Vlastimil was also a respected composer in his own right and always included one of his works (his From Moravia suite was a great favourite), on one occasion giving us the world première of his latest composition.

Another instance of Jiri's determination to aim high came in 2001. In addition to performances at Prague's three magnificent opera houses we always included an opera in Brno. In 2001 the modern Janácek opera house was closed for renovation and performances were transferred to the smaller 19th-century theatre. The evening we were there was the new season's première of Janácek's *Makropoulos Case.* The problem was that in this theatre every first night was reserved exclusively for life patrons. No seats were on sale to the public. I suggested to Jiri that we should arrange a private concert instead – maybe in Janácek's house. I couldn't believe it when he told me he had hired the Janácek Quartet. This world-famous ensemble, the very best interpreters of their namesake's music, regularly fill the Wigmore Hall and are usually on a world tour performing to capacity audiences in Japan or America. Surely they would not play to our little group of 18? I assumed Jiri must have omitted a crucial differentiating adjective and that they were not *the* Janácek Quartet but a kind of local tribute group. This impression was reinforced when our coach broke down and I had to phone them to apologize for the fact that we would be an hour late. 'No problem,' they said. 'It's your recital. Arrive whenever you like.' Obviously one of the most famous quartets in the world would not be so casual and obliging. But no, when they walked into the room where Janácek composed the work they were about to perform, I recognized them as the real thing (see Plate 8, page 120) – what an honour. What's more, Jiri had also managed to persuade 18 patrons to part with their tickets for the opera. So we enjoyed more Janácek the following evening.

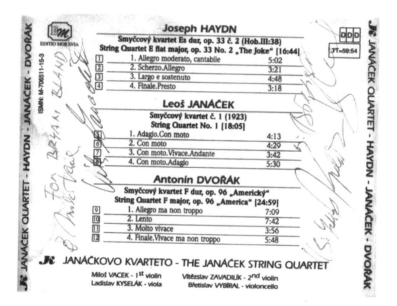

But back to the early days of this tour. Momentous developments were taking place. The major political parties were becoming divided into separate Czech and Slovak groups, and on 1 January 1993 the Czech Republic and the Slovak Republic became without rancour or bloodshed separate sovereign states. Slovakia had not been independent since the beginning of the 10th century and the people were so anxious to proclaim their freedom that, before they got around to printing their own currency, they proudly attached differentiating stickers to all their Czechoslovakian notes. Returning through Slovakia after a reconnaissance trip to the Ukraine that we undertook together in 1993 (see Chapter 13, page 264), Jiri made a fortune by peeling off all the stickers. His Slovakian currency instantly became Czech currency – which at the border immediately increased in value by 10 per cent, Slovakia being considered the poor relation of the divorce.

It was on the last day of the 1994 tour that the back trouble which Betty had been stoically tolerating for five months finally incapacitated her. (Monthly visits to the doctor in Norfolk – usually a locum – had merely resulted in a succession of stronger pain killers.) On the way home from Heathrow we called in on Brian Briggs, a doctor friend at Bushey. He immediately suspected the root cause and wrote a note for our own GP. Still waiting for a hospital appointment two months later it was not until Betty, now in constant agony, became completely paralyzed from the waist down that she was rushed into hospital. On 1 August it was confirmed that she had two large tumours on the spine, secondaries from breast cancer. She died in October. At the following Sunbird board meeting in December Will Russell, over from America, acknowledging that Betty's contribution to the birds and music tours had been crucial in creating that special ambience only possible by having a female co-leader, wondered whether – to maintain this vital gender pairing – there was any lady whose company as co-leader I could tolerate for two weeks at a time (or more to the point who could put up with me). The difficulty was that we were only offering, at the most, a couple of months' employment per year. It so happened that Patty Briggs, the wife of our doctor friend in Bushey, was coming to the end of her three-year contract with the Vincent Wildlife Trust as Bat Officer for East Anglia. She was also a birder and a music lover. On my way home from the board meeting I diverted to Bushey and put the idea to Brian. Patty, by an extraordinary coincidence, was in Norfolk delivering her last lecture – a final commitment – as Bat Officer. She returned the next day a little dejected and out of work. So as a temporary arrangement she accepted Sunbird's offer – a happy association that lasted for 12 years until she retired on her 60th birthday.

For many years our escort and interpreter on these trips was Katka Vozarova. One year she asked if she could be replaced on the last day of the tour so that she could attend the Ride of the King Festival in her village, as her young brother had been chosen to play the king's attendant. It sounded fun so we all went. And indeed it was such a joyful occasion, with folk dancing and cymbalo (dulcimer) ensembles everywhere (see Plate 8, page 120), that we added a day to the tour and made it an annual fixture. Everyone loved Katka – and eventually she fell for a birding friend on my Slovakia birds and bears tour. They were married in Sheringham, Norfolk, in 2005. She then worked in the delicatessen in my village, until the arrival of baby Nicolas (Christmas 2010). Small world. Jiri came over for the wedding and stayed with me. I served him quail eggs for his breakfast. These came from a quail farm at Great Snoring, a nearby village. The box was embossed with the legend 'Great Snoring Quail Eggs'. I asked Jiri whether they had Great Snoring Quails in the Czech Republic. 'What is the scientific name?' he queried. '*Coturnix stentorias*' I replied. 'Worse than Corn Crakes. Keep everyone awake all night round here'. As it was December I couldn't show him one, of course.

One winter, staying at Jiri's Prague flat and then his country cottage to finalize details for the forthcoming spring tour, I experienced great pain in my foot. It was thought that after a week of tramping around Prague I had perhaps broken a bone, and I was taken to the hospital near Jiri's office. 'Don't speak,' he advised me. 'If they ask questions just groan in pain and let me reply.' (I subsequently discovered that I was there courtesy of his company's group insurance policy and was officially a Czech national.) It transpired that I was suffering from gout. A year later, on the Slovakian birds and bears trip, I experienced the same acute pain but realized the cause. I was taken at once to a pharmacy, which prescribed the appropriate pills. The busy chemist turned to my Czech co-leader. 'It's a pity he's a foreigner,' he said. 'It will take me 20 minutes to deal with the administration. Can we say the pills were for you?' My co-leader agreed. Eventually the gout attacked when I was in Norfolk. When I told my doctor I knew what it was from previous occurrences, he tapped away at his computer and told me I had never had gout. I had to explain that I usually get an Eastern European to have it for me.

Once more, there is no better way of conveying the details and delights of these dual-interest tours in the Czech Republic than to end with a few trip reports.

12 May–1 June 1999
Dusk. But still bright. No wind. No sound other than the distant rasp of a Corn Crake, the nearby reeling of a Grasshopper Warbler, and the occasional grunt and sneeze of a roding Eurasian Woodcock. A deer moving into the clearing was surely too dark. Could it be a bear? Now finally exposed it was clearly a bristle-backed Wild Boar. But what a size. So huge that suddenly all the folk stories about this fearsome creature made sense. Along the track a Great Grey Shrike glowed like a light on its treetop

lookout. Then, magically perched on a small conifer beside us, there was the Ural Owl – the male of the only known pair in the Czech Republic (and known only to a few people). It filled the Questar. Unperturbed it gazed back at us. Occasionally with a few deep wingbeats it moved to another perch. In essence it was a huge long-tailed grey Tawny Owl. But so much more. It was one of those memorable moments that will stay with us forever. There had been so many on this wonder-filled trip.

One of the very first birds on our pre-breakfast stroll on day one had been a well-lit Tawny Owl. Tengmalm's and Eurasian Eagle Owls were to follow. And even this obliging Ural fairy on top of the Christmas tree was to be upstaged the following day by another target species doing a weathercock on the church spire: a Black Grouse that chose when flushed not to dive for cover, but to perch on a pine and display. In fact, tree displays were quite a feature in the Sumava Mountains this year – in particular two spectacular finch trees with Common Rosefinch, Lesser Redpoll, Common Crossbill, European Serin, European Goldfinch, European Greenfinch, Linnet, Chaffinch, and Eurasian Bullfinch all arranged for convenient comparison. Even more thrilling was the raptor moment on the Soutok flood plain when a European Honey-buzzard performed its butterfly display directly over our heads with both Black and Red Kites, Eastern Imperial Eagle, and Osprey as supporting cast. (Some supporting cast.) An hour later the centre of the universe was the glaring yellow iris of a Northern Goshawk perched on its nest. Perched White-tailed Eagle filling the Questar and a Peregrine Falcon on Tyn Church in the very heart of Prague were also memorable raptor moments. To these could be added the family of Hazel Grouse at our feet; showy Golden Orioles, European Bee-eaters, and Bluethroats; singing

Despite a proliferation of 'northern' species in the Czech Republic,
European Bee-eaters always evoke the Mediterranean.

River Warblers and Collared Flycatchers; all those woodpeckers;
White Storks and Black Storks; and Red-crested Pochards.

But as ever this trip was so much more than birds. It is difficult
to overestimate the thrill of watching a superb performance of
Cosi fan tutte in the very opera house where Mozart conducted,
or the delightful evening at Bertramka recreating his stay there
before the première of *Don Giovanni* (see Plate 8, page 120).
Other musical experiences ranged from Verdi's *Rigoletto* at the State
Opera House and a Ballet Gala in Brno to our private concerts
in Trebon and Ceský Krumlov and the lively folk ensembles at
the Ride of the King Festival in Moravia and in the wine cellars.

With such a feast for all senses it is little wonder that the tour
remains one of our most popular.

19–30 May 2000

In our annual attempt to experience a complete cross-section
of Czech birds and music, guaranteeing a good balance of
representative composers and compositions might be thought
to be the easier task. Not so. In the preceding months, as each

opera house and concert hall changes its programmes and dates, various balls have to be juggled until a final balanced selection can be made. The eventual result this year was as satisfying as ever. The Pipers of Trebon introduced us to the Bohemian gothic, Renaissance, and classical musical tradition, and set it in a general European and indeed transatlantic context. Vera and Vlastimil Lejsek played for us Dvořák's Sumava suite in the very area that inspired the composer, adding also Brahms's Hungarian dances and Lejsek's From Moravia suite. In Prague we enjoyed Mozart's *Marriage of Figaro* in the opera house where Mozart himself conducted and a chamber version of *Don Giovanni* in the Bertramka, the place he really loved – plus Beethoven's fifth symphony and Lutosławski's cello concerto stirringly rendered by the Czech Philharmonic Orchestra in Prague's main concert hall, the Rudolfinum, and church music at its best with an exquisite performance of the Jesuit Vespers in St Salvator's Chapel in the Clementinum Palace. In Brno a magical production of Dvořák's *Rusalka* proved there is more to this opera than the famous 'Hymn to the Moon'. And in Moravia folk ensembles at the Ride of the King Festival and our final evening in the wine cellar introduced us to the distinctive combination of cymbalo, fiddle, and double-bass. Further exposure to the Czech musical tradition came with our visit to Janácek's home and our musical journey with Smetana as we followed the course of the Vltava.

Persuading the birds to perform on cue was straightforward by comparison. Welcomed on our first evening by a most obliging Eurasian Pygmy Owl, we were entertained during the following 24 hours by roadside Black Stork and Red-crested Pochards, overhead White-tailed Eagle and Black Kite, and a sequence of speciality passerines as we strolled between Trebon's medieval fishponds, from Eurasian Penduline Tit and Icterine Warbler to Golden Oriole and Bluethroat. This delightful area of water, woodland, and wildflower meadows also enabled us to compare Grey-headed and European Green and Middle and Great Spotted Woodpeckers, Firecrest and Goldcrest, Marsh and Eurasian Reed and Great Reed Warblers, and Collared and Pied Flycatchers. European Honey-buzzards, Eurasian Spoonbill, Black-crowned Night Heron, White Stork, and Little Egret added to the variety. Even more excitingly, the Sumava Mountains yielded Black Grouse, Common Rosefinch, Great Grey Shrike, Willow and Crested Tits, Grasshopper Warbler, Tengmalm's and Ural Owls (both close and sustained views), and – a high point in every sense – Eurasian Three-toed Woodpecker. A convenient picnic puddle provided the stage for a serendipitous finch cabaret with non-stop turns from Eurasian Bullfinch, Lesser Redpoll, Eurasian Siskin, European Greenfinch, and Common Crossbill. By contrast Moravia added Mediterranean Gulls, more woodpeckers (Syrian, Black, Wryneck), more warblers (Barred and River performed particularly well), and best of all a wonderful raptor morning with Red and Black Kites, Eastern Imperial Eagles, and Saker Falcons.

Add to this unspoilt countryside, easy woodland walks, attractive mountain scenery, historic castles and parkland, and the architectural splendours of the world's most beautiful city, and there is little wonder that this Czech birds and music tour presents a winning formula that has endured for ten years.

17–28 May 2001

Never before. And maybe never again. The Janácek Quartet playing Janácek in Janácek's house, just for us. We can still hardly believe it, but this world-famous ensemble actually played

Janácek's first quartet and Dvorák's American quartet for the group in the very room where Janácek composed his greatest music. It was a unique and inspiring hour, every bit as exciting as the new season's première of Janácek's *Makropoulos Case* the following evening in Brno's old theatre, where it was first performed, or the three productions in Prague's three sumptuous opera houses on the three previous evenings: Puccini's *Tosca* at the National, Mozart's *Marriage of Figaro* at the Estates, and Verdi's *Aida* at the State. Our other private concerts – by Vlastimil and Vera Lejsek in Ceský Krumlov (another privilege with a respected composer playing his own compositions for us, as well as Dvorák's Sumava suite in the setting that inspired it), by the Pipers of Trebon in the great hall of Trebon Castle (another first – to hear baroque music played in the setting for which it was written), and our cymbalo, violin, and double-bass trio in the Mikulov wine cellars (the lively music and the wine ensuring that dancing was inevitable) – perfectly complemented the Bertramka recital, the folk music at the Ride of the King Festival, and the carefully planned taped music on the coach to give as complete a picture of the Czech musical tradition and its contribution to the music of Europe as is possible in 12 action-packed days.

A similar mix of dramatic spectacle and more intimate moments characterized our birding experiences to give both range and variety. The big white birds and the big black birds performed impressively – the first Great White Egrets to nest in the Czech Republic for 100 years, Little Egret, Eurasian Spoonbill, Squacco Heron, and two unexpected drake Smew; a White-tailed Eagle and a Black Stork low overhead, plus Black Kite and Black Grouse. Even Tyna and Tycho, Prague's resident Peregrine Falcons, were at their aerodynamic best. But other

Our luxurious pied-à-terre near Lednice: the newly converted 200-year-old border palace of Hranichi (plus Golden Oriole).

families were even more popular: Wryneck and Lesser Spotted, Middle Spotted, Syrian, Grey-headed, and Black Woodpeckers and, in particular, the Tengmalm's Owl doing a full body lean out of its hole as though it had a side box at the Estates theatre, the treetop Eurasian Pygmy Owl mobbed by a swarm of Chaffinches, and the massive Eurasian Eagle Owl sheltering her young from the heat of the sun. Equally memorable were the Bluethroat in the reeds, Common Rosefinch in the blossom, Spotted Nutcracker on the pines, roding Eurasian Woodcock, and wing-clapping European Nightjar, and Red-breasted Flycatcher and Crested Tit in the quiet forests.

After more than a decade, this was probably the most integrated and continually satisfying mix of birds and music yet. But the finishing touch was undoubtedly our four homes for the holiday – the baroque-and-renaissance Golden Star in Trebon's photogenic old town square, yet only a short walk from Svet Pond, the gently curving Arnika in Sumava with birds from the balconies, the elegant Magnolia so convenient for Pruhonice park, and especially the newly converted 200-year-old border palace near Lednice, with its dawn chorus of Common Nightingales, Golden Orioles, and a thousand frogs. Pre-breakfast birdwatching at all four locations has never been better.

16–27 May 2002

From the smallest to the largest, from ancient to modern, from the flop that became a favourite and the instant success that fell into obscurity, from the dance of the dead nuns to a sensuous seguidilla, from multicolour to black and white – this year's birds and music tour of the Czech Republic was a compendium of contrasts.

On our first evening we were greeted by one of the Palearctic's smallest owls with splendid views of Eurasian Pygmy Owl in the wetland pines, together with Eurasian Woodcock and European Nightjar. On our final evening, despite the counter-attraction of a hugely enjoyable cymbalo trio, we slipped out to the quarry behind our wine cellar to check for Eurasian Eagle Owl and were rewarded with a magnificent specimen of the world's largest owl perched on a dead tree: a fitting farewell. Completing an exciting trio of owls was an endearing Tengmalm's with a Bank Vole in the Sumava Mountains.

Equally contrasting were our first two private concerts – from the medieval music by the Pipers of Trebon in the fitting setting of a room in the castle where it was first performed 500 years ago, to the world première of a just-written movement from Vlastimil Lejsek's Seasons suite played for us by the composer himself in Cesky Krumlov, when he and his wife Vera also treated us to Dvorák's Sumava suite and other compositions as they celebrated 50 years of playing together and also their golden wedding anniversary: a wonderfully happy occasion.

Our operas in Prague included Bizet's *Carmen*, the most popular opera ever written, though it was not a success in the composer's lifetime, and – conversely – Meyerbeer's *Robert the Devil*, which was an overwhelming success at its première in 1831 but is rarely performed today. A delightfully intimate *Night with Mozart* at the Bertramka, Offenbach's *Tales of Hoffman* at Brno opera house, an Ave Maria concert in the underground chapel of the Church of St Francis of Assisi (Handel, Bach, Vivaldi, Gounod, Albinoni, Frank, and Schubert), a private visit to Janácek's house, and folk music at the Ride of the King Festival in Vlcnov completed our very varied musical offerings.

Even so, we saw more birds than ever before. The favourite five presented a kaleidoscope of colour – European Bee-eater, Eurasian Bullfinch, Common Rosefinch, Bluethroat, and Little Bittern. But black (as in grouse, woodpecker, kite, and stork) was also popular. As was white (particularly our discovery of Mediterranean Gull at a new breeding site). And black and white (Ring Ouzel, Crested Tit, Collared Flycatcher, Lesser Spotted Woodpecker, and spectacularly a close Eurasian Three-toed Woodpecker). Other highlights included Eurasian Spoonbill, Red-crested Pochard, White-tailed Eagle, Red Kite, Saker Falcon, the other woodpeckers (Wryneck, Grey-headed, European Green, Great Spotted. Syrian, and Middle Spotted), an out-in-the-open Common Nightingale, vigorously vibrating Grasshopper and River Warblers, obliging Barred Warbler and Firecrest, Golden Orioles, and Red-backed and Great Grey Shrikes. A selection as varied as the music.

19–30 May 2005

The one common denominator that encapsulates this year's birds and music tour of the Czech Republic seems to be *Rusalka*. The magical misty lake on stage at the State Opera House that so exactly interpreted the vision of both composer and librettist in one of the most perfect productions (of any opera) imaginable also symbolized the recurrent image of our own Czech experience: water (with or without water nymphs but always with waterbirds) – in the ancient fishponds of Trebon, Dvorák's black lake in the Sumava Mountains, the landscaped lakes of Pruhonice and Lednice, the frog-filled ponds at Hlohovec, and the fishponds of Moravia. And reflected in so many mental pictures are Red-crested Pochards, Garganey, Black-necked Grebes, and Mediterranean Gulls; a Bluethroat in the reeds or a Little Bittern clinging to a phragmites stem and stretching more and more vertically until it almost fell over backwards; a Common Kingfisher surrounded by pink and yellow azaleas; and Common Cranes flying, striding, and bugling amongst the waterside vegetation.

It is difficult to evoke any species without recalling the setting, the total context of the landscape. Admittedly there were some isolated cameos – the displaying Firecrest at eye level, the Crested Tit in the pine needles, the Icterine Warbler on its nest, the Tawny Owl squeezing into the broken branch, a Eurasian Penduline Tit or a Marsh Warbler in the sallows, a Common Rosefinch throwing back its head and uttering its cheery song, and Grasshopper Warbler vibrating its whole body in a low bush. But almost invariably an entire scene comes to mind. It is impossible to picture Black Grouse without seeing the misty meadows beneath the wooded hillside or to recall Hawfinch and not remember the castle gardens at Ceský Krumlov. Similarly our first Black Woodpecker and our only Ring Ouzel and Eurasian Three-toed Woodpecker are inextricably linked to the silent vastness of the primeval beech and spruce forest of Boubin Hill – appropriately black-and-white birds in a sombre-hued world largely without colour, but dramatically lit by shafts of silver sunlight. Colourful European Bee-eaters and yellow-eyed Barred

Warblers immediately evoke the sunny vineyards of Moravia; Wryneck and Middle and Lesser Spotted Woodpeckers mature parkland; Golden Oriole a canopy of sun-lit leaves; and Corn Crake brings to mind the source of the Vltava so clearly that Smetana's rippling music can be heard in the background. Eurasian Pygmy Owl and Eurasian Woodcock conjure up an entire scene of silhouetted pines and such non-avian extras as a whole family of Wild Boar trotting towards us along a forest trail. Eastern Imperial Eagle and Saker Falcon evoke the secret woodland of the Soutok flood plain that we were so privileged to visit. And even White-tailed Eagle, European Honey-buzzard, Black and Red Kites, Montagu's Harrier, and Black Stork come to mind complete with their own particular context of the bluest skies.

All in all, a good selection of Czech birds – and some superb views in unsurpassable settings. As equally memorable as the attractive and ever-changing countryside were the charming townscapes – of Trebon, Ceský Krumlov, Prague, Telc, Mikulov – justly meriting their World Heritage status and appropriate settings for our selection of musical experiences from the Pipers of Trebon, Vera and Vlastimil Lejsek, and the Radusov Cymbalo Quartet all performing exclusively for our group to *Rigoletto* and *Lucia de Lammermuir* at the State Opera, the Aloe Trio at Bertramka, *Le Corsaire* at Brno, and the happy succession of folk ensembles at Vlcnov.

These first-hand experiences, together with the excellent film documentaries at Janácek's house and the taped narratives that unfolded during our time on the road, provided as comprehensive a picture of the music of the Czech Republic as any during the 15 years of the trip's operation. Birds. And music. QED.

8. *Midnight sun, midday cello*

In August 1994, the month that Betty's cancer was officially diagnosed, we had originally planned to check out the Savonlinna Opera Festival in Finland as the basis for the next birds and music tour. Exactly one year later Brian and Patty Briggs were staying at my home, evaluating the possibility of conducting bat breaks in Norfolk. They had presented me with a CD of Sibelius songs performed by Jorma Hynninen, Finland's leading opera singer. We were in my kitchen listening to these and I recalled the reconnaissance trip Betty and I never made. I took out the file, noticed that Jorma Hynninen was the artistic director of the Savonlinna Opera Festival, and on the spur of the moment decided to go immediately. All flights from Heathrow to Helsinki were fully booked, but there was a flight from Manchester early the next morning. I phoned the department of tourism in Finland and also spoke to Dick Forsman, Sunbird's chief birding contact in the country. Their helpfulness and efficiency was amazing. Dick met me at Helsinki airport, argued that to amass a good bird list I should also include Lapland, Arctic Norway, and Estonia, and gave me the telephone numbers of some contacts. The director of tourism had paged me both on the plane and on my arrival, and in her office at the airport immediately arranged my itinerary.

I drove to Kerimaki, where the largest wooden church in the world provided the venue for some of the concerts associated with the festival, and whilst there noticed that a concert was scheduled for 7.30pm in Savonlinna Cathedral. I arrived when the cathedral clock was striking the half-hour, abandoned my hire car in the graveyard, and rushed to the door. 'What's the programme?' I enquired. 'No time to tell you. We are just about to start. Come in if you wish.' I noticed Jorma Hynninen standing by the altar. 'If he's singing I'll come in.' They apologized for the fact that all the seats were taken. I would have to watch from the organ loft. Jorma Hynninen sang the first item on the programme from the altar, then transferred to the organ loft. At the end of the concert I explained that I had just been listening to him in my kitchen in Norfolk and had come to arrange group visits to his festival. He gave me a ticket for Verdi's *Macbeth* the following evening, and a pass to have drinks with the directors in the interval to discuss details. All very efficient. Needless to say the music was spine-tingling and the setting spectacular. The operas are performed in the dramatic and acoustically perfect setting of a 15th-century castle on an island in a lake (see Plate 9, page 241). Birds around Savonlinna ranged from Eurasian Bittern and Spotted Nutcracker to Blyth's Reed Warbler and Thrush Nightingale. So far so good.

I checked out the Saimaan wilderness camp (Black-throated Diver, White-backed and Black Woodpeckers, and the attractive possibility of a private recital in the woods). Another satisfactory pairing. And the wardens at Oulu reserve (where I saw Yellow-breasted Bunting and a range of waders) put me in touch with a quartet to play for us whilst we had dinner at the snail farm.

I then flew to Ivalo to meet the Sheriff of Lapland, a fellow birder. I warmed to Heikki Karhu the moment we met, and we spent a happy day trekking through the pine forests and locating Pine Grosbeaks, Siberian Jays, and a range of northern specialities. Excellent birding. But I still needed to arrange a concert featuring kanteles, the Finnish national instrument. I noticed a poster announcing a festival that translated as the Days of the Music Men, due to start in two days' time. In the interim I hired another car and explored Arctic Norway (Varangerfjord, Vadsø, Vardø, and Hamningberg), taking advantage of the 24 hours of daylight each day. There were many complementary bird species (Steller's and King Eiders, White-billed Diver, Brünnich's Guillemot). And Saami *joiku* (primitive songs in the Lapp style) would take care of the music aspect. Heikki had suggested I take some nourishment with me, restaurants being as scarce as Snowy Owls and Gyr Falcons, and had sliced off a portion of dried reindeer from a carcass in his cellar. 'Be sure to eat it with plenty of liquid,' he warned. On the top of Skalluvaara, having located Long-tailed Skuas, I took my first bite. I immediately appreciated the necessity of washing it down. It tasted like someone's old sneaker soaked in rancid butter. I drove down the mountain to the nearest shop, bought a jar of soused herrings, and consumed the entire contents including the vinegar.

The road from Vadsø to Hamningberg (at the end of which a sign overlooking the Barents Sea and faraway Novaya Zemlya proclaimed 'Europe ends here') seemed so remote that I wondered if I would ever see another vehicle. At around 3am (but still in good light) I pulled over to watch some roadside Shore Larks. At last another car approached. So Arctic Norway was not devoid of human lifeforms. The car stopped. 'Are you Bryan Bland?' enquired the driver. Is there no hiding place for a birdwatcher?

Three species of eider in the Varangerfjord: Common, King and Steller's.

I arrived back in Ivalo just in time for the opening night of the Days of the Music Men. I had checked with the organizers that this was folk music with folk dancing and folk costume. Surely this would include kanteles. It transpired to be an evening of tango dancing with the locals in their best suits and dresses. (The tango is more popular in Finland than anywhere in the world beyond Argentina.) Obviously something had been lost in translation. For the first time there was a hitch in this whistle-stop reconnaissance. The following day I had to fly back to Helsinki and take a boat to Estonia. 'Never mind,' said Heikki. 'My son's music teacher has Siberian Tits in his garden and has invited you for coffee in the morning.' The music teacher turned out to be Martti Salo, a celebrated composer and kantele virtuoso. Whilst we waited for the tits he played some of his compositions. Never before had I willed a lifer not to appear. I could have listened all day. When Martti learned that I was devising a birds and music tour he made an outstanding offer. 'Don't worry about a kantele concert. All my life I have fantasized about playing to the midnight sun from the hut at the top of Mount Inari overlooking that vast expanse of lakes and forest. You have given me the motivation. I will gather together all the best kantele players in Finland and we will give you a concert.' This has remained a fixture on every tour and has provided successive groups with many magical moments.

There now remained only the grand finale in Estonia. On my first morning in Finland I had tried to phone another of Dick Forsman's contacts, but he was not in his office in Tallin. I explained to his colleagues that I was intending to catch the ferry at the end of the week, but was left with the feeling that they did not understand. It was therefore a great surprise when we docked at the attractive medieval Hanseatic port to see a young lady holding up a card bearing my name. She was from the local travel agency and asked how she could help. On hearing that I wanted to know what musical events would be taking place there in 12 months' time, during a month when all concert halls and opera houses seemed to be closed, she explained that only one man could tell me (Estonia's leading musical entrepreneur, it seemed) and that she did not know how to contact him. Rounding the next corner, we nearly knocked someone down. 'How amazing,' she said. 'This is him.' He outlined for me the programme for Tallin's International Organ Festival. The wonderful singing that I then heard issuing from the Alexander Nevsky Cathedral (a wedding was in progress) suggested the bonus of a Russian Orthodox sung mass. And Muhu island and a bird reserve nearby yielded such species as Red-backed Shrike and White Stork, which are not found in Finland.

In less than a week a completely blank canvas had become a finished picture. Everything had fallen into place. On the plane back to Manchester I wrote a detailed day-by-day itinerary, which remained substantially unchanged throughout subsequent years.

The only addition was an extension to St Petersburg, primarily to enjoy an opera or ballet at the Mariinsky Theatre (Kirov) and to visit the Hermitage Museum, the impressive palaces, and (en route) the almost legendary bird-rich Lake Ayrapaanjarvi. But before our first tour in 1996, the gift of a CD from friends in Germany served to confirm both the recurring role of serendipity and what a small world this is. The CD in question was a Deutsche Grammophon recording of the Night Vigil St Petersburg Litany, recorded live at Spaso-Preobrazhensky Sobor, the Cathedral of the Transfiguration in St Petersburg, at the Palm Sunday All-Night Vigil in 1994 – a service that lasts for over three hours. Beginning with the chimes of church bells summoning worshippers from all over the city, the recording captured the mesmerizing Orthodox liturgy with all the impassioned chanting and sonorous polyphony that has held visitors to Russia spellbound for

1,000 years. The tingle factor was overwhelming. As I listened I began to read the accompanying booklet. 'The Vigil on Saturday evenings,' began the text, 'consists of Great Vespers, the Litia, Matins and the First Hour, and in its fullest form it would continue throughout the night'. I read the sentence again. Yes, it stated 'Saturday evenings' – not a specific Saturday but apparently every Saturday. And we were scheduled to be in St Petersburg on a Saturday. I immediately phoned the Russian Tourist Board, the Russian Embassy, and numerous other contacts – but no one could confirm this. No one had even heard of the Cathedral of the Transfiguration. I felt frustrated but continued to listen to one sublimely inspiring track after another, following the liturgy in the booklet: Lord have mercy... Blessed is the man that hath not walked in the counsel of the ungodly (in a setting by Chesnokov)... Lord I cry to Thee... The Lord is King... Now lettest Thou thy servant depart in peace (the setting by Rachmaninov)... Blessed be the Name of the Lord... Glory to God in the Highest... The Lord is God... Praise the Name of the Lord... From my youth up, my passions have warred against me... Let everything that hath breath praise the Lord... Rejoice, O Jerusalem... Grant this, O lord... then finally 'After further petitions, the blessing is given and the choir responds by asking God to protect all Orthodox Christians. Even though the service is drawing to a close, the ektenia (continuous prayers) continue throughout the world.' If only I could find out more. I then noticed the author of the explanatory notes: Father Philip Steer. Surely not the same Orthodox priest who was a friend and neighbour at Cley next the Sea? Yes. Another phone call later Philip had recounted how he had been sent over three hours of recording and told to reduce it to half the length and still make liturgical sense of it. More to the point, he had confirmed that this wonderful musical experience was indeed recreated every Saturday evening at the Cathedral of the Transfiguration – as the group discovered for itself on its first visit a few weeks later. Needless to say, the real thing was even more inspiring than the recording.

We were all amazed that this ritual of a divine service had so impressively survived the years of communist suppression. But the following morning was almost surreal. As we drove in our coach from the hotel to the city centre, we became increasingly aware that street after street was filled with pedestrians in their smartest suits and best dresses walking purposefully as if to church. It seemed that the entire population of St Petersburg was on the move. Could they really all be attending Mass? Moreover, there were no other vehicles – and curiously our own coach was stopped at every junction whilst our guide had increasingly more heated discussions with a growing police presence. She seemed quite aggressive in brandishing our papers.

Eventually, when we insisted that this could not possibly be a typical Sunday morning, she explained that this was the 300th anniversary of the founding of the Russian Navy by Peter the Great, and that the President of Russia was scheduled to address the nation from the island fortress of St Peter and St Paul – which, as it happened, was our destination that morning. By some bureaucratic oversight we had been issued with authorization and timed tickets (presumably weeks before, when our itinerary was originally planned), which explained why we were the only vehicle in the city and able to defy the police cordons. (This was as good as a Norfolk Naturalists Trust pass.) I understood the Russian mentality on this point: the imperative of sticking to a prearranged itinerary.

When Sunbird was the only company licensed to run a Siberia and Mongolia tour, I had to travel to London to represent the company and meet with the Mongolian minister of tourism to exchange in person, with witnesses, counter-signed, detailed itineraries. The scene was reminiscent of the signing of the Treaty of Versailles. Deviation from such schedules was not allowed. On one occasion our coach drove past a perched Great Grey Owl, seen by only half the participants, but the driver refused to stop as it was not in his instructions for that morning.

Here in St Petersburg our guide had orders to show us the oldest building in the city, and she was determined to obey. The problem was that we were due back in Savonlinna for a performance of Carl Orff's *Carmina Burana* in Olavinlinna castle that evening, and already our timing was adrift as we progressed with the crowd at walking pace. The River Neva was filled with craft representing 300 years of Russian naval history, the sky was peppered with fly-pasts representing Russia's prowess in the air, and as we reached the bridge to the island fortress – presumably the final checkpoint – a helicopter arrived with the President. Even if we were allowed to join him, I anticipated (at the best) interminable delays in leaving. So I at last convinced our determined guide that she really did not have to complete her assignment, and that rather than embark on a sightseeing tour amidst a battalion of bodyguards, it would suit us to begin our five-hour return journey to Savonlinna. (In subsequent years we flew back to Finland.)

When we arrived back in Savonlinna I commented to our hotel that the packed lunch they had provided for our trip to St Petersburg had been rather nominal. Eager to make amends the next day, they presented us with 16 fully plated meals. This was fine – except we had to fly from Helsinki to Lapland. The security staff at the airport were intrigued to see 16 plates of meat and two veg trundle one by one through the X-ray machine.

Logistically – despite the serendipitous smooth-running of the original reconnaissance – this four-country tour involving so many inter-related bookings of flights and concert/opera tickets remained one of Sunbird's most complex offerings, and each tour, despite the common denominators, offered an entirely different experience, as indicated by the trip reports that follow.

19 July–2 August 1999

'Was that only yesterday?' was the constant refrain on this year's birds and music trip to Finland, Russia, Norway, and Estonia. There were so many different experiences each day (and of course constant daylight north of the Arctic Circle) that conventional clocks and calendars tended only to confuse the issue. 'Relax and enjoy' was as usual the best technique.

The superlatives started the very first day, when after flights to Helsinki and Savonlinna and a meal at our hotel, we attended our first opera at Olavinlinna Castle, the 15th-century fortress on its island on the lake. Appropriately this new production of Gounod's *Faust* was dominated by a giant white wing arching from earth to heaven (with accurately delineated primaries and secondaries), which while acting as the screen for a variety of projected images symbolically emphasized for the Sunbird group the significant role of birds in our lives. Soloists, chorus, and orchestra were superb and the setting overwhelming. So too were the performances of Verdi's *Force of Destiny*, Mascagni's *Cavalleria Rusticana*, and Leoncavallo's *Pagliacci* which thrilled us on subsequent evenings in the castle.

Our mornings and afternoons in Savonlinna were in complete contrast. On the first morning a boardwalk through Siikkalahti reserve to a convenient viewing platform launched our list with a succession of effortless specialities from Eurasian Bittern, Western Marsh Harrier, Osprey, and Eurasian Hobby to Smew, Slavonian Grebe, Tree Pipit, Willow Tit, and Wood Warbler. Nearby woodland added Spotted Nutcracker (the slender-billed

Siberian race), Crested Tit, and our first woodpecker before we took time out from birding (following the example of one truant participant who had been enjoying Savonlinna museum and joyriding in a seaplane) to explore the unique Retretti art galleries with textile artist Kaarina Kellomaki's giant light-fibre installations and Pertti Kekarainen's works exploiting light and movement in the underground grottoes; Edvard Munch in the main galleries; and the illiterate Russian artist Kuindzhi's sunset and moonlight paintings a revelation in the annexe.

A change of pace on the second day was ensured by our private cruise on Lake Saimaa, with splendidly close views of Black-throated Divers and Red-necked Grebes, and our relaxed sojourn at the delightful Saimaan wilderness camp enjoying a variety of activities – birdwatching, of course, a traditional smoke sauna followed by the equally traditional plunge into the lake, archery, swimming, rowing the church boats, eating and drinking, resting in complete silence (a particular favourite with one member of the party), and enjoying a wonderful cello recital with the lapping of the lake and frissons of foliage-rustle replacing the usual concert hall coughs to complement rather than detract from the Bach, Saint-Saens, Merikanto, Jylhä, Järnefelt, and various folk melodies (see Plate 9, page 241).

After an exciting two-day detour to St Petersburg – the splendour of the Hermitage, Peterhof Summer Palace, and numerous churches and cathedrals; *La Sylphide* ballet at the Mariinsky (Kirov); and a fine folk ensemble to complete the authentic atmosphere for our very Russian lunch – flights to Helsinki and Ivalo took us to the heart of arctic Lapland, where in the vast pine forests, bogs, and bare hillsides of Europe's last wilderness we found Siberian Jay, Long-tailed Skua, Brambling,

Eurasian Bullfinch, Little Bunting, Temminck's and Little Stints, Spotted Redshank, Willow Ptarmigan, Velvet Scoter, Little Gull, Rough-legged Buzzard, Hen Harrier, Fieldfare, and Redwing. But again the experience that will live with us all for ever was a musical moment. Our private mountain-top midnight-sun kantele concert overlooking Lake Inari with its 3,000 islands was as magical as ever. Martti Salo's style is gentle, delicate, and ethereal. And what a privilege to hear such a virtuoso play his own compositions just for us in this unique annual fixture.

The balance was redressed in arctic Norway. Although a Saami shaman entertained us with fascinating *joiku* impersonating many sounds of nature – a Great Black-backed Gull was particularly endearing – it is a series of bird images that in retrospect predominates: a Gyr Falcon on the rock above us; a White-tailed Eagle that swept down to interrupt our picnic (and disturb the eiders even more) only to be eclipsed the following day by two adults flying, fishing, and attending their young on the nest; Brünnich's Guillemots amongst thousands of Common

Searching through the Common and Black Guillemots, Atlantic Puffins and Razorbills on Hornøya island for the Brünnich's Guillemot was always a rewarding experience.

Guillemots, Atlantic Puffins, Black Guillemots, and Razorbills; King Eiders; Great Northern Divers; European Golden Plovers; Snow Buntings; Arctic Redpolls; and 55 Red-necked Phalaropes on one small pool. More *joiku* and a fascinating insight into the life of the Laplander followed during our evening with Ulla and Paulus Magga around the log fire inside a traditional circular hut up Mount Kilopaa. But again it was the birds that were the highlight: Rock Ptarmigan and Eurasian Dotterel on our pre-breakfast walk and Siberian Tit in the woodland around our hotel.

Our drive south across the Arctic Circle added more Siberian Jays plus Two-barred Crossbills overhead (which frustratingly refused to perch), and close views of the real Santa Claus who beckoned 'brother' Bryan into his grotto for a beard and knees competition (Bryan lost on both counts). But disappointingly our day at the famous Liminganlahti reserve was very windy, which inhibited many passerines. Even so, 100 Common Cranes, 300 Greylag Geese, various waders – from Curlew Sandpiper to Ruddy Turnstone (despite high water levels) – and a couple of Caspian Terns compensated for the all-too-brief views of Ortolan Bunting, Whinchat, and Mistle Thrush. So once more a non-ornithological experience provided the day's most memorable moments – our own quartet playing Vivaldi, Schumann, Boccerini, Haydn, and a selection of lighter music by several Finnish and American composers, whilst we enjoyed the most gracious meal of the trip at Finland's only snail farm. The sunset and rainbow effects that occasioned so many stops on our homeward journey must surely have been sponsored by Kodak.

Music of a different kind delighted us in Estonia: folk dancing both on Muhu island and at Rocca al Mare open-air museum, the Russian Orthodox sung Mass at Alexander Nevsky Cathedral, and the first three concerts of the 13th International Organ Festival in Tallinn, the soloists from France, Germany, and Estonia accompanied by the Gregorian chant ensemble Vox Clamantis. Our pace eased a little during the final weekend. There was ample time for sightseeing and shopping (even some official free time on the last day). And there were new birds: White Storks on roadside nests and pacing the fields, Red-backed Shrikes annotating the telegraph wires like short musical phrases, Grey Heron, Common Buzzard, European Honey-buzzard, Common Whitethroat, Icterine Warbler, Eurasian Nuthatch, and Goldcrest. But again it was a musical moment that provided the fitting finale for our tour – a meeting in St Nicholas Church with Arvo Pärt, whose self-effacing modesty and charm was every bit as captivating as his wonderful music, which had inspired us not only during that evening's concert but over many kilometres of driving on what remains one of our most action-packed and diverse tours.

As one happy participant put it 'My everlasting thanks for some of the most wonderful memories I could ever have hoped to have. Although I expected it to be exceptional, it far surpassed anything I had imagined.'

17–31 July 2000
The Finland-Russia-Norway-Estonia birds and music trip packs more life into each day than most people's monthly average. (The perpetual daylight north of the Arctic Circle helps.)

Our first day (not including our arrival evening at Verdi's *Force of Destiny*) included Eurasian Bitterns, Whooper Swans, Smew, Western Marsh Harriers, European Honey-buzzards, Ospreys,

Eurasian Hobbies, Slavonian Grebes, Temminck's Stints, and Golden Oriole, plus a sumptuous buffet lunch at a historic hunting lodge built for the Czar in the early 19th century, the artistic delights of Retretti (the main exhibition this year appropriately featuring the ornithological paintings of the three von Wright brothers), and a remarkable modern opera in Olavinlinna Castle, crowned for one participant by a specially arranged meeting with the composer Kalevi Aho.

The castle also topped and tailed our next day – in the morning when we cruised past it on our private launch the *MV Faust*, and in the evening when it was the acoustically perfect setting for Gounod's *Faust*. In between we slid past Red-necked Grebes, Black-throated and Red-throated Divers, Goosanders, and Baltic Gull. At the Saimaan wilderness camp the entire group manned one of the huge church boats Viking-fashion and rowed to a nearby beavers' lodge, where earlier we had seen White-backed Woodpecker, Crested Tit, and Black Grouse, and where no doubt a Eurasian Eagle Owl had seen us. An authentic Finnish smoke sauna followed by a plunge into the lake, wonderful food, and a delightful cello recital in the woods all combined to make this a favourite day.

Our third day was equally eventful – Greater Spotted Eagles at Lake Ayrapaanjarvi in Russia; the overwhelming spectacle of one of the world's greatest museums at the Hermitage; incredible male-voice singing in the Chapel at St Peter and Paul's Fortress St Petersburg; folk music and dancing on our boat restaurant; the Kirov ballet company dancing *Giselle* especially for the group and the surviving members of the Romanov family (there for the reinterment of Czar Nicholas II) in the tiny but sumptuous Hermitage theatre built over 200 years ago for the Russian royal family; and bedroom windows overlooking the *Aurora*, the ship that fired the signal shot to start the Russian Revolution.

More baroque splendour, endless gilt, the amazing Amber Room at Catherine's Palace, our first Eurasian Siskins and Pied Flycatchers in the park, more folk music over lunch at Pushkin, and a sightseeing evening in Helsinki enlivened day four. But could day five really have embraced Eurasian Eagle Owl and Lesser Spotted Woodpecker opposite our seaside hotel in Helsinki, Siberian Tits mobbing Siberian Jay shortly after our arrival in Lapland, magnificent plump Northern Bullfinches, waders at the sewage farm, and a magical mountain-top kantele concert overlooking Lake Inari by the light of the midnight sun?

Two for the price of one: Siberian Tits mobbing Siberian Jay.

Arctic Norway provided more excitement – Bohemian Waxwings, Bramblings, Bluethroats, Velvet Scoters, Gyr Falcons, Rough-legged Buzzard, Steller's and King Eiders, Brünnich's Guillemots, Snow Buntings, White-tailed Eagle... And the day we returned to Lapland added Arctic Redpolls, Red-throated Pipits, a striking summer-plumaged male Lapland Bunting, Red-necked Phalaropes, an out-of-range Grey Heron, and a fascinating Lappish evening with *joiku* and anecdotes before the log fire in our traditional hut.

White-throated Dippers and Grey Wagtails (another out-of-range species) from our bedroom windows up the mountain the following morning and Caspian Tern and Red-backed Shrikes from our hotel windows overlooking Oulu Bay in the evening opened and closed a day that also included pre-breakfast Rock Ptarmigan and European Golden Plover, a clear-blue-sky mountain-top view over hundreds of kilometres of forest and *fjell*, and a visit to the real Santa Claus on the Arctic Circle. Then came Common Cranes, Little Gulls, Spotted Redshanks, Black-tailed Godwit, excellent close comparisons of Eurasian Curlew and Eurasian Whimbrel, but all-too-brief and frustrating Parrot Crossbills and Ortolan and Rustic Buntings, before another day was brought to a memorable close with a fine meal at the snail farm and our own string quartet to serenade us with music by Boccherini, Mozart, Puccini, Sibelius, Merikanto, Palmgren, Kuula, Madetoja, Melartin, Markkula, Mononen, Lehtinen, de Godzinsky, Sherwin, and Shearing. By complete contrast the following evening's music was an overwhelming performance of Bach's St Matthew Passion in St John's Church, Tallinn, Estonia – but not before we had seen Short-eared Owl and Hen Harriers, close Crested Tits, and four airports.

After the many and varied wonders of Finland, Russia, and Norway, our final weekend in Estonia provided the perfect climax. On Saturday yet more new species – White Stork, Mute Swan, Greater Scaup, and European Goldfinch – folk music and dancing on Muhu island, and an organ recital in St Nicholas's Church. And on Sunday the unique experience of a Russian Orthodox Mass with the Archbishop of Estonia in the Cathedral of Alexander Nevsky, more folk music and dancing (and a cabaret of woodland birds) at Rocca al Mare, sightseeing in the attractive medieval Hanseatic port of Tallinn, and another rewarding concert in St Nicholas's Church, this time including Gregorian Chant from Vox Clamantis and their echo Scandicus in the organ loft. But still the experience was not over. As an alternative to a shopping spree on the Monday morning, the avid birders spent four hours around Tuhala reserve adding spectacularly Lesser Spotted Eagle and a male Common Rosefinch to their lists (and less spectacularly Common Chiffchaff, Turtle Dove, Common Crossbill, and Black Woodpecker). And still they came. Even on our way to the airport, a stop at Peter the Great's newly restored palace and the nearby President's Palace gave us more new birds (Garden Warbler and seven Icterine Warblers), so that our brief waits at Tallinn and Helsinki airports only just left us enough time to complete the lists and conduct the bird of the trip contest (congratulations to Gyr Falcon, Siberian Jay, Siberian Tit, White-tailed Eagle, Bluethroat, and Atlantic Puffin).

23 July–6 August 2001

Every year a privileged party of clients agrees that there can be no better end to a perfect day than Martti Salo's kantele concert, by the light of the midnight sun at a mountain viewpoint overlooking Lake Inari and the endless afforested undulations of Lapland – ethereal and enchanting sounds, like an angel passing by, as a respected musician with his own distinctive playing style performs his own compositions for us and explains the circumstances and settings that inspired him: the bay below 'where the waves come to sleep every evening', the Lapland Bunting that chided him for trespassing into its garden. But what makes the rest of the day so memorable? Certainly this year it was to watch, without moving even our feet, Siberian Tits, Siberian Jays, three Lesser Spotted Woodpeckers, Bramblings, Mealy Redpolls, Bohemian Waxwing, and Rough-legged Buzzard – followed by the world's most northerly Little Gulls, Temminck's Stints, Spotted Redshanks and Little Bunting, a selection that would normally entail several kilometres of forest walking in this Arctic wilderness by the Russian border, but that involved no more than 200 metres in total. Then to cap it all a cock Capercaillie walked in front of the coach as we drove up the mountain to our concert and displayed beside us, just as depicted on our 10 Finnish markka coins.

Such double-whammy days were a feature of this tour. We enjoyed superb views of Siberian Slender-billed Nutcrackers opposite the Salvador Dali exhibition at Retretti art galleries, plus Wood and Green Sandpipers, Slavonian Grebe, and our only Whooper Swan

Saimaa (Ringed) Seal sketched from our boat.

of the trip, followed by Verdi's *Rigoletto* in Olavinlinna Castle. We saw Black-throated Diver, Red-necked Grebe, and a Saimaa (Ringed) Seal (one of only 200 in the world) alongside our launch to the Saimaan wilderness camp, where as usual we enjoyed rowing the 16-seater church boat followed by a smoke sauna and a lake plunge, and were enchanted by a cello and violin recital in the woods before returning once more to the castle for the grandest possible production of the grandest grand opera *Aida* (will we ever again see over 300 performers on the stage at once?). And how appropriate to see fellow-birder Timo, one of our hosts for the day, as a most athletic leading dancer. Such daily doubles continued throughout the tour. Seventy Common Cranes, a close eye-level Eurasian Hobby, White-tailed Eagle, Black-tailed Godwits, and Common Crossbills, followed by our private string quartet at the snail farm. Crested Tit, Caspian Tern, and Red-backed Shrike as a warm-up for the opening concert of the International Organ Festival at Tallinn, and a stirring performance by the Estonian National Male Choir of masses and other works by Duruflé and Liszt. Lesser Spotted Eagle, White Storks, 149 Velvet Scoters, Greenish Warbler, and even at this late stage (on our 13th day) four new species for our set of 22 buntings and finches, rounded off by the lush and all-enveloping romantic sounds of the Dome Church's world-famous Sauer organ rendering Handel, Bellini, Gounod, Rameau, Mayerbeer, Liszt, and Guillou.

Every day it seemed that if one experience didn't overwhelm us another one did. Other musical highlights included a spine-tingling *Macbeth* in what must surely be the most appropriate setting imaginable, a delightful *Giselle* performed by the Mariinsky Company in the intimacy of the old theatre in the Hermitage Palace, Nicholas Kynaston playing Bach, Franck, Elgar, and Rheinberger in St Nicholas's Church, folk dancing at Rocca al Mare, Russian Orthodox singing in the Cathedral of Alexander Nevsky, and by complete contrast Saami *joiku* before a log fire in a Lappish hut as we learned of the life of the Laplander. We could have listened longer had it not been for our early walk to the mountain top the following morning for the closest possible Rock Ptarmigans – and later that day Two-barred Crossbills, more Siberian Jays, and the real Santa Claus at the Arctic Circle. Memorable also were the snowy-white Arctic Redpoll and crushed-raspberry Mealy Redpolls, the blue-throated Bluethroat, the Lapland and Snow Buntings, Red-throated Pipits, Common Rosefinches, the juvenile Shore Lark that was so much more intriguing and attractive than any field-guide illustration, and the preening pink-rumped Twite on Hornøya island, which was presumably the most easterly individual in Europe and 2,500km distant from the next (Caucasian and Asian) population. Large flocks of Steller's Eiders and Red-necked Phalaropes at close quarters also delighted us, as did Smew, Jack Snipe, White-billed Diver, King Eider, Long-tailed Skuas, Brünnich's Guillemots, White-tailed Eagle on four days, and increasingly fine views of Gyr Falcon until one nearly parted our hair.

So many birds, so much music, and all in the context of wonderful scenery and the splendours of St Petersburg, Tallinn, and Savonlinna. Europe's end certainly never disappoints.

22 July–5 August 2002

On our first evening, as we walked across the pontoon bridge to Olavinlinna Castle with the President of Finland, we knew it was going to be a special trip. That first opera, Merikanto's *Juha* (now recognized, 80 years after its conception, as the first operatic masterpiece by a Finnish composer with word-setting and speech-rhythm melodic fragments recalling Janácek) was a new and exciting experience for all of us. Wagner's *Tristan and Isolde* and Verdi's *Rigoletto* – two very different productions – followed. Operas in Olavinlinna Castle are certainly spectacular. But this year on our fourth evening the opera in St Petersburg was even more breathtaking – the production première of Puccini's *Turandot* at the Mariinsky Theatre: a dazzling production that is surely destined to become a jewel in the Kirov's crown. Yet equally memorable musical experiences were our more intimate private recitals – our introduction to the kantele in the woods at the Saimaan wilderness camp shortly after our chance encounter with the forest fairy Metsänpirkko (see Plate 9, page 241), our magical midnight-sun concert with the gentle composer virtuoso Martti Salo, the Saami *joiku* during our Lappish evening around the log fire, our string quartet at the snail farm, our accordion ladies on Muhu island. Plus Russian Orthodox singing in the Cathedral of Alexander Nevsky, three very different organ recitals with the Gregorian-chant group Vox Clamantis, the Estonian Television Girls' Choir, and St Michael's Boys' Choir and instrumental group, and authentic folk dancing in Estonia.

Our ornithological encounters were equally memorable – and similarly ranged from massed spectacles to solo performers. On the one hand, a thrilling wader show including Little and Temminck's Stints and 100 pirouetting Red-necked Phalaropes in arctic Norway. Or hundreds of crossbills in a three-species flock. Or a cliff-full of Black-legged Kittiwakes and auks including Brünnich's and Common Guillemots, Razorbills, and Atlantic Puffins. On the other, a silky plumaged and brightly bejewelled Bohemian Waxwing feeding quietly on the forest floor. Or a Greenish Warbler in the birch leaves. An Ortolan Bunting surrounded by Red-backed Shrikes. A Siberian Tit at a feeder. A scolding Siberian Jay. Or a summer-plumage male Long-tailed Duck preening on a rock outside our hotel window.

As usual Varangerfjord had much to offer, both passerine (Shore Lark, Red-throated Pipit, Snow and Lapland Buntings, Twite, Arctic Redpoll, Bluethroat) and non-passerine (White-tailed Eagle, Rough-legged Buzzard, and after much searching in a year when they hardly put in an appearance, single King and Steller's Eiders). Siikalahti yielded perched Eurasian Hobby,

Osprey, Eurasian Bittern, Smew, and Red-necked and Slavonian Grebes, and nearby Punkaharju Slender-billed Nutcracker, Willow Tit, Eurasian Bullfinch, and Redwing. Other highlights included Black-throated and Red-throated Divers, Common Cranes, White Storks, Barnacle Geese, three species of harrier, Caspian Terns, and Icterine Warbler. But for many the most abiding image was the pre-breakfast scene up Kiilopaa with a clear blue sky, hundreds of kilometres of undulating Lapland forests as far as the eye could see, and nothing but strokable Eurasian Dotterel and Rock Ptarmigan and a single pure white Reindeer for company – such a contrast to the Hermitage, where we were not the only visitors.

Contrasts, indeed, were the essence of this tour – not just the birds and music already itemized, but also the vastness of the tundra, the bustle of St Petersburg, the quietness of the silver birch and spruce forests, the dramatic craggy beauty of Europe's End, the gilt and splendour of Peterhof, the Gothic charm of Tallinn, church-boat rowing, smoke saunas and swimming in the lake... The one common denominator, this year at least, was the quality of the light. You'd think with so much of it about, 24 hours a day, it would wear thin. But the opposite seemed the case. The photographs looked great.

9. *Five a day (concerts, count-down lifers, and -putt aszu)*

'Imagine a music festival with some of the best European orchestras and ensembles performing high-quality concerts in some truly wonderful castles, churches, and palaces. Then imagine that this location is in the very heart of the best birding habitats to be found in Eastern Europe, including the world-famous Hortobágy National Park – a must for every birdwatcher interested in European birds. Well, this combination really does exist in the magical country of Hungary.'

So read the announcement for the next birds and music pairing. The Zemplén festival takes place every August in the Zemplén foothills of the Carpathians on the border with Slovakia. This wonderful mosaic of small peaks, forested slopes, beautiful valleys, and rivers meandering through countryside dotted with tiny villages and castles creates an unforgettable atmosphere of peace and tranquillity. The Carpathian castles that are a feature of the area represent a transition between medieval fortresses and baroque mansions. No less than three-dozen venues host the concerts, and each village regards it as an honour to be chosen. Consequently the villagers delight in serving (at no charge) local cakes and wines – even the four- and five-putt aszu. The performers attend each other's concerts. A relaxed and informal atmosphere is inevitable, and visitors are welcomed with genuine pleasure. In fact, as the first foreigners to discover the festival, our little group was usually officially welcomed from the stage. On one occasion we discovered that our front-row seats had been especially vacated for us by the President of Hungary and his party, who transferred to the rear – a gracious gesture typical of a most charming and cultured leader. At our first festival a beautiful young woman offered her seat at a well-attended open-air concert to an elderly participant – another gracious gesture that was the beginning of a lasting friendship. It was some time before we discovered that Lúcia Megyesi Schwartz was Hungary's leading operatic mezzo soprano and the celebrity star of many subsequent concerts and a magnificent *Carmen* when the festival produced Bizet's opera. (In fact we eventually realised that she had delighted us years before we met her in Hungary as a soloist at the Haydn Festival in Austria.) As at the Haydntage in Austria, the all-pervading friendly face of this festival cannot be overemphasized.

In 1998 the Franz Liszt Chamber Orchestra and its conductor János Rolla, the founder and prime mover of the festival, produced a souvenir book to celebrate its 30th anniversary. It included a blank page 'for autographs'. So we all signed a copy and presented it to the orchestra. Appreciating the joke, they reciprocated and inscribed theirs 'To Sunbird who recognize the songs of all the birds, from the Franz Liszt Orchestra who only have their instruments'. Included in the book was a full-page photograph taken the previous year, which showed the Sunbird group in the front row of the audience at an open-air concert. The photographer recalled that as he took the picture we all lifted our binoculars. For 12 months he had wondered why. We enlightened him with the simple explanation that a Northern Goshawk had flown past. Such bonuses were a regular feature of the alfresco concerts.

Many concerts run concurrently. But with careful planning and nifty driving between locations it is possible to attend at least three (sometimes four and on one occasion five) each day, during the heat of the afternoon and throughout the evening, when the birding is slow.

To complement the landscape and birdlife of the Zemplén area we always begin and end our tour with several days in the Hortobágy, that small piece of Asia inside Europe where the vast steppe reaches its

Great Bustards in full foam-bath display.

western border. Here magnificent Great Bustards still roam, while the huge wide-open skies are the domain of such raptors as Saker Falcon, Long-legged Buzzard, and White-tailed Eagle. The extensive wetlands and ancient man-made fishponds are home to an incredible variety of waterbirds from Eurasian Bitterns and Pygmy Cormorants to a selection of ducks, waders, and terns.

One year, on the flight from Heathrow to Budapest, an American client mentioned that he was only five species away from his 3,000th bird. I decided that for such an impressive milestone it should be an impressive bird. Great Bustard seemed the obvious candidate, so that evening I prepared a certificate appropriately worded and including a sketch of a strutting male. The following day the countdown began. I discovered that, just as difficult as producing the required lifers (Temminck's Stint, Little Crake, Ferruginous Duck, and Eurasian Penduline Tit) was ensuring that no extras crept in to usurp the Great Bustard. (Fortunately, Pallas's Gull, Glossy Ibis, Common Crane, and Stone-curlew were already on Cliff's list.) As soon as 2,999 was reached we drove to a spot where we had always seen Great Bustard.

But not this year. A second trusted stake-out. Another dip. This was disastrous. Any moment now a Red-footed Falcon might appear and ruin everything. Happily a third location produced the goods. 'Three thousand' announced Cliff, whose surprise and delight at seeing the bird was then eclipsed when a certificate, champagne, and glasses were produced in this remote and uninhabited stretch of endless puszta. Hardly the traditional setting for an award ceremony but a suitably celebratory moment. Nonetheless, I shall think twice before I tempt fate in this way again. I should know by now that in birding nothing is predictable. (Years later when I visited Cliff in Pennsylvania I was delighted to see the certificate mounted and framed on his wall.)

Once more, the flavour of these birds and music tours can only be conveyed by examining a few in detail.

16–26 August 2000

August in Hungary this year was unprecedentedly hot. The temperature of 41.7°C (107°F) recorded during our stay (but fortunately not where we were staying – for us it was a steady 33–38°C, usually 35°C or 95°F) was the highest in the country for over 100 years. So it was particularly ironic that the very first music at the opening concert of the Ninth Zemplén Festival was Britten's Ceremony of Carols. Yet as the cooler evening air blew through the courtyard of Sárospatak castle, the crystal-clear sounds of the celebrated Pro Musica Girls' Choir seemed entirely appropriate.

With members of the choir positioned not only on the stage but also on every stairway, balcony, terrace, and window on all four sides of the courtyard, the full surround sound was truly amazing as one exquisite performance followed another with pieces by Kodály, Bartók, Koscár, Petrovics, Karai, and Enescu. The evening certainly lived up to the programme's promise that this choir performing with the Russian State Philharmonic Orchestra of Morosvásárhely would be 'a new unforgettable experience for the listeners'. For the group this was the perfect end to a day that had started with Little Bittern, Common Kingfisher, and Great Reed Warbler on the pool outside our hotel, and continued with Eurasian Hoopoe, Icterine Warbler, Tawny Pipit, perched Northern Goshawk, Great Black-headed Gull, Middle Spotted Woodpecker, and Short-toed Treecreeper.

A popular pre-breakfast bird: Little Bittern at Trofea hunting lodge.

And so it continued. Indeed, for the birds and music lover it would be difficult to conceive a better series of double-whammies. The following evening we were back in the castle courtyard enjoying the Renaissance music that accompanied our Renaissance banquet (roast carp stuffed with spiced spawn, hand of pork stuffed with sheep's cottage cheese and baked in bread, brisket coated with horseradish, pie filled with cottage cheese and dill, summer fruits – washed down with Tokaj wine, home-made beer, and home-made brandy). Earlier we had been outside Pácin Castle (happily most of the concerts were outdoors) for a sequence of Hungarian dances by the Franz Erkel Chamber Orchestra augmented by two very vocal and visible Syrian Woodpeckers. But before that, Ural Owl, Eastern Imperial Eagle, Hawfinch, and Woodlark had all performed for our delight.

The following day brought Eurasian Eagle Owl and a male Rufous-tailed Rock Thrush (both filling the Questar), a close Lesser Spotted Eagle, and the only Red-breasted Flycatcher of the trip, before we sat outside Károlyi Castle for the most extraordinary Tamás Hacki's whistling concert with the Ex Antiquis Ensemble. Vivaldi, Paganini, Handel, Mozart, Mendelssohn, Beethoven, Bach, Verdi, Bizet, Liszt, Saint-Saens, Morricone, and Mancini have never sounded quite like this before. But how delightful. Similarly different were the concerts by the Weiner Quintet and the New Classy Four Saxophone Quartet outside Kokapu hunting castle – the two venues linked by a ride through the forest on a narrow-gauge railway.

A welcome return to Sárospatak castle courtyard the following evening gave us our favourite concert – the world-famous Franz Liszt Chamber Orchestra with ravishing performances of Bach's Brandenburg concertos. Before that we had two contrasting musical events at the churches of Olaszliszka and Tolcsva – the Vagantes Trio with Hungarian Rhythms ('thanks to the 20–26 special instruments and historical costumes their musical and literary production constitutes a picturesque historical chronicle') and the Zoltan Kodály Children's Choir with exquisite choral works by Palestrina, Martini, Franciscus, Fischer, Koscár, Kodály, and others. But the abiding image of the day was the White-backed Woodpecker on the dead tree beside the forest track.

More contrasts the next day: a programme of traditional folk music by the Galga Ensemble in the garden of the Greek Catholic Church at Komlóska, the Kalyi Jag Gypsy Folk Ensemble in Sárospatak cultural centre, and between the two a lecture in Sárospatak Old Palace aiming to provide insight into the creative process of producing literary musical products or artefacts – and although we only 'understood' the vocal and piano illustrations by Schubert and Beethoven, we could during the spoken moments reflect on our birds of the day – 26 Black Storks, Wryneck, Lesser Spotted Woodpecker, European Bee-eaters, and Golden Oriole.

The double-whammy to beat all must have been our final day at the festival. In fact for the gourmet it was probably a triple-whammy – and for the wine-buff a quad-whammy. Before breakfast, a Eurasian Eagle Owl flying, circling, landing. After breakfast, a Grey-headed Woodpecker displaying beside the road – only to be eclipsed by a Ural Owl catching an Edible Dormouse and consuming it shred by shred. For over an hour we watched it in the telescope until, replete and relaxed, it slept on its branch. Options in the afternoon ranged from swimming at the river lido to shopping and visiting the museum.

Then a wine-tasting of the famous Tokaj wines in the 16th-century cellar of the Hungarian King János Szapolyai, capped by a lavish baroque evening in Sátoraljaújhely, a Bach concert by the Franz Erkel Chamber Orchestra in the ornate Piarist Church, and a baroque feast of dishes made according to the old recipes with the Lavotta Chamber Orchestra periwigged and in period dress.

The Zemplén Festival really is a uniquely enjoyable experience. With events scattered in so many locations throughout the

Ural Owl with Edible Dormouse prey.

Zemplén countryside, with its wooded hills, hidden villages, castles, vineyards and flower meadows, a relaxed and informal atmosphere is inevitable.

This happy core week of a seemingly endless variety of both birds and music (from classical to folk) was sandwiched between two two-night stays in the Hortobágy, where the music was limited to gypsy cymbalo ensembles. But the birds were even more varied – 11 species of heron and stork (plus Eurasian Spoonbill); Pygmy Cormorant; thousands of wildfowl including Ferruginous Duck and – surprisingly – Smew; raptors ranging from Montagu's Harrier, European Honey-buzzard, Long-legged Buzzard, and White-tailed and Short-toed Eagles to a flock of nearly 100 Red-footed Falcons and a close perched Saker Falcon; Little Crake; hundreds of Common Cranes plus Great Bustards, Stone-curlews, and Eurasian Dotterels on the puszta; a further 22 species of wader on the fishponds, including Broad-billed Sandpiper, Temminck's Stint, and Red-necked Phalarope;

comparisons of Yellow-legged and Caspian Gulls; European Rollers and shrikes (Lesser Grey and Red-backed) lining the roadsides; and a seasoning of other passerines for daily variety, from Collared Flycatcher to Eurasian Penduline Tit.

But potentially the bird of the trip was one of the first we saw, en route from the airport to the hotel – an immaculate Chinese Pond Heron (if accepted, a first for the Western Palearctic). A happy instance of being in the right place at the right time, since it stayed only a few days. And Sunbird serendipity lasted until the end. On our final day when we declared the birding over and adjourned to a *czarda* (Hungary's answer to a British pub) for a last session of gypsy cymbalo, violins, and double-bass, a Long-eared Owl was discovered roosting in a tree outside. Neither did the music end there. En route to Budapest airport, sightseeing outside Matyas Church and the Fisherman's Bastion, we were surprised by the arrival of a marching band playing the stirring tunes of the 1848 uprising whilst a company of mounted Hussars in mid-19th-century uniform performed intricate manoeuvres around us. A fitting finale.

15–25 August 2001

As soon as we cleared customs at Budapest airport the Saker Falcons came out. Admittedly they were on the 50-forint coins required for the luggage trolleys. But they proved excellent talismans and very soon, despite their scarcity this year, we were enjoying the real thing, both perched and in flight. Also en route to our hotel we saw Montagu's Harrier, roadside European Roller and Red-footed Falcon, Eurasian Hobby, Temminck's Stint, and Marsh Sandpiper. Appropriately celebrating our fine start with Hungary's national bird their national instrument, the cymbalo, welcomed us to dinner and evoked the Kodály, Bartók, and Liszt that had accompanied our journey. Even so the most memorable tune that evening was the violinist's spirited rendering of The Lark in our individual ears.

More gypsy music (and another version of The Lark) followed the next day over lunch at the Hortobágy *czarda*. But the appropriate celebratory tone of this continually celebratory trip was set by the surprise champagne toast in the field as one participant, Cliff, saw his 3,000th bird.

Happily there never seemed to be a mealtime without something to toast and fortunately the Zemplén Festival is based in the famous Tokaj wine region. The special appeal of this dual-interest tour is best conveyed by considering the birds of the day, which were still fresh in our memories during the afternoon and evening concerts. For instance, as we sat in the courtyard of Sárospatak castle at the opening concert watching the Black Redstarts fly around Shlomo Mintz as he played Beethoven's violin concerto, and the celebrated Franz Liszt Chamber Orchestra performed Mozart's *Marriage of Figaro* overture and Handel's Fireworks music (with fireworks) with the brass sections positioned on the gallery and at the upper side windows (clever stuff – the conductor had to bring them in slightly ahead of the musicians on the stage), we could dream of our first Pygmy Cormorant, Little Bittern, Red-necked Phalarope, Middle Spotted Woodpecker, Short-toed Treecreeper, Bearded Tit, and Lesser Grey Shrike. Or the following evening, first in Hercegkút Catholic Church for a baroque evening of Bach, Handel, Marcello, and Albinoni played by a flute, guitar, and double-bass trio, then in Sárospatak castle church for the Budapest cello ensemble with music by Bach, Vivaldi, Haydn, Rossini, Barber, Klengel, and Hollós Máté to accompany our mental images of the magnificent Eurasian Eagle Owl beneath us in a quarry, the close perched Short-toed Eagle, nine Black Storks, or the Lesser Spotted Woodpeckers at our lunchtime *czarda*.

The next day we had a concert of Palestrina, Telemann, Dusek, Myslivecek, Debussy, Fiala, Haydn, Gebauer, and Bodnár by the Kosice Wind Trio in Erdobénye Reformed Church. That evening came a Renaissance banquet with dishes of the age and authentic Renaissance music and dancing from Musica Profana and the Company Canario: four hours of eating (stuffed pike, duck 'with drunken apple', turkey, pork, lamb, various poppy-seed and squash and cottage-cheese pastries, and fresh fruits) washed down with unlimited wine, beer, and home-made brandy. So it was fortunate we had so many birds to toast – the only male Rufous-tailed Rock Thrush on the Zemplén, the most centrally European Syrian Woodpecker in the world (which joined our group photograph at the monument marking this spot – but who worked out what is the exact centre of Europe?), our first Ural Owl and our first White-backed Woodpecker flying through a beechwood where we also saw several Lesser Spotted Woodpeckers and a very obliging Grey-headed Woodpecker, our first European Bee-eater, and our only Black Kite.

Music in two very different styles the next day – folk music from Zemplén, Szamár, Bodrogkoz, and Transylvania played by the Szeredás Ensemble at Vágáshuta up in the hills, and film music by I Salonisti, the ensemble that appeared as the ship's orchestra in the film *Titanic*, on the steps of the newly restored Károlyi castle. Two colourful concerts. There was much colour too in the birds of the day: 140 European Bee-eaters, 12 Golden Orioles, four Common Kingfishers, and 80 Red-backed Shrikes.

'Parlagi sas' to the locals: Eastern Imperial Eagle to us.

But the brown moments were just as exciting: a Common Quail flushed twice by a feeding White Stork, two Corn Crakes, Woodlarks, Eastern Imperial and Lesser Spotted Eagles, and European Honey-buzzard – though the biggest surprise was a Great Grey Shrike, a rare record in August.

Twenty-four hours after our first flight views it was another Eastern Imperial Eagle that became bird of the day – indeed bird of the trip – by gliding over our coach, flushing two Common Buzzards from their prey in a roadside field, and providing a majestic subject for our scopes. A close second was the White-backed Woodpecker (one of three), which remained motionless long enough for 14 people to enjoy the same scope view. Two images that remained with us throughout our three concerts that afternoon and evening: the Ukrainian Cantus vocal ensemble in Komlóska Greek Catholic Church singing Bortnyánszky, Vedely, Dilecky, Lyudkevics, Verbicky, Sztecenkó, Strumszki, and particularly Rachmaninov's Vespers and two pieces by Arvo Pärt; Sárkozy Gergely playing Purcell exquisitely on his baroque guitar in Erdohorváti Reformed Church; and the wonderful Franz Liszt Chamber Orchestra once more in Sárospatak castle courtyard playing Handel, Bach, and Mozart with Emmanuel Pahud ('the Rampal of the 21st century') as the brilliant solo flautist. All this we were able to toast with Tokaj's very best wines (including the 5-putt aszu: 'the wine of Kings, the King of wines', according to Louis XIV) at our dinner in the wine cellars.

Our final day at the festival gave us a perched Ural Owl, Black Woodpeckers, two European Honey-buzzards alongside the coach, and a trio of contrasting concerts: the Rákóczi Tárogató (a sort of shawm) ensemble at the ruins of Füzér fortress (music of the 1848 uprising); the Accordion Ensemble of the Conservatory of Kosice in the fields below (Binge, Bernstein, Gershwin, Strauss, Svendsen, Cuchran, and Smetana); and more magic from the Franz Liszt Orchestra in Sátoraljaújhely Catholic Church as it played Handel, Bach, and a Haydn cantata with Zandra McMaster as the mezzo soloist. We then discovered with typical serendipity that the *czarda* we had selected for our final dinner in the Zemplén had also been chosen by this superb orchestra, which founded and still organizes this amazing festival. In the happiest of ambiences we discussed the performances and they marvelled at the number of birds we had seen between concerts – even though our final total of 183 had not yet been reached. This was to come, along with more gypsy music, back in the Hortobágy with Eurasian Hoopoe, Eurasian Dotterel, Tawny Pipit, White-tailed Eagle, Long-legged Buzzard, Broad-billed Sandpiper, Spotted Crake, Caspian Tern, Long-eared Owl, and Red-necked Grebe. Finally enough was enough and we found time on our last day for several hours of shopping and sightseeing in Budapest before leaving our excellent local guide János Oláh at the airport to join his friends on a twitch to see Hungary's second-ever Sabine's Gull.

14–24 August 2002

As so often seems the case, the gods smiled throughout this tour. A phone call on our departure warned us that it had been raining continuously for two weeks. But before we touched down in Hungary the rain had stopped and we were treated to increasingly warm and sunny weather culminating in temperatures in the 90s. Dirt tracks that had been impassable by four-wheeled vehicles dried out before our eyes. And despite widespread flooding in Eastern Europe our visits to Budapest were before the sandbags were out and after the waters had subsided. Moreover, the delayed opening of the Zemplén Festival which had persuaded us to spend more time than usual in the Hortobágy at the beginning of the tour and less at the end, proved especially fortuitous as this year passage was unprecedentedly early, peaking during the first three days of our tour. Consequently we had the time just when we needed it to find close Broad-billed and Marsh Sandpipers, Red-necked Phalaropes, Temminck's Stints, both Little and Spotted Crakes (including the latter in flight showing the white leading edge to the wing), Ferruginous Duck, Eurasian and Little Bitterns, Common Cranes, perched Saker Falcon, Long-legged Buzzard, Short-toed and White-tailed Eagles, and Red-footed Falcons, Eurasian Hoopoes, European Rollers, and Lesser Grey Shrikes on the wires, Pygmy Cormorants, comparisons of Yellow-legged and Caspian Gulls, and of course magnificent Great Bustards.

Even so, our return to the Hortobágy at the end of the tour still yielded new species – Eurasian Dotterel (a magical experience in the early-morning silence of the Great Hungarian Plain), Glossy Ibis, Tawny Pipit, Bearded and Eurasian Penduline Tits – and a flock of over 100 Black Storks.

*Ten heron species have delighted us in Hungary,
including the 'Vörös gém', or Purple Heron.*

Our more leisured Hortobágy prologue also gave us an extra
night there to enjoy a new feature – a traditional evening of
authentic folk music and dancing just for us at a farm in the heart
of the puszta, accessible only by horse and cart – and a complete
contrast nevertheless to the zither ensemble at our final (outdoor)
meal together on our return, and the gypsy cymbalo, violin, and
double-bass trio that accompanied our *czarda* lunches.

The Zemplén Festival itself was as charming as ever and the
musical events we chose (usually two or three in quick succession
despite the 36 widespread locations on offer) as contrasting
as possible – from the exciting opening concert by the Pécs

Symphony Orchestra and the Kodály Choir of Debrecen with its scenes from Kodály's comic opera *Háry János* (how wonderful to hear more of that typically Hungarian work than just the familiar suite) to the final 4½-hour hunting feast on the terrace of Kokapu hunting castle with the talented and inventive Daniel Spear brass quintet entertaining us with a repertoire both classical and modern, including a remarkable and hilarious parody of Bizet's *Carmen.*

Other highlights included two concerts by the superb Franz Liszt Chamber Orchestra in the courtyard of Sárospatak castle – symphonies by Haydn and concertos (for piano, clarinet, and bassoon) by Mozart – and an inspiring and beautiful 'Ave maria' selection by the Jubilate girls' choir in Hercegkút Catholic Church with works by Caccini, Dufay, Fauré, Bruck, Palestrina, Friderici, Gallus, Strohbach, Halmos, Bárdos, and others. Filkeháza Greek Catholic Church hosted a concert of Byzantine liturgical music by the Byzantine men's choir of Rózsák Terei; Erdobénye Calvinist Church a flute and harp recital; Bodrogkeresztúr Church a programme of religious music from the court of Lajos II by the Voces Aequales ensemble; Erdohorváti a tárogató (Turkish pipe) and harpsichord recital of music from the palatial courts and *kuruc* camps (particularly fascinating as a prelude to the solo clarinet, bassoon, and oboe later that day), the Degenfeld Palace a marimba recital (Bach, Chopin, Schubert, and Joplin), and Károlyi castle a tea party with the Blue Danube palm court orchestra recalling life in the castle in its prime with the classical saloon music of 100 years ago, a transition between symphonic and dance music incorporating waltzes, overtures, opera medleys, and entertaining character pieces.

The selection of birds was just as varied and many memorable images linger in the mind's eye: Ural Owls sitting quietly amongst the foliage, a Eurasian Eagle Owl filling the scope yet still managing to blend in with the rockface behind it, colourful European Bee-eaters perched on the fence beside our vehicle and circling overhead, a male Rufous-tailed Rock Thrush still dappled orange and blue, a Lesser Spotted Eagle dangling a hamster, Eastern Imperial Eagles both perched and in flight, European Honey-buzzards, Red Kite (a rarity in the Zemplén), Golden Orioles, Thrush Nightingale, Barred and Great Reed Warblers, and satisfyingly nine species of woodpecker including Wryneck, Black, Lesser, and Middle Spotted, and a couple of White-backeds.

All in all, such a feast of birds and music that it is surprising we found time for eating and drinking in sampling the best of Hungarian cuisine and the celebrated Tokaj wines. But above all the happiest memories are of people – not just our own particular congenial group and the unsurpassable efficiency and helpfulness of our hosts János and Mariann, but also the warmth of all our friends in the orchestra and festival office, and indeed the entire population of the Zemplén, which always seem as delighted to welcome its British and American guests as we are to attend this joyful festival.

14–24 August 2003

The very essence of a Sunbird birds and music holiday was encapsulated on a balmy evening in August: sitting in the courtyard of Sárospatak castle being caressed by a gentle breeze whilst listening to the brilliant Franz Liszt Chamber Orchestra play Haydn and Mozart, as the Black Redstarts flitted against an unblemished blue sky and the birds of the day surfaced in succession from the subconscious – a female Ural Owl perched alongside the forest track, a Short-toed Eagle hovering just above our heads and snatching a Slow-worm from our feet, an edge-of-range Rufous-tailed Rock Thrush posing for photographs with European Bee-eaters circling overhead, Black Kite and Black Stork with the Whiskered Terns and Curlew Sandpipers at the fishponds... Sheer bliss. And the happy rapport of the soloists was such that it came as no surprise to learn that they were newly married. They even exchanged instruments (violin and viola) for their encore. Our sense of well-being had already been prepared by two earlier concerts that afternoon: the Hungarian Harp Duo playing Bach, Campra, Nardini, Handel, Pachelbel, Albinoni, and Grandjany in Taktabáj decorated Lutheran Church, and the celestial Pro Musica Girls' Choir singing Koscár Orbán, Bartok, and Bárdos in Mád Reformed Church. Little wonder we slept so well.

God was in his heaven the previous evening too as we listened to Mozart, Haydn, Chopin, Rachmaninov, and Bartók in the Lavotta House, Sátoraljaújhely (again tingling in the aftermath of a concert by the Pro Musica Girls' Choir in Erdobénye Reformed Church performing Lotti, de Lassus, Surianus, Gallus, Mendelssohn, Fischer, Kodály, Bartók, Koscár, and Karai) and dreamed of the birds of the day – five Eastern Imperial Eagles, European Honey-buzzard, Syrian and Grey-headed Woodpeckers, Hawfinch, Woodlark, and our first Black Stork. And all was right with the world the following day, when after enjoying a range of birds in the flower meadows of the Bodrog flood plain and nearby woodland – from Long-tailed Tit and Red-breasted Flycatcher to Great Grey Shrike and Lesser Spotted Eagle – we drove into Slovakia for a concert at Borsi castle by the Lavotta

Chamber Orchestra with Csaga Nagy (tárogató) playing Bengráf, Farkas, and Berlioz, followed by wine and cakes, another concert at Királyhelmic Catholic Church (baroque religious chamber music by Monteverdi, Hume, Frescobaldi, Schütz, Weiss, Purcell, Ortis, Sances, and Dalla Casa) and rounded off by dinner and wine-tasting at the Klastrom cellar, Tokaj.

Other such double-whammy days at the Zemplén Festival included the Matáv Hungarian Symphony Orchestra playing Rossini, Brahms, and Beethoven – to memories of the day's Great Snipe, Little Bittern, Icterine and Wood Warblers, Short-toed Treecreeper, and Middle Spotted Woodpecker; the Sola Scriptura Symphony Orchestra and Choir playing religious music by Haydn, Schubert, Fauré, and Mendelssohn in Pálháza cultural centre and the complete contrast of a lively Renaissance banquet at Sárospatak castle with authentic tárogató accompaniment – and images of White-backed and Lesser Spotted Woodpeckers, Ural Owls, and Lesser Spotted Eagles (all perched and posing); and concerts at Károlyi castle (quintets by Haydn and Mozart) and Sátoraljaújhaly Piarist Church (the Esterházy Ensemble of baryton, baroque violincello, and baroque viola playing works by Haydn and Tomasini) whilst we relived our views of Eurasian Eagle Owl, Black Woodpecker, Common Nightingale, and yet another Ural Owl proving that an Edible Dormouse was just that.

Our prelude and epilogue in the Hortobágy were just as satisfying. Here the more folksy sounds of gypsy cymbalo trios evoked Pygmy Cormorant, Little Crake, Great Bustard, Stone-curlew, White-tailed Eagle, Long-legged Buzzard, Saker and Red-footed Falcons, European Roller, Eurasian Hoopoe, Golden Oriole, Common Kingfisher, and Eurasian Penduline Tit; the slambuc (traditional shepherd's dish) tasting and alfresco dinner with the Forget-Me-Not Zita Ensemble evoked Common Cranes, Eurasian Spoonbill, Red-necked Grebe, Ferruginous Duck, Broad-billed Sandpiper, Temminck's Stint, Pied Avocet, Montagu's Harrier, and Tawny Pipit; and the private dinner-dance at Vólkony Farm with the Hétlépés Egyuttes Folk Band evoked the day's Red-necked Phalarope, Eurasian Whimbrel and 111 Eurasian Dotterels surrounded by the stillness and space of the Great Hungarian Plain.

12–22 August 2004

'Why have we been going on ordinary birdwatching tours all these years and doing nothing in the evenings and on hot afternoons when we could have been enjoying these wonderful concerts when the birding stops?' This observation by one of this year's participants encapsulates the appeal of these unique dual-interest tours and the double-whammy effect: reliving the exciting ornithological highlights of the day whilst experiencing such magnificent music.

Our first day was a typical example. Starting before breakfast with Little Bitterns and Common Kingfisher right outside our hotel in the Hortobágy, we continued with no less than 20 species of wader at Kaba sugar factory, including Terek Sandpiper, Temminck's Stints, Red-necked Phalaropes, and Marsh and Curlew Sandpipers, and even added Lesser Spotted Woodpecker, Common Redstart, Red-backed Shrike, and Marsh Tit over an outdoor lunch in Debrecen, before continuing to the luxury of the newly restored Degenfeld Palace hotel and the opening concert of the Zemplén Festival.

Here in the relaxed setting of Sáraspatak castle courtyard we could relish these superb birding experiences whilst enjoying the

Danubia Symphony Orchestra playing Rossini's Semiramide overture, Shostakovich's second piano concerto, and a particularly exciting performance of Dvorák's eighth symphony.

The following afternoon and evening we had plenty of time, over Andrea Henkel's piano recital in the salon of Károlyi Castle (Bach, Beethoven, and Liszt) and the four-hour Renaissance evening in the Rákóczi Old Palace (with vocal and instrumental music, poems, pantomime, and an eight-course banquet including stuffed starlet with cream and spices – see Plate 9, page 241 – pheasant soup with quail's eggs, oven-baked duck in a liqueur and fruit sauce, and roasted pork stuffed with cottage cheese and mushrooms) to relive the day's ornithological highlights. They included Black Storks, Black Kites, our first Lesser Spotted Eagles, Wryneck, Grey-headed and Middle Spotted Woodpeckers, and a range of woodland passerines from Eurasian Treecreeper to Long-tailed Tit and Hawfinch. The pattern was repeated the next day with an organ recital in Kovácsvágás Calvinist Church and a folk-dance performance by the French group La Farigouleto, followed by a concert by the Orfeo Chamber Orchestra in Sátoraljaújhely Catholic Church. To the strains of Purcell, Lully, Tessarini, Telemann, and Bach's transcriptions of Pergolesi's Stabat Mater, we could relax and savour the day's excitements: more Lesser Spotted Eagles plus the first Eastern Imperial Eagles, a huge female Eurasian Eagle Owl sitting on an open branch, Black Woodpecker, Thrush Nightingale, and Barred Warbler. The next day brought options – *either* a Rosemary Hardy recital at our own hotel (Schubert, Schumann, Britten, and Kodály) followed by dinner there and the chance for an early night *or* two outdoor events: the East European World Music Festival in the garden of the Rákóczi Castle, Sáraspatak, followed by the opening concert of the International Folk Dance Festival in Sátoraljaújhely Park (the programme promised 'frantic dance': the Eurasian Woodcock was a bonus). But the common denominator was the shared bird images of the day: comparisons of Northern Goshawk and Eurasian Sparrowhawk, a distant Short-toed Eagle, and a pair of White-backed Woodpeckers.

Next came everyone's favourite concert. Just to look at Lúcia Megyesi Schwartz is satisfaction enough (and particularly in the intimate setting of the Oremus Hall salon). But she also sings, exquisitely. And after the Milhaud, Berio, Copland, and de Falla came fine wine and food in the garden. Then an amazing and staggeringly exciting selection of ethnically inspired sacred oratorio from all over the world in the courtyard of the Rakoczi cellar Tokaj (Handel, Tan Dun, Bacalov, Lloyd Webber, Gil Shohot, Fanshawe, and Szentpáli), followed by a fully staged performance by the choir and orchestra of the Kolozsvár Hungarian Opera (the oldest Hungarian-speaking music theatre) of János Vajda's popular opera buffa *Leonce ét Léna* in Sáraspatak cultural centre (happily with well-upholstered comfy chairs as the opera continued until midnight). Again, there was the opportunity to opt out of the latter for an earlier evening. But the shared experiences included close European Honey-buzzards, comparisons of Willow Warbler and Common Chiffchaff, European Serin, more woodpeckers, and yet more woodland birds from Goldcrest to Coal Tit.

Our final day in the beautiful wooded valleys and cool forests of the Zemplén finally brought us the hitherto-elusive Holy Grail of all our woodland walks – three Ural Owls, finally disproving the winning entry in our acronym competition (claiming that the abbreviation stood for 'unreasonably reclusive avian loner'). Other memorable moments that day were the male and female

Eastern Imperial Eagles giving flying lessons to a juvenile, and the perched Grey-headed and Lesser Spotted Woodpeckers and Hawfinch. These indeed were lingering images to match the inspired concert performance that evening of Puccini's first opera *Le Villi* back in the Sáraspatak castle courtyard (with surely the largest chorus ever assembled for any Puccini opera – the combined forces of the Budapest Academic Choral Society and the Honvéd Male Choir). What a finale!

Nor did these double-whammy days cease when we traded the Zemplén Festival and its charming landscape for the fishponds of the Hortobágy and the indescribable silent vastness of the open puszta. Here the music was more exclusively folk: gypsy cymbalo, violin, and double-bass trios as we ate our *czarda* lunches; zither ensembles or folk-dance groups in the evenings. But the bird images, which surfaced from our subconscious as we enjoyed the traditional tunes, were just as memorable. Specialities included Long-legged Buzzard, Pygmy Cormorants, Ferruginous Ducks, Lesser Grey Shrikes, Bearded and Eurasian Penduline Tits, Common Cranes, Squacco and Purple Herons, Eurasian Spoonbills, Stone-curlews, Tawny Pipits, Bluethroat, White-tailed Eagles, Montagu's Harrier, Caspian and Yellow-legged Gulls for convenient comparisons, Little Owls, and that most colourful trio European Bee-eater, European Roller, and Eurasian Hoopoe. But the cameos that remained most vivid even after the music stopped must be the tree in Balmazujvaros flowering with Long-eared Owls (plus a single intrusive Golden Oriole); the flock of Eurasian Dotterels tripping across the early-morning puszta and the flock of Great Bustards striding majestically past a bush where Red-footed Falcons perched; the roadside Broad-billed Sandpipers so close that the split supercilium and unique bill shape were clearly visible; the single Saker Falcon on the closest pylon; and most of all the muddy inlet where at least a dozen Little Crakes and 20 Water Rails (plus a single Spotted Crake) fed unconcernedly at minimum-focus range – a breathtaking experience that lasted for 90 minutes.

Throughout this tour with both the birds and the music it was a selection of popular favourites and new and rare discoveries that – combined with an endless succession of imaginative and hearty meals and fine wines – sent us to bed happy and inspired and looking forward to the next exciting day.

10. *Wearing white for Eastertide*

When I first visited the Easter Beethoven Festival in Poland it was held in Kraków, the capital from the 11th century until 1596 and an exquisitely beautiful city – small enough to walk around in 20 minutes and still completely encircled by a broad open area of the former moat, now grass and trees with breeding Fieldfares. Old churches and museums abound and the architecture is endlessly photogenic. The central market square is the largest in Europe and offers angle after angle for the tourist's camera. Local birding opportunities were offered by the amazingly beautiful Ojców National Park with its two old castles and picturesque landscapes of gorges and Jurassic limestone rocks, where the deciduous forest ensured a variety of woodland species; by the Gorce, Tatra, and Pieniny National Parks; and by the numerous fishponds and parks. All this changed in 2004 when Warsaw became the host city. Although this was initially disconcerting, we soon realized that this gave us the opportunity to visit the world-famous Biebrza marshes and Białowieza forest in the north whilst still including some time in and around Kraków: the best of both worlds.

We could still retain such typical exclusives as a private concert of Polish Renaissance lute music, plus a selection of pieces by England's famed John Dowland, in the context of a special meal (just as the composer intended) at Wysoka manor near the Polish Carpathians, home of the Old Polish Lute Foundation. But we could also attend a Sunday service at a Russian Orthodox church on the Belarus border renowned for its choral excellence and with a number of CDs to its credit.

A significant factor was (and is) the timing. Since Easter Day falls on the first Sunday after the full moon following the vernal equinox, this feast can move by a month or so – which is critical when trying to provide a mix of winter visitors and summer migrants. Easter may be symbolic of new life, rebirth, and spring...

Loveliest of trees, the cherry now
Is hung with blossom along the bough,
And stands about the woodland ride
Wearing white for Eastertide.

... but the white is not always blossom. On our pre-breakfast walk in the Białowieza forest on Easter Day 2007 large snowflakes began to fall and by the following morning the core area was deep in snow. As usual, despite the common denominators, every year is different.

9–21 April 2006
The 2006 Poland birds and music tour once more confirmed this destination as equal to any of our established dual-interest tours to Austria, the Czech Republic, Hungary, Finland and Estonia. Although based largely on the Easter Beethoven Festival the selection of music was wide ranging (from Vivaldi to Penderecki), and every single performance was definitive. The selection of birds, too, was impressively comprehensive, featuring both winter visitors and summer migrants.

The excitement started on the first evening with a performance in the Warsaw Opera House of Khachaturian's ballet *Spartacus*: a perfect blend of testosterone and tenderness that thrilled us from the moment when Crassus ran into view along the carefully aligned shoulders of his legionaries – an amazing entrance – and completely captivated the British participants when the familiar love theme evoked memories of *The Onedin Line*.

The following morning, just around the corner from our hotel, a Peregrine Falcon perched on the Palace of Culture launched our birding list, to be followed by Black-necked and Great Crested Grebes and Short-toed and Eurasian Treecreepers at Razyn fishponds. A highlight of our city-centre picnic park was a pair of Syrian Woodpeckers at the very north-west periphery of their limited world range – a significant sighting that set us on a course to see all ten European woodpeckers, a quest that continued apace in the other city parks with Great Spotted, Middle Spotted, and European Green, together with a wealth of birdlife ranging from Goosander and Mandarin Duck to Tree Sparrow and Eurasian Hoopoe. Rudolf Buchbinder's playing of Beethoven's Diabelli Variations and four Schubert impromptus in the Warsaw Philharmonic Hall that evening was the perfect finish to a happy day.

The very first bird we saw as we disembarked from our coach on our second day was a magnificent adult White-tailed Eagle, completely dwarfing the Hooded Crows standing beside it on the small island in the flood plain of the River Bug. But our attention was also taken by seven Caspian Terns, Whooper Swans, a selection of ducks including Garganey and Northern Pintail, and our only Marsh Tits of the trip. Buchbinder delighted us again that afternoon, performing with the celebrated Shanghai Quartet Schumann and Dvořák piano quintets in the Grand Hall of the Royal Castle. Even more joyous was the evening Concerti della Natura (how appropriate) by Dorothee Oberlinger (flute) and I Sonatori de la Gioiosa Marca. This was Vivaldi at his most delightful and with Il Cardellino gave one (American) participant his second Goldfinch lifer of the day.

Kampinoski National Park the next day delivered our

first Black Woodpecker and Woodlarks and an obliging pair of Eurasian Hoopoes; the grounds of Chopin's birthplace a further selection of woodpeckers and finches; and the Famulki wet meadows our first Common Cranes and Black Storks. Musical treats included Chopin scherzos and Brahms rhapsodies played by Alexander Kobrin, winner of last year's Van Cliburn piano competition (another afternoon recital in the Royal Palace) and (in the Philharmonic Hall) Beethoven's symphony no 7, Prokofiev's Classical symphony, and Shostakovich's cello concerto thrillingly rendered by Natalia Gutman and the St Petersburg Philharmonic.

Maundy Thursday brought more waterbirds at Modlin, plus Eurasian Curlews, European Serins, Whinchat, and Eurasian Bullfinch at Bronisławka and Stawinoja. But perhaps the most intriguing sight of the day was the striking blue frogs at the latter location. A return to the opera house gave us a brilliant production of Penderecki's opera buffo *Ubu Rex* – a fitting finale to our days in Warsaw.

En route to the Biebrza marshes a visit to Drozdowa manor, the home of Lutosławski, for coffee and cakes, a tour of their nature museum, and a private concert by the Podlasie Quartet added not only more Chopin but also Wieniawsky, Koszewsky, Mozart, Piazzolla, and even Lennon/McCartney. Then followed more clangorous Common Cranes, thousands of

Greater White-fronted Geese, Great White Egrets, and a pair of Eurasian Otters. Our constant searching for Bewick's Swans and Bean Geese (two of the very few lifers possible on this trip for one American participant on the countdown to 4,000) was finally rewarded by two distant Bewick's, only to be followed at our next (and final) stop by a further 220 at close range, plus 250 Bean Geese that obligingly joined them just as we were about to call it a day (see Plate 10, page 242). The spectacle of so many target birds against a backdrop of Elk and Red Deer in beautiful evening light will surely be an abiding memory.

A morning walk along the Wulka road from our hotel reinforced our fondness for Biebrza marshes, with Lesser Spotted and Booted Eagles, Rough-legged Buzzard, and Black Storks, but at our next stop a passerine stole the show – the first Bluethroat of the year, displaying to us in all its technicolour glory. It was also a passerine – the delightful Eurasian Penduline Tit – that gazumped the Red-necked Grebes as the star of Dojlidy fishponds. But bird of the day was the last one of the day – a charming Eurasian Pygmy Owl that posed in the last rays of the sun on our arrival in the Białowieza forest.

Easter Sunday in the Białowieza forest is always a memorable day. It began (at -3°C with much frost and ice) with a pair of Lesser Spotted Woodpeckers (and a Lesser Spotted Eagle overhead just to confuse matters), and ended with Eurasian Three-toed and White-backed Woodpeckers sharing the same trees. Other delights were three Hazel Grouse, 31 Bohemian Waxwings, Crested Tit, and two hours of mesmeric singing at Hajnówka Russian Orthodox Church – a splendidly theatrical Palm Sunday (by their calendar) service conducted by the bishop of the diocese.

Then, on cue, came spring – warm sun (up to 19°C) and

The first Wryneck of the year completed our set of all 10 European woodpeckers.

the first Wryneck of the year quickly following Grey-headed Woodpecker to complete our woodpecker set. On our walk in the restricted core area of this ancient forest along the Belarus border it was obvious that the monotones of winter were already enlivened by yellow catkins, blue *Hepatica nobilis*, pink *Daphne mezereum*, and touches of scarlet *Sarcoscypha coccinea* like tiny earthenware bowls of tomato soup abandoned by fairies on the forest floor. By the time we reached Kazimierz Dolny ('the pearl of the Polish Renaissance'), the spring sunshine lent this attractive town all the atmosphere of a summer holiday resort.

Beginning our day with an hour's river-watch at nearby Meçniera on the Vistula we added perched Woodlark, convenient comparison of Northern Goshawk and Eurasian Sparrowhawk, and a pair of Eurasian Oystercatchers heading for the Baltic. And the sun was still out for our history walk through photogenic Kraków that afternoon.

Then came a fascinating three-hour tour of Wieliczka salt mine (including Chopin at 110m below ground); a choice of crossing the peat bog for Black Grouse or walking the woodland edge for Common Crossbill, Eurasian Bullfinch, Mistle Thrush, Rough-legged Buzzard, and a flurry of spring butterflies – Brimstone, Comma, and Camberwell Beauty; White-throated Dipper, Grey Wagtail, Common Sandpiper, and a field of crocus at Koniówka; a photostop for the wooden houses of Chochotów; the briefest of visits to Slovakia; and a wonderfully intimate visit to Wysoka manor for a delicious home-cooked meal and a memorable lute concert.

Finally, and appropriately, spring arrived quite indisputably with the temperature rising to 21°C and the songs of migrants everywhere – Blackcaps, Willow, Eurasian Reed, Great Reed, Sedge and Savi's Warblers (the latter vibrating in full view so close that it was voted bird of the trip, the first time ever that this honour has gone to an LBJ). Other new birds for our list included Black-crowned Night Heron, Spotted Redshank, Common Greenshank, Little Ringed Plover, Long-tailed Tit, and European Stonechat. Our afternoon activities were concluded by a walk around more fishponds or an optional visit to Auschwitz and Birkenau – a moving experience that gave added poignancy to the tapes of Kilar's Requiem of Father Kolbe and Gorecki's Symphony of Sorrowful Songs as we rode home, but which was put into perspective by our happy evening in the Jewish Quarter and our fine meal of yet another fantastic soup, tender meat, and fancy sweet, complemented by joyous klezmer music.

All in all, a very satisfying two weeks with a wide-ranging selection of music and a tally of over 140 species of birds, including a remarkable number of specialities and all seen very well. Next year we plan to arrive at the Beethoven Festival a day earlier. But this year will be a hard act to follow.

31 March–13 April 2007

The Poland birds and music tour always centres on the Beethoven Festival during the days leading to Easter – which of course is a movable feast. This year it was a critical week earlier than last, depriving us of some summer migrants. But more than compensating for this were the six extra concerts we managed to attend. This was achieved by arriving in Warsaw on a Saturday (rather than on Palm Sunday) – thus giving us the opportunity to attend three concerts on our first full day (in addition to the Saturday evening concert performance of Verdi's *Otello*) – and by restructuring the Kraków days to give us three very contrasting musical evenings there too (plus more time exploring the Carpathians on the Slovakian border, thanks to a later flight home that enabled us to visit Wieliczka salt mine on our last day).

The Beethoven, needless to say, was superb: six string quartets, five piano sonatas, piano concertos, piano trios, variations for piano and cello, and a stirring performance of the eighth symphony. But so too were the Berlioz Damnation of Faust, Wagner's Valkyrie, Mahler's ninth, the Liszt Years of Pilgrimage, the Szymanowski songs, Richard Strauss A Hero's Life and Don Juan, and the Frank Martin and Schönberg – all performed in the splendid acoustics of the Warsaw Philharmonic Concert Hall or Chamber Hall, the Polish National Opera House, or the Grand Hall of the Royal Castle.

In Kraków, too, the settings perfectly complemented the music: Vivaldi, Handel, Bach, Corelli, and Mozart in the gilded glitter and baroque splendour of St Bernard's Church; Chopin, Liszt, and Schumann in the most beautiful chamber in Poland (decorated with baroque stucco by Baltazar Fontana in the 17th century); and Jewish klezmer music in the 19th-century décor of

THE PROFIT IN PICTURES (PART II)

Plate 9 (page 241): *The Saimaan wilderness camp in Finland has been the setting for many alfresco recitals accompanying wholesome buffet picnics – such as the cello-and-violin and kantele interludes depicted here (note the forest fairy Metsänpirkko on the extreme left). Rowing the church boat is also a regular feature. Beyond the Arctic Circle, composer/virtuoso Martti Salo always delights us with a kantele recital by the light of the midnight sun. Other splendid settings for magnificent music include St Petersburg and Savonlinna castle. The road to Hamningberg and the fish-drying racks at Nesseby evoke the more basic Saami throat music. In Hungary, at the Zemplén Festival, appropriate music accompanies our Renaissance banquets, but our favourite mezzo soprano is Lúcia Megyesi Schwartz, one of Hungary's leading opera stars.*

Plate 10 (page 242): *'Wearing white for Eastertide' (one way or the other: see page 233) sums up the Beethoven Festival in Poland, where extras in the Białowieza forest include European Bison and* Sarcoscypha coccinea. *Also featured are a private recital at Lutosławski's manor, scanning for Bewick's Swans and Bean Geese in the Biebrza marshes, and a baroque concert in a Kraków church. Even more glittery are the baroque and Renaissance concerts in Bolivia's restored Jesuit cathedrals. The phone booths throughout the country suggest a strong rapport with nature. Birds featured are Tataupa Tinamou (in full view), Southern Screamer, Red-fronted Coot (another unprepossessing species but significant as it was the first record for Bolivia), Toco Toucan (as in the Guinness ads), and Blue-and-yellow Macaw. The impressive mountainscape is Los Volcanes in the foothills of the Bolivian Andes.*

Plate 11 (page 243): *Sunbird's latest birds and music tour is the Indian Summer Festival in Slovakia. Spis castle is the largest in Eastern Europe and the domestic architecture is as fine as any in the Eurozone (Levoca town square and a typical country church are shown here). The autumn colours render the woods just as attractive and are a bonus when searching for Black Woodpecker and Spotted Nutcracker. The Tatras are also looking their best. On our 2010 tour the very first bird we targeted (Eastern Imperial Eagle; both adult and juvenile flying just over our heads below tree-top height) was still voted bird of the trip at the end of the week. Slovakia is also a popular destination on our spring tour. Here the group is shown crossing the bridge to a bear hide with the dramatic Krivan peak as a backdrop. The centuries-old Russian Orthodox wooden churches on the Ukrainian border are a non-ornithological attraction, and one year a Hazel Grouse (usually a fleeting glimpse) actually posed for our instamatics. When voting for creature of the trip, however, it is always a close-run contest between the endemic Carpathian Blue Slug and Brown Bear. (There's only one way to find out. Fiiiiiight.)*

Plate 12 (page 244): *Romania is another country which offers two bites at the cherry: either Transylvania sandwiched between two stays on the Hortobágy, Hungary (where the sunsets embrace thousands of flying Common Cranes), or the Danube Delta combined with the painted monasteries of northern Moldovia. Sighisoara was the real home of Dracula (though those are birds, not bats, in this picture) and the Bicaz gorge is the best place in Europe to view Wallcreeper. (The Fire Salamander was also in this gorge, on the same rock as a White-throated Dipper.) Transylvanian mountains and forests are as attractive as all those film locations would have us believe, and on one occasion the almost mythical Ural Owl (a particularly dark brown individual) flew out of the trees to perch alongside our coach (page 291). The Danube Delta offers a quite different experience as a comfortable ponton is towed through the channels by a salupa past such typical birds as Great White Pelican and Pygmy Cormorant. The painted monasteries were described by Sacheverell Sitwell as 'among the most impressive revelations of the whole Byzantine world'.*

(continued on page 249)

PLATE 9

PLATE 10

PLATE II

PLATE 12

PLATE 13

PLATE 14

PLATE 15

AMERICAN AGRESSION

PLATE 16

(continued from page 240)

Plate 13 (page 245): *The Guatemalan tourist board promotes its country, with justification, as Soul of the Earth. Lake Atitlán was regarded by Aldous Huxley as 'the most beautiful lake in the world'. The view looking down on the town of San Juan La Laguna was taken from the halfway point of the relentless climb up San Pedro volcano to the habitat of Horned Guan, a popular icon. When you see the flowers and fruits of the Canek tree* (mano de leon) *on the path (the bird's favourite food) look up (pages 333-334). San Juan is famous for its murals and at the 2010 Encounter (page 329) one of the artists unveiled his latest work, confirming that birds and birdwatchers are now a significant element of local culture. The top of a temple at Tikal is an excellent vantage point for viewing Orange-breasted Falcon whilst 'elusive and wary' Ocellated Turkeys stroll over the ruins below. The coffee* fincas *along the southern volcanic slopes are joining forces to create a continuous biological corridor throughout Central America (page 331). The bird line-up shows Black-and-white Owl, Grey-necked Wood Rail, Pink-headed and Red-faced Warblers, White-throated Magpie-jay, and Collared Trogon. The Guatemalan age-old affinity with them is encapsulated in the embroidery on a local's trousers. Antigua, the ancient capital, is a delight of Spanish colonial architecture.*

Plate 14 (page 246): *Japan must surely be the best country in the world to see a selection of crane species, but other star attractions are Swan Goose, Steller's Sea Eagle, and Blakiston's Fish Owl. Despite the deep snow and sub-zero temperatures, hot springs (note the steam) provide warm and comfortable pools for the Snow Monkeys. In 2009 there was even snow on the roof of the Golden Temple at Kyoto. But the ultimate snow-and-ice terrain has to be Antarctica. The fellow waiting for a bus is the only Emperor Penguin I have ever seen. King Penguins and Yellow-nosed Albatrosses were more approachable. Also depicted are the graceful lines of a boat on Ushuaia beach, neck-straining photographers in the South Atlantic, Tristan da Cunha (the most remote community in the world), and steep stairs on St Helena.*

Plate 15 (page 247): *Libya offers some remarkable historic sites – not only the Greek and Roman ruins at Leptis Magna, Ptolemais, Cyrene, Apolonia, Sabratha, the Temple of Zeus, and Castle Libya, but also the ancient fortified granaries of the Jabul Nefusa (resembling a setting in a* Star Wars *film) and one of the very oldest mosques in North Africa at Awjilah. Billboards of Colonel Gaddafi were everywhere. Also on this page Sunbird groups are shown looking for Rufous-bellied Seedsnipe in the High Andes, Ecuador, Cape Rockjumpers in South Africa, and Macqueen's Bustards in the Rann of Kutch. There's also the wonderful profusion of wildflowers in Oregon, a castle in Spain, the Hermitage in St Petersburg, a river trip so typical of birding in the Amazon, and the magical city of Jaiselmer rising like a mirage out of the Thar Desert.*

Plate 16 (page 248): *To counter the cries of 'Osama bin Laden' that followed me since 9/11, various clients have pointed out a profusion of other look-alikes all over the world (page 50-51): Omar al Mukhtar on the Libyan 10-dinar note, a Scandinavian goblin, an unknown ancient Greek, Cronus in a Polish palace, the founder of the Bishnoi faith which a lady in the Thar Desert insisted could be my twin brother, Noah, St Christopher, Dracula, St John the Baptist, and even half a mountainside in Namibia. For an explanation of the 'show them the field guide' sequence see page 100. The selection of local ladies in India complements the images on Plate 3 to confirm what a colourful country that is. And finally there's some on-coach tuition: Sunbird's answer to an in-flight movie.*

the celebrated Klezmer Hois (where Spielberg stayed when making *Schindler's List*). In the intervening days our musical fare ranged from a private concert by a wonderful piano quartet in Lutosławski's manor to the sonorous and mesmeric singing of the Russian choir in Hajnówki Orthodox Church on the Belarus border at its Easter Day service (which happily this year coincided with ours).

Our selection of birds was equally wide-ranging. For the second year running our bird list was launched on day one with a Peregrine Falcon which flew over our minibus as we left the hotel. The Warsaw city parks then added a variety of delights – from exotic Mandarin Ducks and Indian Peafowl to more tickable Fieldfares, Eurasian Jays, Goosanders, and woodpeckers (Lesser, Middle, and Great Spotted, plus two edge-of-range Syrians). Chopin's birthplace gave us our first Black Woodpeckers, Firecrest, Blackcap, and Common Cranes, and our only Common Kingfisher. Lutosławski's manor gave us a very close pair of Black Woodpeckers at a nest hole. And also between concerts in Warsaw we saw White-tailed Eagle, Bewick's Swan, White Stork, Black-necked Grebe, Garganey and Common Goldeneye, European Green Woodpecker, Marsh and Willow Tits, Woodlark, and Hawfinch. In the Biebrza marshes we were welcomed by thousands of Greater White-fronted Geese, plus Bean Geese, Whooper Swans, and both Lesser Spotted and Greater Spotted Eagles. Red-necked Grebes were also a highlight in this area.

The Białowieza forest seemed to be full of Bramblings and Redwings, but our traditional Easter Day trio of Eurasian Three-toed and White-backed Woodpeckers and Hazel Grouse gave us only the briefest of glimpses this year (due to the extraordinary

A Black Woodpecker at its nest hole entertained us in the grounds of Lutosławski's manor after our private concert there.

weather conditions), though a Grey-headed Woodpecker was particularly obliging, as were numerous Great Spotted and occasional Lesser and Middle Spotted and a pair of Blacks, plus both Marsh and Willow Tits. The much-desired Crested Tit failed to show itself at all (not even a call), but this was put into perspective a few days later when at the edge of Podczerwome peat-bog near the Slovakian border a particularly energetic and charismatic individual put on such a show a few metres in front of our eyes that it was voted bird of the trip – well ahead of the other specialities at the same location: an equally close Firecrest, our only Great Grey Shrike, three Black Storks, and 21 Black Grouse (the most we have ever seen there) – plus White-throated Dippers and Grey Wagtails just a few kilometres away. Runners-up were an equally obliging pair of Eurasian Penduline Tits (another species that had eluded us earlier) at Spytkowice fishponds, where Great White Egrets, Western Marsh Harriers, Black-crowned Night Herons, Ruffs, Temminck's Stints, Wood and Green Sandpipers, Black-tailed Godwits, a proliferation of grebes, and the first Yellow Wagtail of the year also competed for our attention.

In addition to the birds and the music we visited many beautiful and historic buildings, as well as some magnificent natural habitats with cloudless blue skies setting off vast vistas of marsh and reedbed, pure white blossom cumulus-clouding the hedgerows, and ancient woodland carpeted with blue hepatica and pink anemonies. But in a year when the first three months had been particularly mild in Poland, with anticyclonic weather, warm temperatures, and clear blue skies throughout March, the most memorable aspect of the trip was the Białowieza forest deep in snow and even more mysteriously silent than usual – a rare and magical experience and such a contrast with the eventual arrival of summer (and a temperature of 22°C) on the day we left.

II. *Glittering cadenzas, sparkling mica, burnished gold*

With more than 1,400 bird species recorded to date, Bolivia is one of the last undiscovered dream destinations for watching birds. This friendly country has a huge range of habitats from puna and salt pans in the High Andes to Amazonian forest and vast flooded grasslands in the lowlands with an equally dazzling avifauna.

Bolivia also hosts a largely undiscovered music festival. For about 100 years from the late 17th century, great areas of the country's eastern lowlands were effectively ruled by Jesuit missionaries. They brought local indigenous cultures together in mission towns, built elaborate churches, composed sacred music, and taught their congregations to play and sing it. After the Jesuits were expelled from South America in 1767 their musical tradition was lost, but in the 1980s an ambitious project restored the surviving Bolivian missions, employing the techniques with which they had originally been built. The restorations led to the discovery of lost archives of Bolivian baroque music. This in turn triggered the launch in 1996 of a biennial Festival of International Renaissance and American Baroque Music, during which international and Bolivian musicians perform a richly varied repertoire of period music in the seven mission churches that were granted World Heritage Status by UNESCO in 1992.

This combination seemed to offer an excitingly different addition to our Old World birds and music tours, so we combined the sixth Festival of International Renaissance and American Baroque Music in 2006 with birding in the diverse forests and savannas around the peaceful historic towns in which the concerts are held. The tour also included a brief trip to Los Volcanes, in the foothills of the Bolivian Andes, allowing us to see many new birds and the chance to relax in one of Bolivia's most scenic wildlife refuges. It surpassed all expectations.

26 April–9 May 2006

Our first birds and music venture in the New World was unanimously voted a resounding and unqualified success: two weeks of sheer joy, providing a feast for all the senses, with excellent food and drink, luxurious hotels, a succession of outstanding concerts in exquisitely beautiful settings, and a bewildering variety of birds. Even the Renaissance-and-baroque aficionados were amazed at the range of musical experiences encompassed by what some might consider a limited and esoteric context. Yet each concert was so different (and so thoroughly enjoyable) that every one was a contender for 'best of trip', the top professional ensembles from all over the world (Argentina, Belgium, Bolivia, Brazil, Chile, Colombia, England, France, Germany, Holland, Israel, Italy, Japan, Mexico, Paraguay, Poland, Spain, Switzerland, Uruguay, and the USA) intermixed with indigenous choirs and orchestras that made up in enthusiasm and infectious happiness anything they lacked in polish and technique.

It is difficult to explain the heightened sense of ecstasy and complete satisfaction brought on by listening to glittering chords and cadenzas whilst gazing on the burnished gold and sparkling mica of the Jesuit altarpieces. The tingle factor was ever-present. And not just for the familiar Vivaldi, Bach, Handel, Purcell, Biber, Telemann, Monteverdi, Schütz, Corelli, Sweelink, and Praetorius, but also for the lesser-known Zipoli, Basanni, Gletle, Frescobaldi,

Between concerts we saw no less than
17 species of parrot and macaw.

Perez, da Silva Gomes, do Monte Carmelo, and most of all a wealth of unknown but thrilling works by the prolific Anónimo. Alfresco jamming sessions of local dances, a surprise impromptu concert of exciting modern music by a passing Brazilian orchestra, and a rare chance to see an 18th-century Bolivian opera featuring an encounter between St Ignatius of Loyola and the Devil (actually hugely enjoyable) all added to the variety.

The birds were equally varied and equally colourful – parrots and macaws (17 species), hummingbirds (10 species), trogons, motmots, jacamars, kingfishers… The relentless succession of exciting specialities started as soon as we arrived at Santa Cruz airport (with Greater Rhea, Red-legged Seriema, and Red-winged Tinamou) and continued until the very last morning, when new birds were still being discovered near our hotel (White-eared Puffbird, White-bellied Seedeater, Sooty-fronted Spinetail) and even, as we were about to leave for our flight check-in, a Common Potoo in the hotel grounds – a new record for the area. A big surprise to all, including co-leader Nick Acheson who has lived in Bolivia for the last nine years, was the number of easy birds by the roadside en route to every concert, without recourse to arduous forest treks.

So many cameos come to mind: the Bolivian (Southern White-crowned) Tapaculo fully exposed on a log, the White-tailed Goldenthroat feeding its chick (the first time any of us had witnessed this in a hummingbird), the Small-billed Tinamou that flew from cover into the road and the Tataupa Tinamou that similarly shunned concealment, the party of 50 Nacunda Nighthawks alongside our coach, the Andean Condors above our hammocks, the Red-billed Scythebill and the Swallow-tailed Hummingbird, the Toco Toucan just like the Guinness advertisement, prehistoric Hoatzins and noisy Southern Screamers, Saffron-billed Sparrow, elegant Capped Herons, Bat Falcon, Long-winged Harrier, Black-capped Donacobius, Red-fronted Coot (the first for Bolivia)… It is significant that every participant chose a different species as bird of the trip, though proportional representation gave that accolade to the delightful Peach-fronted Parakeet, which was a popular runner-up.

Other forms of wildlife ranged from the Giant Hunting Ant (described in the *Travellers' Wildlife Guide to Brazil* as 'probably the most dangerous animal you will encounter during your trip to the rainforest in Brazil… if all you do is see it, consider yourself lucky, because the sting of this animal is considered one of the most painful in the entire world – it may even cause hallucinations in some people'), to Brown-throated Three-toed Sloth and the Tayra which, unaware of our presence above it as we watched a Yungas Manakin, paused to drink at a forest stream.

Memorable images also must include the splendid pink-blossomed Toborochi trees adding a splash of colour to both forest and savanna, and the spectacular sandstone cliffs and 'Lost World' landscape surrounding Los Volcanes in the Amboro National Park.

Our only regret is that the Festival of International Renaissance and American Baroque Music is biennial – which means we have to wait 24 months before we can return to this happiest of festivals in a delightful country inhabited by the loveliest of people, whose courtesy and welcome to visitors knows no bounds.

12. *Old Wives, young virtuosos*

Ever since my first visit to Slovakia 20 years ago I considered Levoca to be the most attractive old town in the country. Every year on the birds and bears tours we included one lunch there so that we could admire the Gothic architecture and visit the magnificent 500-year-old carved wooden altars of Master Paul. I was therefore delighted when it became the venue for a new music festival: the Babie Leto (literally Old Wives'/ Grandmothers' Summer, or as we would say Indian Summer). When I attended the inaugural concerts in 2008 the weather lived up to its name and the clear blue skies and bright sunshine brought out the best in the autumn colours. As it happened Queen Elizabeth II was following in my footsteps a week later and the British Ambassador was busy preparing the way, but not too busy to attend the concerts featuring his wife as piano soloist. For the first group's visit in 2010 the temperatures were unprecedentedly low, but the warmth of our welcome was ample compensation. This is yet another unpretentious, friendly, and intimate festival with a wonderfully human scale. The right note was set on the opening night when we received our personalized programmes (every client was registered as a patron). But a typical incident was when one of our American participants, on leaving Jonathan Powell's recital, expressed her appreciation of the Scriabin sonata he played as an encore and wished he had included more in his programme. She hummed a snatch of her favourite. 'Ah, number 4,' said this celebrated composer and pianist, and despite being exhausted and still dripping with sweat after his virtuoso two-hour performance added, 'I'll play it for you,' and took Cecile back into the Congress Hall for a private recital. It was also satisfying to sit just two metres in front of Julian Lloyd Webber to appreciate fully every nuance of his sensitive playing – compensation for three of our group who, when they last saw him perform (at Great Yarmouth Hippodrome in Norfolk), were seated behind the orchestra as far from the soloist as possible, despite having booked the best seats. (This was due to a 180-degree reorientation in the circular arena but when we asked Julian Lloyd Webber over lunch why this had happened he couldn't remember.) In short, the Levocské Babie Leto was a satisfying mix of familiar works superbly performed and completely unfamiliar works, some of which were attractive revelations. And although the bird list was the shortest ever of all our birds and music offerings, the quality made up for the length. Let's hear it again for the perched nutcrackers and woodpeckers, the not-so-shy Spotted Crake, the chubby dippers, the nine species of tit, and most of all the low-flying Eastern Imperial Eagles.

29 September–6 October 2010

The new birds and music trip to Slovakia certainly started with a bang. The first bird we looked at (apart from pre-breakfast Common Kingfishers, Grey Wagtails, Common Chiffchaffs, and Blackcaps in the little bay behind our hotel on a promontory in Zemplínska Šírava lake) was Eastern Imperial Eagle – in fact both adult and juvenile low over our heads offering excellent photographic opportunities. Needless to say, 113 species later it was still voted bird of the trip, and only one point short of the absolute maximum of 110. Despite the unseasonably cold weather for this Indian Summer in Levoca festival, other specialities quickly followed, including Grey-headed, European Green, Great Spotted, and Middle Spotted Woodpeckers, white-headed Long-tailed Tits, Spotted Flycatcher, Eurasian Nuthatch, and Great Grey Shrike. Nor did we ignore the most famous non-avian speciality of the area: the celebrated Tokaj wines. Our private tasting in the five kilometres of barrel-lined tunnels, carved centuries ago as a hideaway from invading Turks, left us all with a warm inner glow, whatever the thermometers said.

Our second full day was the epitome of a birds and music tour: spectacular birds in the morning and a memorable concert in the evening. Senné ponds held a wealth of waterbirds from Eurasian Spoonbills and Purple Herons to Temminck's Stint and Wood Sandpiper. Highlights included Spotted Crake, Eurasian Hobby, Peregrine Falcon, perched Northern Goshawk, Eurasian Penduline and Bearded Tits, Ruff, Little Gull, Black Tern, 150 Great White Egrets, Red-backed Shrike, and four species of grebe in the same field of view. Even our stop at Tesco for toilets and money changing provided Crested Larks, an overhead flock of Common Cranes, and another Eastern Imperial Eagle being mobbed by Common Ravens. Bidding farewell to our local guide Milos Bala and transferring to our base for the remaining five nights of our stay, we arrived in the UNESCO world heritage site of Levoca, with its Gothic town houses, churches, and ancient town wall, in time to shower, sample more satisfying Slovakian cuisine, attend a talk by festival director Dr David Conway, and enjoy a faultless performance by the Czech Stamic Quartet of works by Smetana and Schulhoff and, together with Ivo Kahanek, Schumann's piano quintet in E flat op 44.

The continuing cold weather persuaded us to have a cultural morning the following day. Nevertheless, Spis Castle (another UNESCO World Heritage Site and at over four hectares the largest castle complex in eastern Europe) held birds new for the trip and several that we did not subsequently see elsewhere (Northern

Wheatears, Dunnocks, Eurasian Siskins, Yellowhammers), plus the delightful little European Souslik. The monastery village of Spisska Kapitula provided European Greenfinches and ubiquitous Black Redstarts and Tree Sparrows, and our walk from there to our lunch restaurant in the woods yielded Common Redstart and European Stonechats (see Plate 11, page 243).

Arriving back at our hotel at 1.45pm gave us time to change and drive to nearby Makusovce for an amazing lieder recital in the spectacular Dardanelles summerhouse (an outstanding monument of rococo architecture) by Klara Kolonits (soprano soloist at the Hungarian National Opera in Budapest, famous for her roles as Violetta, Gilda, Fiordiligi, Mimi, and the Countess in *The Marriage of Figaro*). There was also the option of relaxing or sightseeing in Levoca and another pre-concert talk at 6pm. But we were all gathered again in the attractive 200-year-old theatre at 7pm for another concert by the Stamic Quartet, one of Europe's leading chamber ensembles, playing works by Dvorák, Ives, and Schumann. The day was rounded off with a 9pm dinner at the Three Apostles.

A leisurely walk through the Levocské hills the following morning produced both target birds – Spotted Nutcracker and Black Woodpecker – with a supporting cast of Eurasian Sparrowhawk, a flock of 70 Stock Doves, Mistle Thrush, Willow Tit, Eurasian Treecreeper, and a mixed flock of European Serins, Eurasian Siskins, and Yellowhammers (many of these were lifers for our American participants). After another rest-and-recuperation hour back at our hotel or birding from the town walls (Hawfinches, Fieldfares), we gathered again at 1pm to view the magnificent 500-year-old carved altars by Master Paul in the Church of St James, followed by a light lunch, and the option of a 3pm recital by the exciting young Czech pianist Ivo Kahanek (playing works by birthday boys Schumann and Chopin, plus Klein and Martinu) or more birding with Martin in the Levoca hills (Crested Tit being the star attraction). Dinner at 5.30pm was followed by a moving and thrilling cello recital by Julian Lloyd Webber, a satisfying close to another day of birds and music.

A pre-breakfast return visit to the town walls gave us another opportunity to scope Hawfinches and Fieldfares (with a mammal bonus of Red Squirrel), and our morning walks in the Slovak Paradise ensured that the whole group caught up with Crested Tit when a particularly obliging individual performed at close eye-level height together with an instructive tit flock comprising Long-tailed, Marsh, Willow, Coal, Great, and Blue. Equally engaging was our first White-throated Dipper and an overhead Northern Goshawk, but the hoped-for Eurasian Three-toed Woodpecker taunted us with flight views only, whilst the Hazel Grouse was an even more frustrating 'heard only'. Lunch at the Hotel Stela was followed by Jonathan Powell's piano recital of works by Suchón, Feinberg, and Rachmaninov (or alternatively free time in Levoca); afternoon tea at the Conways' and a guided tour by Nadia of their beautifully restored medieval home; an evening concert of works by Beethoven, Zagar, Godar, and Zemlinsky by the Aperta Trio; and supper at our hotel.

Our final day brought a rise in temperature, but with clouds and intermittent drizzle. Even so, it was our last chance to visit the High Tatras and to find a perched Eurasian Three-toed Woodpecker. Our local guide Marian Janiga led us through the attractive beech and coniferous woodland of Tatranska Javorina to the alpine zone with its chamois-dotted slopes and dipper-decorated mountain stream until we finally achieved our goal:

a Eurasian Three-toed Woodpecker clamped onto the trunk of a close pine. What's more, at the same spot was a completely unexpected and exciting extra: the equally scarce and much-sought-after White-backed Woodpecker – a fitting reward for our effort and the grand finale of our birding quests. A male Hen Harrier back down at the meadow provided the final ornithological punctuation point but, to equalize the score somewhat for the short-walkers who had taken the cable car with Martin to 2,000m only to discover that cloud deprived them of the view and construction work deprived them of the birds, a female Hen Harrier obligingly flew alongside our bus as we returned to Levoca. After our showers, a quick change, and a three-course meal, we settled in the Evangelical Church to finish as we started with a big bang: the 52-strong Slovak State Philharmonic Orchestra with Julian Lloyd Webber performing Beethoven's Egmont overture, Elgar's cello concerto, and Schumann's second symphony, followed by an opportunity to discuss performances and say goodbye to all the musicians who had so splendidly entertained us at a reception in the Congress Hall given by the mayor.

13. *Whatever happened to Ruthenia?*

The Slovakia birds and bears tour is one of Sunbird's most popular offerings. But it came about almost by default. When the Ukraine parted company with mother Russia and declared independence in 1991, the possibility of a tour there seemed an attractive option. So, together with Jiri (our excellent ground agent for our Eastern European tours), a Slovakian birding colleague, and a Dutch friend interested in developing birding tours from Holland, I embarked on a reconnaissance over Easter 1993. Knowing that there were teething troubles in the newly independent Ukraine, we took with us a large amount of food which we gave to Dr Gorban, our birding contact at the University of Lviv. We accepted his invitation to share some of it with him and his family on the first evening whilst we discussed logistics, but insisted that on subsequent days we would eat at our hotel. We discovered that our hotel had two restaurants but both of them were locked. No problem. Lviv was a large city. However, not one restaurant was open. Eventually we received a tip-off that there was food at the railway station. En route our interpreter said that there would probably be tea or coffee. 'I think I'll have tea,' I said. 'But we don't know which it will be until we get there,' he explained. In the event it was pre-sweetened coffee, without milk, served in jam jars. The food ration was a cube of bread and some slices of sausage. For this we had to join a queue that snaked around the entire station. The irony was that I had in my pocket the equivalent of two years' university lecturer's salary, in American one-dollar bills. This was because the Ukraine had gleefully abolished the Russian rouble but had not got around to printing any money of its own. There were coupons (available on the black market). But for most transactions American currency was acceptable – and all in one-dollar bills because, of course, there was no such thing as change.

We knew that Dr Gorban earned only US$20 a month at the university, yet our hotel was charging us US$200 a night. 'How can this be?' we asked. 'Because the hotel is run by the mafia.' 'Can't something be done about it?' 'The manager of the hotel next door tried to do something but they murdered him last week.' We began to wonder whether the Ukraine was ready for a birding group.

This feeling was reinforced during our days in the field with Dr Gorban. He would mention that there was a White-tailed Eagle nest '200 metres down that track,' or a pair of Red-necked Grebes 'on the reservoir just over that bank' – but always continued driving until he reached a farm where he would engage the farmer in conversation, park the car, then lead us back on foot to the stake-out. 'Is it illegal to park by the roadside?' I eventually enquired. 'No. But we would be away from the vehicle for 20 minutes or so. In that time someone could have removed all the wheels.' That is why we had been advised to leave our vehicle overnight in a secure compound guarded by Alsatian dogs.

With all the restaurants still closed due to lack of food, we decided to head for Poland. At the border we exchanged all our coupons for 10,000 złotys. All those zeros. We headed for the first restaurant on the Polish side. Yes, it was open. Yes, they had food. But 10,000 złotys bought one bar of chocolate. We carried on to Slovakia, enjoyed a wonderful meal, and decided to restrict our Carpathian tour to the Slovakian side of the mountain range. And so it has remained.

The birds were abundant from the start (ten species of woodpecker, Wallcreeper, Alpine Accentor, Rufous-tailed Rock Thrush, Lesser Spotted Eagle, Hazel Grouse, Black Stork, Spotted Nutcracker,

Pygmy Cormorant, Thrush Nightingale, Collared and Red-breasted Flycatchers, and various owls – Ural, Eurasian Pygmy, and Tengmalm's). The bears came later. We learned that the foresters had built several hides in the forest and were putting out dead cows and horses to attract the bears when they emerged from hibernation. For several years, on three or four consecutive evenings, our groups had the opportunity to view them. Then one year conservationists persuaded the authorities to outlaw the practice 'because it is not natural' (a curious point of view). 'No problem,' said Jiri. 'I will put out a box of mice.' We considered that, for a bear anticipating a dead horse, a mouse would hardly be a satisfactory substitute. But the penny dropped when we were looking for Saker Falcons. 'The Sakers come here to catch the Woodpigeons,' said Jiri 'and the Woodpigeons come here to eat the mice.' But Woodpigeons don't eat mice, we argued. 'Yes, they do and it makes the farmer angry,' insisted Jiri, pointing to a field of maize. So that was the bear bait: maize laced with honey. It worked a treat and excellent photographs were obtained.

That extra vowel makes all the difference. Katka, our escort in Slovakia as well as the Czech Republic, was always annoyed when I told her that both her countries were too impoverished to afford vowels. Even the place names look like bad hands at Scrabble. Vlcnov and Plzen are typical examples with a 5:1 or 4:1 consonant:vowel ratio. And even well-endowed names like Vlkolínec and Svitavy still have twice as many consonants as vowels and always contain at least one penalty V or Z, sometimes both (Zvolen, Nové Zámky). Rich countries like Finland amassed all the vowels, so many that they have lots to spare. Their place names can even afford to double up on the vowels in a most wasteful and ostentatious manner. The vowel count there is at least equal to the consonant total and usually more: Kankaanpää, Haapajärvi, Riihimäki, Naantali, Elisenvaara, Vaasa, Kajaani, Äänekoski. Vowels for vowels sake. Conspicuous consumption. It's a pity the Common Market can't introduce a vowel-sharing system.

Coinciding with the addition of bears to the trip in 1996 was the routing of the tour via Budapest rather than Vienna. The tour report gives more detail.

> Imagine spending four nights at a hotel set amongst dramatic snow-clad mountains and conifers where the pre-breakfast birds from your window include Ring Ouzel, Fieldfare, Common Crossbill, Eurasian Siskin, Brambling, and Spotted Nutcracker. Somewhere in the far north perhaps? Now imagine another hotel in a wooded promontory on a lake where a glimpse out of your window could reveal Black Stork, Black Kite, Lesser Spotted Eagle, Golden Oriole, Eurasian Hoopoe, European Bee-eater, Common Nightingale, and European Serin. Maybe somewhere in southern Europe if it were not for the eastern species? In fact these two hotels were our bases for a week in Slovakia, a little-known country which offers a spectacular cross-section of European avifauna in wonderfully photogenic settings.
>
> Snow-clad peaks and primeval beech forest, rolling countryside, wetlands, and limestone gorges provide some of the most exciting birdwatching on offer, including Pygmy Cormorant, Squacco Heron, Tengmalm's, Ural, Eurasian Pygmy and Eurasian Eagle Owls, all ten European woodpeckers, Wallcreeper, Barred and River Warblers, Rufous-tailed Rock Thrush, Thrush Nightingale, Collared and Red-breasted Flycatchers, Alpine Accentor, and Rock Bunting.
>
> The 1996 tour recorded most of these and much more besides, but in addition to the 175 bird species there was an impressive bonus this year – European Brown Bear. We set aside three

Our first day in Slovakia had something for everyone: three Tengmalm's Owls,
Eurasian Pygmy Owl, White-backed Woodpecker, two Eurasian Three-toed Woodpeckers,
Fire Salamanders among the Soldanellas, Giant Pasque Flowers, Camberwell Beauties,
and five close European Brown Bears against the dramatic backdrop of Kriván peak.

evenings for bear watching and were rewarded with exciting
views on each occasion: breathtaking finales to three different
and stimulating days in the field.

Another variation on the 1996 tour was routing the trip via
Budapest rather than Vienna. This gave us the opportunity to
see one of Europe's most beautiful capitals as we began our drive
through Hungary. At the border crossing, our first Black Stork
landed on the Hungarian side and our first Black Redstart sang
us into Slovakia, with a roadside White-throated Dipper along

the way. But the abiding image of the journey was perhaps the hordes of Fieldfares among the vivid crocus meadows.

Our first day is summed up by the caption to the accompanying illustration (see opposite). Each subsequent day had its highlights – the Wallcreepers out-flashing the butterflies on a sunlit cliff-face; the two European Honey-buzzards being mobbed by a Golden Eagle; the Eastern Imperial Eagle perched and then flying by the roadside; the Barred Warbler which performed so well and for so long that whilst we were standing there we were able to watch Short-toed Eagle, European Bee-eaters, and Common Quail; the Wryneck in an old orchard; and the summer migrants that had just arrived – River Warbler, Red-breasted Flycatcher, and Lesser Grey Shrike.

But for sheer quantity and quality combined, our day at Senné ponds is worth a special mention – well over 100 species including Red-necked Grebe, Glossy Ibis, Purple Heron, Great White Egret, Common Crane, a profusion of Ruffs, Marsh Sandpipers, all three marsh terns, Bearded and Eurasian Penduline Tits, and numerous Red-footed Falcons hawking overhead and perched on the wires.

Added to this were daily non-ornithological extras: the photogenic old wooden Russian Orthodox churches on the Ukrainian border (see Plate 11, page 243), the highest carved wooden altarpiece in the world in Levoca, the evocative atmosphere of Vlkolínec village (a World Heritage Site), and the largest castle in Eastern Europe.

The tour continued to run successfully to this formula until the millennium and it is worth including the 1997 tour summary if only to record the typically hospitable gesture by the Mayor of Kasov.

Once more, our Slovakia tour opened with a first day that had something for everyone – pre-breakfast Spotted Nutcrackers, a morning Wallcreeper, an afternoon Northern Goshawk-on-nest, and an evening European Brown Bear. All this interspersed with Fire Salamander, Camberwell Beauty, and Giant Pasque Flowers. Spectacular views of Tengmalm's Owl and Eurasian Three-toed Woodpecker followed, and the views of bears improved on each of three consecutive evenings, culminating in a five-year-old individual performing non-stop on a dead cow for an hour-and-a-half at a distance of only 40 metres (and indeed at one point a heart-stopping five metres away).

This one-week trip is timed critically to begin in winter (better for the bears, owls, woodpeckers) and finish in summer (with the arrival of all the migrants). This year spring was three weeks late and our Slovakian hosts were dismayed on our arrival by the still-deep snow and the absence of birds. Nevertheless, within days the snow and ice had gone, our clouts were completely cast (to the very bounds of common decency), and the first European Bee-eaters, Barred and River Warblers, Thrush Nightingales, and Lesser Grey Shrikes had arrived. This week of contrasts was once again typified by the birds we could see from our bedroom windows – at the first hotel Spotted Nutcrackers, Ring Ouzels, Bramblings, and Crested Tit; and at the second, Golden Oriole, Common Nightingales, Common Kingfishers, Hawfinches, and Red-necked Grebes. Highlights included close views of White-backed, Grey-headed, Black, and Syrian Woodpeckers; a Wryneck that eventually compensated for innumerable glimpses by sitting on a nearby branch until we walked away; Common Crossbills in a Celtic hill fort, a family of Eurasian Eagle Owls (parents, two fluffy chicks, and egg) on a ledge just below us; plus

*White-winged Terns amongst the Black
Terns are always striking.*

Eurasian Hobby, Saker Falcon, and Eastern Imperial, Golden, Short-toed, and Lesser Spotted Eagles. As usual our day at Senné ponds was the most memorable for quality and quantity – thousands of birds of 121 species, including all five grebes, Little and Great White Egrets, Purple Heron, Black Stork, Eurasian Spoonbill, Ferruginous Duck, Pied Avocet, Marsh Sandpiper, all three marsh terns, and Bearded and Eurasian Penduline Tits. Appropriately symbolic was the Eurasian Bittern that greeted us on our arrival by freezing on the roadside verge as we drove right up to it, cameras clicking. This remarkable range of European species – including so many specialities – meant that everyone in the group had at least one lifer (even a regular client who had covered the Western Palearctic from Finland and Poland to Austria and Israel), and more than one member of the group notched up 50 lifers during the week.

Such contrasts within so few kilometres and so few days are difficult to imagine, but Slovakia really is a country of contrasts – dramatic snow-clad mountains, alpine meadows, powerfully primeval beech forests, rolling countryside, limestone gorges, lakes, vineyards, and small-scale agriculture. And encapsulating the friendliness of the place was the gesture by the Mayor of Kasov, who crossed the fields to us in his best suit whilst we were watching Short-toed Eagle, Northern Goshawk, and Eurasian Hobby to say, 'We are a small community but a hospitable one; we invite you to drink some wine with us.' That was on 1 May – election day in Britain. The mayor would have got our vote.

Then in 2000 the sequence was reversed from west-to-east to east-to-west:

Slovakia, unknown and unspoilt, lost in the middle of eastern Europe, is a ravishingly beautiful country of snow-clad mountains, wooded hills, primeval beech forests, limestone gorges, clear streams golden-edged with marsh marigolds, country roads lined with white plum trees in blossom, fields of dandelions, and open plains where horses still plough and babushkas hoe and weed by hand. The endless variety of trees in the mixed coniferous and deciduous landscape ensures that each vista contains every green from almost-black to almost-yellow. Romanticized memories of childhood become a living reality. Indeed, the terrain is the archetypal setting for all those fairytales of our infancy. To visit the country is to step back in time. And late April is the very best time to enjoy this magical experience.

This year the weather was exceptionally hot (30°C), the mountains were free of cloud, and bright blue skies were the norm. In fact, the midday lull in bird activity was reminiscent of the tropics and freed us to include more non-ornithological extras than ever before – with visits to Vlkolínec (a typical example of an old Slovak mountain village), Liptov village museum at Pribylina (valuable examples old folk architecture moved from the villages flooded by the reservoir of Liptovská Mara), Havronec Celtic village and hill fort (representing life in the area 2,500 years ago), and Banska Stiavnica (the amazingly photogenic old mining town – the oldest documents on gold and silver mining are dated 1075 – with its gothic, baroque, and Renaissance architecture).

Nevertheless we still saw as many birds as last year (one more, in fact) and enjoyed a succession of exciting specialities. For once we started at the eastern end of the country and spent our first day in the primeval beech forests on the borders of the Ukraine and Poland. This meant that our first woodpecker in our annual quest for the full European set of ten was the much-sought-after White-backed (usually our last), quickly followed by Grey-headed and two male Lesser Spotteds, which performed at close quarters beneath the 300-year-old wooden Orthodox Church of Rusky Potok. Great Spotted and Wryneck were virtually the first birds on our second day, Middle Spotted and Syrian on the third, and European Green on the fourth. But the climax appropriately came on our last day when, as we waited at a Eurasian Three-toed nest hole, the hitherto elusive Black hurtled towards us like a cannonball and clamped itself onto a nearby tree for breathtaking views – earning itself a first-equal placing as bird of the trip along with Wallcreeper. This latter species, just as the woodpeckers evoke the variety of Slovakian forests, sums up the images of Slovakia's rocks and mountains, with the pair displaying, singing, nest building, and fluttering like butterflies against the sunlit cliff-face. Runner-up in the contest was Eastern Imperial Eagle, not only because of the grandeur of this magnificent bird, but also because of the excellence of the views as we watched a pair in flight, perched, and copulating. Golden Eagle, Lesser Spotted Eagle, Short-toed Eagle, Saker Falcon, Eurasian Hobby, Northern

'Lesser Spotted' was the ambiguous and inadequate call at Rusky Potok Church when two woodpeckers were displaying as an eagle flew overhead.

Goshawk, Osprey, and Montagu's Harrier also provided us with many enjoyable raptor moments.

Other favourites – again because of the wonderful views – were Hawfinches feeding on the path, Eurasian Penduline Tit building its nest, and White-winged Terns dipping and twisting amongst the Whiskereds and Blacks at Senné ponds. Highlights there also included Red-necked and Black-necked Grebes, their summer plumage intensified by the bright sunshine, a pair of Smew, Ferruginous Ducks, Pygmy Cormorants, Eurasian Bittern, Black-crowned Night Heron, Purple Herons, Great White Egrets, Marsh Sandpiper, Savi's and Great Reed Warblers, and a flight of Common Cranes calling low overhead. Quantity as well as quality: we saw over 100 species that day. Then came the owls – the Tawny mobbed by Common Blackbirds, the female Eurasian Eagle Owl mantling two white owlets in the heat of the day, the

Tengmalm's peering out of its tree hole, and the Ural flying large, grey, and silent through the White Firs. A perched and posing Spotted Nutcracker was also popular, as were the Crested Tits and Ring Ouzels on the same sentinel spruces. Other favourites ranged from the White-throated Dippers on every rushing mountain stream and the summer-plumaged Water Pipits around the top station of the High Tatras cable-car to the newly arrived Collared Flycatchers, the Rock Bunting, and the Barred Warbler.

Slovakia really is an amazing place. Just as it was the crossroads and melting pot of the Old World for human migration, where else could you see such a Mediterranean, northern European and eastern mix of birds?

And as usual, for the general naturalist, the supporting cast was superb: Fire Salamander, Montandon's (endemic to the Carpathians) and Alpine Newts, Eastern Green and Sand Lizards, European Souslik, Red Fox, Red and Roe Deer... numerous butterflies from Camberwell Beauty to Scarce Swallowtail... and everywhere a delightful selection of wild flowers – *Soldanella, Daphne, Adonis,* Spring Crocus, Pasque Flower... But in choosing a non-avian 'creature of the trip' most clients will have to think long and hard in deciding between the 200kg male European Brown Bear and the endemic Carpathian Blue Slug. (No, it didn't talk so it wasn't really a substitute for a Norwegian Blue Parrot.)

Then in 2001 came another development. Although the tour had remained popular, usually fully booked, throughout the 1990s, the American participants often observed that it was a long way to come for just one week. So we devised a back-to-back week in Hungary. Each country provided a holiday that was a perfect entity in itself, but to yoke these two countries together in a comprehensive Carpathian Basin tour was logical. And there was a certain irony in the fact that Slovakia had only just become an independent country again after over 1,000 years. The formula was another winner. Here's the combined tour report for 2001.

For a two-country birding holiday in Eastern Europe, the combination of Slovakia and Hungary offers an unbeatable pairing. In 2001 each country yielded about 180 species (Slovakia a few less, Hungary a few more). Each country offered a wetland area with over 100 species in one day. But the differences were significant and the combined total of 222 species was a record (for any tour in the two countries by any company). For one participant this meant 200 lifers (again, surely a record for two weeks anywhere in Europe) – though as he was on a genealogical research pilgrimage to visit the Slovakian homeland of his grandparents no doubt his genes knew the birds. Selections from the list would probably leave most birders pondering the location – and the time of year. On the one hand, Mediterranean species such as Rock Bunting, Rufous-tailed Rock Thrush, Eurasian Scops Owl, Squacco Heron, Short-toed Eagle, Collared Pratincole, Glossy Ibis, European Bee-eater, and European Roller (plus even Wallcreeper and Alpine Accentor, which are at the northern limit of their range here). On the other, northern and/or eastern species such as Thrush Nightingale, White-tailed Eagle, Ural Owl, Eurasian Three-toed and White-backed Woodpeckers, Steppe, Eastern Imperial, and Lesser Spotted Eagles, Pallid Harrier, Red-footed and Saker Falcons, Pygmy Cormorant, Black Stork, Red-breasted and Collared Flycatchers, and Aquatic, River, and Barred Warblers. Great Bustard, Spotted Nutcracker and Long-legged Buzzard only confuse the issue. Alternatively surely winter meets summer when Smew, Bohemian Waxwing, and Great Grey Shrike are seen alongside Common Quail, Corn Crake, and Golden Oriole.

Slovakia

This country always delights with its stunning natural beauty and infinite variety, but never before have the mountains been so clear and the views so breathtaking. And what an amazing selection of birds. Hazel Grouse, for instance, often features as a 'heard only', but this year, in addition to a pair that posed all too briefly in the Questar, one female tolerated pocket instamatics at a distance of one metre (see Plate 11, page 243). Similarly a pair of Eurasian Three-toed Woodpeckers was still in full view as we walked away (as were Lesser Spotted, Middle Spotted, Grey-headed, Black and Wryneck) – rivalled only by the lingering Ural and Eurasian Eagle Owls and Saker Falcons. As for the Eastern Imperial Eagles, not only were they still performing as we departed, but one of them seemed to escort us from the premises, flying low alongside us as we left. Even the Thrush Nightingale chose to sing from an exposed perch.

From the very moment we arrived at the border and watched a brief skirmish between a migrating Pallid Harrier and a Booted Eagle, the birds performed on cue: Alpine Accentor, Water Pipit, and a close pair of Golden Eagles in the snows of the High Tatras; Rock Bunting and Common Redstart in a southern gorge; waders and wildfowl (plus Glossy Ibis, Eurasian Bittern, and White-winged Tern) on Senné ponds; European Bee-eaters and Eurasian Hoopoe on the Hungarian border; Red-breasted Flycatcher and Black Stork in the eastern forests. And as usual the contrasts were emphasized by the 'window birds' from our first and last hotels

– on the one hand Spotted Nutcracker, Ring Ouzel, Crested Tit, and Common Crossbill; on the other Golden Oriole, Common Nightingale, and Common Kingfisher.

But also as usual, it was not a bird but a mammal that stole the show. European Brown Bears were back on form, with their evening cabaret starting long before dusk this year.

Hungary

Within an hour of leaving Budapest airport, superb Questar-filling views of Great Bustards (enhanced by a complete lack of heat haze) were delighting the group. The supporting cast included a colony of Collared Pratincoles, magnificent Red-footed Falcons, a couple of Eurasian Bitterns flying close by, Savi's Warbler, Red-backed Shrikes, Ferruginous Duck, European Rollers on the wires, and White-winged Terns. A fine and instant start to an exciting week. Yet the best was still to come.

Subsequent days brought close views of Pygmy Cormorant from Sunbird's own hide towering above the Hortobágy fishponds; Aquatic Warbler, Bluethroat, and Little Crake at Nagyivani puszta; a Little Bittern nest building at the Trofea hunting lodge; and Rufous-tailed Rock Thrush, Eurasian Hoopoe, European Bee-eater, Greater Short-toed Lark, Eurasian Scops Owl, Lesser Grey Shrike, and a flock of 100 Common Cranes all performing on cue. A rare-bird alert gave us the hot news that, amazingly, there was a Steppe Eagle just 500 metres ahead of us and within minutes we were treated to low overhead views of this magnificent raptor. Long-legged Buzzard and White-tailed, Eastern Imperial, Short-toed and Lesser Spotted Eagles also obliged. A memorable hour by the wet meadows before we checked into our hotel at Tokaj yielded Corn Crakes (two in flight) and definitive views

Pygmy Cormorants viewed from Sunbird's own hide towering above the Hortobágy fishponds.

of Barred, River, and Marsh Warblers. Our woodland tally included Ural and Tawny Owls, and White-backed and the other woodpeckers. And new birds continued to appear right until the very last minute, including a perched Saker Falcon beside the motorway as we approached the departure terminal. Happily no police appeared to debate the definition of 'emergency' and forbid the use of a Questar on the hard shoulder.

Little wonder that the selection and the quality of views surpassed every participant's expectations and left a legacy of memories that seemed like several holidays rolled into one.

The differences are also summarized in the 2002 and 2003 tour reports:

Slovakia 27 April–6 May 2002

As ever it was a mammal that stole the show. The views of European Brown Bear this year were breathtaking – and in bright sunlight, leaving the photographers particularly happy. But equally engaging was the Forest Dormouse that shared our bear-watching hide. And for some participants the optional batting session with Greater and Lesser Horseshoe, Schreiber's, Mouse-eared, Daubenton's, and Noctule (some of them in the hand) was an unexpected bonus. Eastern Hedgehog, European Souslik, Fire Salamander, Fire-bellied and Yellow-bellied Toads, the endemic Carpathian Blue Slug, and a profusion of butterflies and wild flowers also vied for attention.

The birds too provided endless images for the photographers. On the very first morning, from the comfort of his bed, one participant videoed a Spotted Nutcracker on his balcony. And even en route to the airport on our last day we added Black Kite, a local rarity. In between, we enjoyed Alpine Accentor on the dramatic snow-clad peaks of the High Tatras; Wallcreeper and Rock Bunting amongst the Pasque Flowers, anemones, and *Adonis* of sunny limestone gorges; Black, Eurasian Three-toed and White-backed Woodpeckers in magnificent ancient beech forests; a charismatic Tengmalm's Owl peering out of its hole, and a mighty Eurasian Eagle Owl with young; Eastern Imperial Eagles on the nest and flying low overhead; Saker Falcons on the pylons; Red-breasted and Collared Flycatchers calling from the canopy; Thrush Nightingale singing in the open; and a wealth of waterbirds, from Little Bittern and Spotted Crake to Savi's Warbler and Eurasian Penduline Tit, around the lagoons and reedbeds of Senné ponds. Plus the old Russian wooden churches, the historic Vlkolínec village, and all those buttercup and dandelion meadows.

The range of birds to be seen in Slovakia in so short a time is remarkable. And their habitats present the most varied and attractive sequence of settings imaginable. Slovakia is a ravishingly beautiful country in which to spend winter, spring, or summer – which is just what we do every year in the space of nine days.

Hungary 6–13 May 2002

Within an hour of leaving Budapest airport we were watching 19 Great Bustards in full foam-bath display together with Red-footed Falcons, Montagu's Harrier, Collared Pratincoles, and Moustached Warbler: a good start. Once more it was a week that embraced both winter and summer. Amazingly both Greater and Lesser White-fronted Geese still lingered. Yet all the warmth of the Mediterranean was evoked by European Roller, Eurasian Hoopoe, European Bee-eater, and Rufous-tailed Rock Thrush. Little Bittern, Squacco and Purple Herons, Glossy Ibis, Ferruginous Duck, and a profusion of Pygmy Cormorants graced the fishponds; Little and Corn Crakes actually showed themselves; and raptors included Eastern Imperial, White-tailed, and Short-toed Eagles, Saker Falcon, Pallid Harrier, and Long-legged Buzzard. Warblers ranged from River and Marsh to Icterine and the scarce Aquatic. A chance visit to an atmospheric expanse of classic puszta coincided with a rare spring stop-over by a party of Eurasian Dotterel. Other waders, besides the to-be-expected Temminck's Stints, Curlew Sandpipers, Spotted Redshanks, and Common Greenshanks, included Kentish Plover, Stone-curlew, Ruddy Turnstone, and Sanderling (so far from the sea), and Hungary's first-ever Semipalmated Sandpiper.

In the forests we enjoyed definitive views of all the woodpeckers possible – plus, spectacularly, a Ural Owl perched beside the path (and another the following day from the coach). Yet despite all those riches the species that won the accolade of bird of the trip hasn't even been mentioned yet. That honour went to Eurasian Eagle Owl, presumably because a magnificent specimen posed so majestically on an open branch.

Two hundred species in one week is a remarkable total for any country in central Europe. But the lasting impression is not one of 'Never mind the quality, feel the width': here it was the quality – on every single day – that left the abiding memories.

Slovakia, 26 April–5 May 2003

Every year for at least a decade Slovakia has amazed and delighted groups by being 'even better than expected', with so many surprise extras that it has become one of our most popular destinations. The country itself is strikingly beautiful and varied – dramatic snow-capped mountains, sunny limestone gorges, rolling hills, primeval beech forests, and dandelion meadows. The birdlife is similarly diverse. And for the all-round naturalist it is impossible to walk more than a few paces without discovering another point of interest – Fire Salamander, Greater Horseshoe Bats hanging at a cave entrance, European Sousliks peering Meerkat-like out of the short grass, an Eurasian Otter ambling past our bear hide, Oil Beetles, Camberwell Beauties, Southern Festoons, and flowers, flowers everywhere: Yellow Pheasant's Eye, Yellow Anemone, Spring Crocus, Star of Bethlehem, Angled Solomon's Seal, Pasque Flower, Hungarian Snowbell. Yet this year even one of the keenest birders voted as his highlight of the tour not a bird or even a bear, but the historic World Heritage Site old village of Vlkolínec and the ancient wooden churches on the Ukrainian border. So many experiences were packed into our ten days that the holiday seemed much longer.

Even so – and despite the close and prolonged views of European Brown Bears on all three evenings set aside for this exciting privilege – it was the birds, and the incredible views of one target species after another, which left the strongest abiding images. Our local guides (after considerable preparation) surpassed themselves in producing a succession of wonders. Our lists were launched with pre-breakfast sightings of Spotted Nutcracker and Ring Ouzel from the balconies of our first hotel. Thereafter each day brought new ornithological highlights (literally, thanks to the acclivities which are feature of Slovakia): Alpine Accentor and Water Pipit at 2,200m; Wallcreeper, Eurasian Three-toed Woodpecker and Eurasian Pygmy Owl; Rock Bunting, Rufous-tailed Rock Thrush, and White-backed Woodpeckers; Barred Warbler and Middle Spotted Woodpecker; Eurasian Eagle Owl, Short-toed Eagle, Eurasian Hoopoe, Tawny Pipit, and Black Kite; Thrush Nightingale in full song and our tenth woodpecker species; and White-winged Tern, Ferruginous Duck, Pygmy Cormorant, Eastern Imperial Eagle, and Saker Falcon, which distinguished itself by flying directly towards us (concentrating on a feral pigeon immediately in front of us), thus ensuring that it was not only the final target highlight but also overall bird of the trip. There was a full supporting cast of equal stature, of course – Red-necked Grebe, Little and Great White Egrets, Purple Heron, Eurasian Spoonbill, White-tailed and Lesser Spotted Eagles, Peregrine Falcon, Common Crane, Pied Avocet, Mediterranean and Caspian Gulls, European Bee-eater, and Great Grey and Red-backed Shrikes – yet the extraordinary realization is that for every one of those key target species a glance at the European atlas confirms that it is at the very edge of its breeding range, whether it is a Mediterranean faunal type or predominately northern or eastern. This makes for a remarkable mixture. It is significant that from the mountain below us on our first day one river begins its journey to the Baltic, another to the Mediterranean. Slovakia is not only the watershed of Europe; it also offers a unique selection of the best of Europe's birds.

Hungary, 5–12 May 2003

For the last three years a spring week in Hungary has been offered as an extension to our popular Slovakia tour or as a holiday in its own right. Each country yields roughly the same number of species, but the differences are such that our Carpathian Basin total is always well over 200 (between 214 and 230 in fact) and has set several records. Pride of place this year went to Ural Owl, not only because conditions have led to only a few individuals breeding in Eastern Europe, but also because one female delighted us with particularly definitive views. Other owls ranged from Eurasian Eagle, Long-eared, and Tawny to Little and Eurasian Scops.

As usual, our birding began within an hour of leaving Budapest airport with Red-footed Falcon, Montagu's Harrier, Moustached Warbler, and 50 displaying Great Bustards. It concluded a week later on the way back to the airport with a brief diversion to the Hor Valley in the Bükk Hills for instant views of Rock Bunting. In between we enjoyed what in retrospect seems like far more than just one week of magic moments and exciting birds – the happy hour spent in the shade of an oak tree in Erodbénye Valley, where without moving our tripods we scoped European Honey-buzzard, Eastern Imperial Eagle, Eurasian Hoopoe, Grey-headed Woodpecker, Woodlark, Barred Warbler, Red-backed Shrike, and Hawfinch; the sunny evening and early morning along the Dongér bank with Ferruginous Ducks, Squacco Herons, and Little Crakes; the phragmites-fringed fishponds that yielded not only a wealth of waders and waterbirds (from Kentish Plover and Marsh Sandpiper to Little Bittern, Glossy Ibis, and Pygmy Cormorant), but also Bluethroat and Bearded and Eurasian Penduline Tits; our convenient comparison of Syrian and Great

Spotted Woodpeckers in Kerekegyháza cemetery; that most exotic foursome in any European field guide – Eurasian Hoopoe, Common Kingfisher, European Bee-eater, and European Roller; nine species of woodpecker; one exciting raptor after another – White-tailed, Short-toed, and Lesser Spotted Eagles, Long-legged Buzzard, Saker Falcon; Collared Pratincoles in the paddyfields; Greater Short-toed Lark and Short-toed Treecreeper on the same day; excellent views of a range of warblers – Aquatic, River, Savi's, and Marsh; a Corn Crake that was actually seen; Black Storks, Common Cranes, Mediterranean, Caspian and Yellow-legged Gulls, White-winged Terns, Collared Flycatchers, Lesser Grey Shrikes, and a colourful male Rufous-tailed Rock Thrush singing below us on a quarry ledge.

Little wonder that when participants listed their top ten birds no fewer than 44 species were itemized. It is indeed difficult to choose from such riches.

Finally, here is a summary of both Slovakia and Hungary in 2004.

Our combined tour saw 224 species, a remarkable total for a fortnight anywhere in Europe, especially for countries with no coastline. A good number were seen in both countries but sightings of course cannot be divorced from setting. Each country offered so many contrasts – from the snow-clad High Tatras in Slovakia to the vast open space of the puszta in Hungary. As usual the astonishing variety of habitats in Slovakia was highlighted by the birds seen from the balconies of our first and last hotels: on the one hand Spotted Nutcracker, Ring Ouzel, and Common Crossbill; on the other Common Nightingale, Golden Oriole, and Common Kingfisher.

*A Wallcreeper overhead seemed
more butterfly than bird.*

Despite Slovakia being a land-locked country a passable illusion
of a vast ocean greeted us when the cable car and chairlift took
us above the cloud layer to a warm and sunny 'island' mountain
peak where a family of Alpine Accentors gave us astonishingly
close views. These same snow-clad High Tatras thereafter formed
a dramatic backdrop to a succession of memorable experiences,
the most exciting of which had to be three European Brown Bears
enjoying their honey-soaked maize. Our walk through the spruce
and beech forest yielded both Eurasian Pygmy and Tengmalm's
Owls and Eurasian Three-toed and White-backed Woodpeckers;
a Wallcreeper overhead seemed more butterfly than bird; and it
was no surprise to learn that the dramatic crag-clasping castle

where we saw our first Black Stork was the location for the original (silent) film of *Dracula*. Crested Tit, Firecrest, Golden Eagle, Hen Harrier, and even the daily White-throated Dipper all remained exclusive to this area. In the south of the country the ruined Turniansky Castle and its population of European Sousliks attracted Eastern Imperial Eagle, Montagu's Harrier, Northern Goshawk, and Eurasian Sparrowhawk; a nearby quarry hosted a fine male Rufous-tailed Rock Thrush; and the beech forests provided delightful Red-breasted Flycatchers.

Further east one star attraction followed another with Long-eared Owl, Eurasian Penduline Tit, Black Kite, Short-toed Eagle, Saker Falcon, Thrush Nightingale, Red Kite, and finally the almost mythical Ural Owl. Our stay ended with a magical morning in a clearing that afforded views not only of eastern Slovakia's first and only pair of breeding White-tailed Eagles, but also of displaying Lesser Spotted Eagles, Eurasian Hobby, Black Woodpecker, and Eurasian Hoopoe, with a soundtrack provided by Corn Crake and Grasshopper Warbler – an extraordinary selection.

Within an hour of Budapest airport were 76 Great Bustards, plus Stone-curlew, White-winged Tern, and a variety of waders not seen in Slovakia the previous week. Even more new shorebirds were added on the following two days, ranging from Kentish Plover to Collared Pratincole, together with the equally new and exciting European Rollers, Glossy Ibis, Red-footed Falcons, a Eurasian Bittern posing alongside the coach, Little Crake, Pygmy Cormorants, a perched Long-legged Buzzard, and magnificent Common Cranes. Both Aquatic and Moustached Warblers teased us for some time before they surrendered to perched scope views, although other species were more instantly obliging – the male Little Bitterns, Red-crested Pochard, Eurasian Eagle Owl, European Honey-buzzard, Woodlark, Greater Short-toed Lark, Bluethroat, Thrush Nightingale, River and Barred Warblers, and Rock Bunting.

And then there was the raptor morning with Black Kite (a rarity in Hungary), Short-toed, Lesser Spotted and Eastern Imperial Eagles, Northern Goshawk, and a power-charged Saker Falcon just missing a dove a few paces in front of us.

And in case you're wondering, that region on the southern slopes of the Carpathian Mountains known as Ruthenia was dominated by Hungary from the 10th century, part of Austria-Hungary until World War I, divided between Czechoslovakia, Poland, and Romania in 1918, then (uniquely) was independent for a single day in 1938. It was then immediately occupied by Hungary, captured by the USSR in 1944, and subsequently became incorporated into the Ukraine Republic.

14. *Red List tally, Transylvanian count*

Our tours to Slovakia and Hungary proved very popular, but many clients pointed out that too much happens in the spring. So in 2005 we introduced an autumn tour that combined elements of our Carpathian Basin offerings with another location whose very name was excitingly evocative: Transylvania. The beautiful landscape of mountainous Székelyland (actually in Romania but in reality an intact Hungarian community of two million) offered a largely unexplored destination and almost virgin territory for birdwatchers. Target species – in addition to the all-important European Brown Bears – included Western Capercaillie, Wallcreeper (the largest European population, in Bicaz Gorge), and all the woodpeckers, owls, and higher-elevation specialities of Slovakia. And the Hortobágy National Park in Hungary could deliver not only the wealth of waders, wildfowl, and waterbirds that delighted our clients in the spring, but also 'winter' species such as Common Cranes in their thousands and Lesser White-fronted Geese. It was another winning combination.

24 September–2 October 2005

Seldom does a pioneering trip immediately set the standard against which all future tours will be judged. But our first Transylvania and Hortobágy pairing was just that. Perfect weather, luxury hotels, great food, all major targets met, almost every bird on the hypothetical list seen well (plus some exciting extras), nine successive days, each of which seemed paced to perfection, and a cumulative total experience that even with hindsight could not have been better planned – thanks largely to the excellent support of our ground agents, their first-rate guides and driver, and the behind-the-scenes team effort of some 30 or 40 helpers.

Our afternoon arrival in the Hortobágy and our first full day there launched our trip well, with over 100 species, including such specialities as Pygmy Cormorant, Eurasian and Little Bitterns, Cattle Egret (the only European heron not regularly seen in Hungary), Black Stork, Ferruginous Duck, Hen and Pallid Harriers, Long-legged Buzzard, Short-toed and Eastern Imperial Eagles, Saker and Red-footed Falcons, Little Crake, the spectacle of thousands of Common Cranes bugling in to roost, Great Bustard, Eurasian Dotterel, Stone-curlew, and Common Kingfisher (just to list some of the exciting non-passerines).

We were sorry to leave Hungary behind, and also to leave behind our Hungarian co-leader János Oláh (taken to hospital with a fever and high temperature that transpired to be a virus infection and not the suspected malaria from a previous bird tour in Indonesia). But happily Romania was to be equally rewarding and our new Hungarian co-leader Zollie Escedi just as proficient at producing the birds. Even this travelling day gave us superb views of Syrian Woodpecker and our only White Stork of the trip (plus our only Common Greenshanks, Green Sandpipers, and Whiskered and Black Terns). Our first full day in Transylvania, however, was when the excitement really began. A morning walk in the beautiful pine forest on Madarasi-Hargita Mountain gave us glimpses of three Western Capercaillies, Crested and Willow Tits, and perched Spotted Nutcrackers, Hawfinches, and Common Crossbills (a total of 160) – plus Water Pipits as we picnicked at 1,700m. Even so, the real high spot was our evening visit to two bear-watching hides. At one a magnificent Ural Owl perching on the feeding trough held our attention until four European Brown Bears appeared at dusk. And although the other group dipped on the owl, they were compensated by unexpected views of a bear in the forest, in bright sunlight, as they walked to their hide.

The next day left us even more ecstatic. An early start (involving a pre-dawn drive and walk up another mountain under a cloudless canopy of more stars that any of us could remember) rewarded us with a perched cock Western Capercaillie, which stayed long enough for everyone to enjoy sustained scope views, and several Eurasian Three-toed Woodpeckers, including views of white-backed, black-backed, and barred-backed individuals. White-throated Dippers delighted us on our way down. But the best was yet to come. In dramatic Bicaz Gorge two Wallcreepers – one of the most desired and elusive European birds – performed instantly by the roadside, one or two metres away at eye level.

That was a hard act to follow. And, anyway, the following day was decreed the official leisurely day – a lie in, a late breakfast, some easy birding at fishponds in attractive lower-altitude countryside, and a long lunch at the hotel. But the owl-dipping bear-hide group included two American owl aficionados who had already enthused so much over three Little Owls that we couldn't let them go home without a sighting of the near-mythical Ural Owl. So an afternoon visit was arranged in another forest 'to see another Ural Owl'. In autumn, of course, needles in haystacks are easier. So no one was more surprised than the leaders when, whilst we were still driving up the track, we flushed from the roadside a magnificent specimen that not only perched on an open branch, but also proceeded to give increasingly more breathtaking views until it finally flew towards us and sat on a log in bright sunlight. The bird of the trip. And again no walking required.

With all our Transylvanian targets met, we could afford time for a non-birding interlude and were able to enjoy Sighisoara with its romantic castle, film-set main square, and (genuine) Dracula's house before the town was fully awake and before the tourists arrived (see Plate 12, page 244). On then to the beautiful Küküllö Valley to picnic with a Golden Eagle flying just above our heads and – most unexpectedly – four Red-rumped Swallows. Our search for Rock Bunting took longer than expected: happily so as it produced two more close Golden Eagles and increasingly attractive views of our home for the night – the UNESCO World Heritage Site village of Torockó with its 200-year-old houses (some of which were about to house us) still intact. Here we were served a quite delicious home-cooked meal and a variety of local brandies. We slept well.

Our return to Hungary added Middle Spotted Woodpecker and a roost of 18 Long-eared Owls. But one target bird remained: Lesser White-fronted Goose. Although a flock of 20 had arrived before our tour began, there had been no sightings since. So the quest on our final morning was predestined: a long (but easy) walk to the main Hortobágy fishpond, where we gambled that the geese might come to roost after their morning feed. Early morning mist added to the atmosphere as the supporting acts began to perform – our first Squacco Heron, wonderful views of 350 Bearded Tits and 180 Eurasian Penduline Tits, European Robins for our American participants. Then at literally the eleventh hour, as the mist lifted and the sun was revealed to be in partial eclipse (a magical moment), the geese flew in – 20 Lesser White-fronts and a single Barnacle. Our bird list closed on a big one. The catfish soup at Tiszacsege *czarda* had never tasted so good. And our plane arrived at Heathrow ten minutes early.

24 September–2 October 2006

Once more our Transylvania and Hortobágy tour proved the perfect pairing. The two habitats – vast open atmospheric puszta and fishponds on the one hand, dramatic mountain scenery, gorges, and high-elevation conifer forests on the other – offer a satisfying contrast; the hotels are comfortable; and the food and wines remarkably good.

Our first 24 hours in Hungary constituted, by any standards, a classic European birding experience – 112 species including several on the IUCN Red List and eight of world conservation importance: Lesser White-fronted Goose, Greater Spotted and Eastern Imperial Eagles, and Great Bustard (all globally threatened species), plus Pygmy Cormorant, Ferruginous Duck, White-tailed Eagle, and an unexpected Buff-breasted Sandpiper, only the second record for the Hortobágy (all 'Near Threatened'). Staggering. Even the supporting cast was impressive: Squacco and Purple Herons, Black and White Storks, Eurasian Spoonbill, Bean Goose, Long-legged Buzzard, Red-footed Falcon, Common Crane, Red-throated Pipit, Bearded and Eurasian Penduline Tits, and Bluethroat. It was indeed a tremendous kick-start to a holiday in which every day brought a new and memorable experience.

Even our travelling day, transferring to Transylvania, added new species – our only Common Kingfisher (right outside our hotel before breakfast), Red-necked Grebe, Whiskered and Black Terns, Common Sandpiper, and Lesser Whitethroat, and our first Syrian Woodpeckers and Northern Goshawk and Eurasian Sparrowhawk at the same location (a useful comparison). We even found a Blue-winged Teal, a new species for Romania.

Our first full day in Transylvania added Spotted Nutcrackers, Hazel Grouse (two pairs, frustratingly only glimpsed in flight), and Water Pipits at 1,700m. But the 'bird' of the day was without doubt European Brown Bear, with six individuals performing in good light and providing the photographers with some excellent images.

The one target bird that eluded us was Western Capercaillie, which tantalized us with footprints, faeces, and a feather. But ample compensation came the following dawn, when we watched a cock in full strutting, jumping, and gurgling display for over half an hour at an autumn lek (a feature that doesn't seem to be recorded in the books). Little wonder that this was voted bird of the trip, leaving our next target species (Wallcreeper – which we saw the moment we arrived at Bicaz Gorge: too easy) to trail in thirteenth place. Back-up birds included another Long-legged Buzzard (a new species for our Romanian guide), White-throated Dipper, a flock of Fieldfares, Firecrests, Crested Tits, and Common Crossbills. The most photographed bird of our Transylvanian days, however, was a Eurasian Three-toed Woodpecker that obliged us by flying onto a dead spruce the moment we were about to enter the forest to begin our search.

Just as last year, with all our Transylvanian targets met we were able to enjoy a non-birding interlude in atmospheric Sighisoara with its film-set main square, romantic castle and clock tower, and photogenic old houses, still looking largely as it did when Dracula lived there in the 15th century. Equally photogenic were the houses in the UNESCO World Heritage village of Torockó, some of which housed us for our final night in Transylvania – a happy evening of home-cooked produce, local brandies, and reminiscences of the birds of the day: overhead Golden Eagles, Rock Buntings, and (as far as our American participants were concerned) a pole-dancing European Green Woodpecker.

A cock Western Capercaillie in full strutting, jumping, and gurgling display, accompanied by a pair of Eurasian Three-toed Woodpeckers.

Back in the Hortobágy, the epilogue was just as rewarding as the prologue: several well-photographed Middle Spotted Woodpeckers, white-headed Long-tailed Tits, a pylon-perching Saker Falcon, and a thrilling climax to our final evening – 22,000 Common Cranes coming in to roost and flying over and around us in unending lines, first into a red sunset and then under a bright moon. Quite magical.

Our last morning began with Hawfinch (curiously the first of the trip), bringing our total to 160. This left us four short of last year's tally, but the countdown continued with Grey Partridge and Stock Dove (which gave these humble species as much significance as the three more Great Bustards in the same fields), a typically tame Eurasian Dotterel, 25 Long-eared Owls roosting in a town garden (the equalizer), and finally 11 Greater White-fronted Geese – full circle from our first day in the Hortobágy, when its smaller cousin was our first target bird. Satisfyingly this gave us one more species than last year.

23 September–1 October 2007

Once more our Hortobágy-Transylvania pairing proved to be the perfect coeliac sandwich: one with no bread either side, just three layers of filling.

Our first 24 hours in Hungary provided the by-now traditional combination of quantity and quality – over 100 species including several on the IUCN Red List and six of world conservation importance: Lesser White-fronted Goose, Eastern Imperial Eagle, and Great Bustard, plus Pygmy Cormorant, Ferruginous Duck, and White-tailed Eagle. The equally impressive supporting cast ranged throughout the whole spectrum of both non-passerines and passerines, from Eurasian Bittern to Corn Bunting and including Black-crowned Night Heron, Eurasian Spoonbill, Common Shelduck, Garganey, Pallid Harrier, Saker Falcon, Common Crane, Pied Avocet, Stone-curlew, a trip of 22 Eurasian Dotterel, Little Stint, Spotted Redshank, Whiskered Tern, Little Owl, Common Kingfisher, Red-throated Pipit, Bearded Tit, Eurasian Penduline Tit, and Great Grey Shrike. It would be difficult to imagine a better day's birding anywhere in Europe.

Even so, our travelling day that followed added 17 new species: Little, Great Crested, and Red-necked Grebes, Little Egret, Black Stork, Tufted Duck, Eurasian Sparrowhawk, Common Greenshank, Common Sandpiper, Ruddy Turnstone (a rarity so far from the coast), Common Gull, Syrian Woodpecker, Long-tailed Tit, Marsh Tit, Eurasian Nuthatch, European Greenfinch, and Hawfinch. And our arrival at our destination in Transylvania, as in all the best stories and films, coincided with a full moon.

Our first walk in Transylvania yielded a classic high-altitude coniferous-forest selection: Northern Goshawk, Eurasian Three-toed Woodpecker (satisfying scope views), close comparisons of Goldcrest and Firecrest and Marsh and Willow Tits, Crested Tit, Coal Tit, Eurasian Treecreeper, Spotted Nutcracker (both in flight and perched), Eurasian Siskin, Common Crossbill, a pair of obliging Eurasian Bullfinches beside the track, and over 100 Hawfinches – plus Water Pipits and Grey Wagtails on the mountain top. Our one less than satisfactory view was Western Capercaillie. As in 2006 there was tantalizing evidence with footprints, faeces, and feathers. But our frustration was furthered this year (and the alliteration intensified) by a female French flusher and a fleeting fly-by. Nevertheless we went to bed happy and content as the day closed with views of a magnificent tawny-shouldered European Brown Bear.

Memorable images from the following day included a singing Ring Ouzel perched like a fairy on a Christmas tree and a White-throated Dipper posing on a mid-stream rock with a Fire Salamander at its feet. But bird of the day (indeed voted bird of the trip, only two points short of the possible maximum) was a Wallcreeper – understandably known in China as the 'rock flower' – which semaphored close and continuously until we eventually walked away.

Another full moon later saw us back in the coniferous forest at 1,500m with another picnic breakfast, but a change of pace (and lunch in the hotel) was followed by a visit to Szentpáli fishponds (another Eurasian Bittern plus Eurasian Hobby and Purple Heron, which were new for us) and to Kaloda beech forest and meadows (Woodlarks, European Green Woodpeckers, and Fieldfares).

Then came atmospheric Sighisoara and equally photographic Torockó where we were able to enjoy not only the usual home-cooked produce and local brandies, but also optional music and dancing well into the night. Others preferred to dream of the day's birding highlights – Rock Buntings, and another Woodlark, Peregrine Falcon and European Green Woodpeckers, one of which narrowly missed being grabbed by a Northern Goshawk just metres in front of us.

Back in the Hortobágy, our tight schedule worked to perfection: almost instant Middle Spotted Woodpeckers and Short-toed Treecreepers in Debrecen great wood; 30 Long-eared Owls in Balmazújváros town centre and Wood Sandpiper at the sewage farm; and Long-legged Buzzard and Northern Wheatear at Szeg – leaving us time to drive out over Cserepes puszta to await in absolute silence the evening flight of the Lesser White-fronts from the fishponds to a grazing area. On cue they came – a flock of 50 with four more following (half the European population of Europe's rarest breeding bird). Carefully we stalked and scoped until we were close enough to see not only the curving white on their baby-face profiles, but also the yellow orbital-rings around their eyes. A magical moment with the silence now broken by the thrilling bugling of endless lines of Common Cranes strung out above us.

This alone would have made a sufficient grand finale. But our final morning was no anticlimax. A return visit to the Hortobágy fishpond where we began on our first full day presented us not only with a welcome reprise of a range of species from Eurasian Spoonbill to the requested Bearded Tit (over 100 of them and feeding on the path just metres ahead of us), but also a Great White Pelican (a new bird for Bryan's Hungary list and only the second for Zoltan) and the first Tundra Bean Goose of the winter flying in to join thousands of Greylags and a smaller flock of Lesser White-fronts in the morning sunlight. A wonderful finish.

A significant feature of this year's trip was our amazing luck with the weather – dry sunny days that enabled us to drive to many localities inaccessible in wet conditions (despite the four days of continuous rain in the Hortobágy between our two visits). This, and the coincidence of the full moon, gave us magnificent sunrises and sunsets and thrilling moon views – at times as red as the sun, at others as pale as a primrose. Other bonuses were the fine lunches at Hortobágy *czarda* (with gypsy cymbalo, violin, and double bass trio entertaining us with a virtuoso rendition of The Lark) and the Tiszacsege *czarda* (surely the tastiest fish soup ever), together with the varied evening meals washed down with surprisingly fine wines, local beers, and fruit brandies. Mountains and puszta looked equally photogenic in the clear light, and never have the autumn colours looked more splendid.

15. 'The most impressive revelations of the whole Byzantine world'

On the final evening of the Hungary birds and music tour in 2002 I received a phone call with the shocking news that James Roberts, scheduled to lead our birds and history tour of Romania (the Danube Delta and the painted monasteries of northern Moldovia) a few days later, had quite unexpectedly died in bed. Could I take over at such short notice? As it happened I had to attend an (unrelated) inquest in Norwich, but the following day I flew to Budapest. The birds of course were all familiar, but the painted monasteries were indeed a revelation. How could such vivid colours survive for centuries on outside walls?

30 August–7 September 2002
First and last impressions obviously count. A noisy Spotted Nutcracker perched atop a spruce before breakfast outside our first hotel in Sucevita proved runner-up in our bird of the trip contest – topped only by the final spectacle of our tour: 200 Collared Pratincoles on our last evening. Between the two were many memorable moments: the deserted house in the forest with Red-breasted Flycatcher, Common Redstart, and more Spotted Nutcrackers in the garden; the wooded ridge at 1,200m with Common Crossbill, Crested Tits, Collared Flycatchers, and Montagu's Harriers, Lesser Spotted Eagle, and Peregrine Falcon passing by; the roadside orchard with Grey-headed, Syrian, and Lesser Spotted Woodpeckers all in the same small tree; and the amazing painted monasteries of northern Moldavia

with their Black Redstarts, Common Chiffchaffs, and Fieldfares.

At a lower elevation, there can be no more pleasant way to indulge a penchant for birdwatching (beginner and expert alike) than to relax with a drink in one hand and binoculars in the other under the canopy of the observation deck of a houseboat gliding along the old channels of the Danube Delta whilst an ever-changing selection of specialities presents itself for inspection: Squacco and Purple Herons, Glossy Ibis, Pygmy Cormorant, Great White and Dalmatian Pelicans; perhaps a Little or Spotted Crake or a Little Bittern along the edge of the reeds; Red-footed Falcon, Eurasian Hobby, or even White-tailed Eagle in the riverside trees; European Rollers, European Bee-eaters, and Common Kingfisher at regular intervals; and thousands of Ferruginous Ducks on the lakes – until dusk and an increase in the numbers of Black-crowned Night Herons signals time for a shower and a fine three-course meal in the dining room/bar followed by a silent night in the well-appointed cabins (see Plate 12, page 244)

High water levels this year deprived us of muddy edges for waders. But hundreds awaited us on the pools south of the delta when we left our boat: Marsh and Curlew Sandpipers, Red-necked Phalarope, Little Stint, four species of plover, Pied Avocet, Spotted Redshank... plus Caspian and Gull-billed Terns, Little Gulls, and further inland Sombre Tit, Pied Wheatear, Lesser Grey Shrike, Levant Sparrowhawk, Long-legged Buzzard, and male Pallid Harriers. It is remarkable that on that last day we added 34 species to our trip list, with surely more undiscovered before saturation set in and the rival temptations of facilities and food won the day. This was indeed a spectacular grand finale to a holiday which – despite the tragic death of its only begetter just days before the trip began – was a joyful and rewarding experience for all of us and a fitting tribute to James and the legacy he left behind.

29 August–6 September 2003

Last year the water levels in the Danube Delta were the highest ever; this year they were the lowest. The common denominator was that in the last 24 hours of the trip we saw over 40 new species for our list. It seems that the shores of the Black Sea always have something else to offer – and not just list-padders, but such star attractions as Collared Pratincole, Kentish Plover, Marsh and Terek Sandpipers, Temminck's Stint, Levant Sparrowhawk, Long-legged Buzzard, Pied and Eastern Black-eared Wheatears, Bearded Tit, and Paddyfield Warbler. European Bee-eaters and European Rollers became commonplace and at one point the sky was filled with 1,000 migrating White Storks. All this seemed a far cry from our more gentle introduction to the birds of Romania on our first day when, less than an hour from Bucharest airport, we called at Caldurasani monastery (welcome shade in the 40°C heat – and such beautiful music) and discovered a varied selection around the nearby lake, including our only Osprey and Icterine Warbler plus Red-necked Phalarope, Ferruginous Duck, Whiskered Tern, and Squacco and Purple Herons.

Despite the fact that the old channels had only a few centimetres of water our *salupa* crew managed to take us almost everywhere we requested, gliding alongside a single Dalmatian Pelican (as opposed to the 1,500 Great White Pelicans that were ever present) and a magnificent Wild Cat, plus hundreds of Pygmy Cormorants and Squacco and Black-crowned Night Herons and numerous Common Kingfishers. So obliging were the crew, in fact, that eventually – manoeuvring the bulky vessel over a mudbank – we became grounded and the rudder was torn away. Help was close at hand, however, and three delightfully jolly fishermen transported the whole party back to our scheduled 8pm dinner on our moored houseboat. In fact this sunset cruise in a small boat was quite a bonus. A second *salupa* and crew brought the staff-to-participant ratio at this point to 14:8, or even 19:8 counting our various co-opted white knights. Other species obligingly came to us and our houseboat was overflown by thrillingly close Eastern Imperial and White-tailed Eagles, Caspian Tern, Black and Syrian Woodpeckers, Black Stork, and Red-footed Falcon. Shore excursions added Eurasian Hoopoe, Little Owl, Red-breasted Flycatcher, and Grey-headed Woodpecker.

By contrast the mountains of Bucovina with their beech and coniferous forests offered perched Spotted Nutcracker and Common Crossbills, close Lesser Spotted Eagles both overhead and chicken-strutting in the fields, Great Grey Shrike, Collared Flycatcher, Firecrest, and Grey Wagtail. They also produced the bird of the trip (by popular vote): a Middle Spotted Woodpecker that posed for us at length alongside our vehicle as we left Agapia monastery after admiring the 19th-century frescoes of the country's foremost painter, Nicolae Grigorescu, and being granted a privileged peep at the nuns carpet-making and icon-painting and giggling at that strange bearded priest in North African robes who allegedly belonged (according to Tudor) to the Order of Passerines. Other monasteries visited included Moldovita, Humor, Veronet, and Neamt. But without doubt the most exciting and memorable moment of the trip (for almost everyone) was our first view of the exquisite 16th-century frescoes

*Both Great White and Dalmatian Pelicans
can be found in the Danube Delta.*

of Sucevita. Just as Sacheverell Sitwell wrote in the 1920s 'The
first view of the painted church of Sucevita is among the most
impressive revelations of the whole Byzantine world'.

27 August–5 September 2004

Last year the water levels in the Danube were the lowest ever.
The year before they were the highest ever. This year they were
just right – which, combined with perfect weather and migration
coinciding with both the lingering summer and early winter
visitors such as Smew, ensured the highest ever number of species
for this trip. From the 140s a few years ago, the total has now
climbed through the 150s in 2002 and the 160s in 2003 to an
amazing 190 this year. What's more, the views of individual
specialities, both perched and in flight, and the sheer spectacle of
hundreds (and indeed thousands) of such species as Great White

Pelican, Pygmy Cormorant, Squacco Heron, Ferruginous Duck, Spotted Redshank, Wood Sandpiper, and Whiskered Tern were surely the best ever.

From the Long-eared Owls that gazed down at us from their roosting trees at Caldurasani monastery on our first afternoon to the fierce Little Owl that out-stared us in Cheia Dobrogea gorge at the end of our trip, our 11 days were filled with one spectacular sighting after another. The numbers and variety of raptors was outstanding – White-tailed and Eastern Imperial Eagles overhead, Saker Falcons on the pylons, Long-legged Buzzard, Red-footed Falcons, Short-toed, Booted and Lesser Spotted Eagles, a hefty perched Northern Goshawk, and four species of harrier for convenient comparison. Both Great White and Dalmatian Pelicans obliged on the water and in close flight views.

Then there was that most colourful quartet of Common Kingfisher, European Bee-eater, European Roller, and Eurasian Hoopoe; all the woodpeckers possible; White-throated Dipper and Grey Wagtail; Pied, Isabelline and Eastern Black-eared Wheatears; Glossy Ibis, Black Stork, and so many different herons; Eurasian Penduline, Sombre, Bearded, Crested, and Willow Tits; amazing views of Spotted Nutcrackers; and a remarkable selection of waders including Marsh, Broad-billed, and Curlew Sandpipers, Collared Pratincole, Red-necked Phalarope, Temminck's Stint, and Stone-curlew.

In addition to this bird-fest our multi-national group (British, Irish, American, Canadian, Australian, and Romanian), with an age range of 14 to 80, managed no less than eight monasteries – many spectacularly decorated both inside and externally with frescoes in the brightest blues, greens, and reds despite exposure to 500 winters; the historic ruins at Histria, the oldest settlement in Romania and inhabited for 1,300 years; and a variety of non-ornithological and non-historical experiences ranging from Count Dracula's Club in Bucharest to the charming egg-lady demonstrating her lost-wax technique. Once more a highlight of the trip was the time on our luxury houseboat exploring the channels of the Danube Delta, relaxing on deck with a drink in one hand and binoculars in the other. And this year the extra day at the end of the tour added immeasurably to the whole experience by allowing us to explore at a more leisurely pace the delights of the Vadu and Histria pools, Cheia Dobrogea gorge, Babadog forest, the Black Sea coast, and the vast plateaux inland.

For such a wealth of European birdlife and such a sequence of special cameos, Romania would be difficult to surpass. But equally overwhelming and abiding memories are the exquisite 16th-century frescoes in the monasteries of Bucovina.

26 August–4 September 2005

Despite sound reminders that Romania is still the poorest country in Europe and in many ways comparable to a Third World country – indeed part of its charm is the feeling of stepping back in time and experiencing a way of life unchanged for centuries – our ten days in the mountains of Bucovina and the reedbeds and channels of the Danube Delta gave us a daily sequence of happy memories. With a group of so many old friends (representing for the leader a cumulative total of 200 years of friendship) and new ones who quickly became equally special, the group was from the outset a bonded family. Birthday parties on the first night in Count Dracula's Club and our last night on the houseboat reinforced the family atmosphere. And with the presence of a few non-birders we were assured of a multi-interest experience.

Within a few kilometres of Bucharest airport, Caldurasani monastery offered delightful Long-eared Owls staring down at us from their daytime roost and also our first exposure to the work of Nicolae Grigorescu, Romania's leading painter, and numerous historic vestments, chalices and icons.

Our first day in Bucovina, too, provided not only a perfect walk along Obcina Mare ridge with rolling hayfields, blue remembered hills, and pine and beech forest, but also a private visit to the home of the most celebrated artist specializing in decorative eggs. Visits to two of the amazing painted monasteries – Moldovita and Sucovita – vied for our attention with a series of bird-pair comparisons (Willow Warbler/Common Chiffchaff, Northern Goshawk/Eurasian Sparrowhawk, Goldcrest/Firecrest, Montagu's/Western Marsh Harrier, and Northern Wheatear/ Whinchat), plus our first glimpses of Black Woodpecker and Spotted Nutcracker. An even more thrilling view of the nutcracker came the following day with a pre-breakfast individual dealing with a nut at eye-level just a few metres away. After breakfast an exciting sequence of birds followed: Lesser Spotted Eagle, European Honey-buzzard, Eurasian Hobby, Red-backed and Great Grey Shrikes, Black Stork, Icterine Warbler, Red-breasted Flycatcher, and Fieldfare. But the perfect combination of history and ornithology was the Grey-headed Woodpecker drumming on the roof of Neamt monastery – though the painted splendour of Humor and Veronet (and particularly the *Last Judgement* on the western façade of the latter) provided perhaps the most abiding memories.

The following day there were more birds (perched Hawfinch and Lesser Spotted Eagle and splendid views of Middle Spotted

Woodpecker to distract us from our woodland picnic), but the highlight was surely the peace of Agapia monastery and the paintings of Nicolae Grigorescu, plus our visit to the museum and carpet and icon workshops – a fulfilling two hours to round off our mountain experience before we transferred to the delta and our houseboat.

The first pre-breakfast birding session as we were towed along the Sulina channel could hardly have been bettered. A blood-red sunrise was the backdrop to a rolling sequence of Great White and Dalmatian Pelicans, Pygmy and Continental Cormorants, Purple and Squacco Herons, Glossy Ibis, Eurasian Spoonbill, White-tailed Eagle, Eurasian Hobby, European Roller, and even a late Common Cuckoo on the wires. A walk around the Russian village at Mila 23 added Collared and Red-breasted Flycatchers, great looks at Syrian and Grey-headed Woodpeckers, and a handful of Golden Orioles. But perhaps the birds of the day were at our overnight mooring, when Little Crake and Little Bittern performed against a sunset as blood-red as the sunrise. The following day exploring the channels cutting through the world's largest reedbed was endlessly breathtaking for both the numbers and the variety of birds – about 40,000 including over 10,000 Pygmy Cormorants, 15,000 Eurasian Coots, and 4,000 Squacco Herons, and with choice birds including Red-necked Grebe, Red-crested Pochard, Ferruginous Duck, White-winged Tern, Black and Lesser Spotted Woodpeckers, Black Storks perched at our evening mooring, and a final Barn Owl as we ate our dinner.

Back on land the next day, Celic Dere provided yet another monastery and a very photogenic windmill, plus for the birders Long-legged Buzzard, both dark and light morphs of Booted Eagle, and our target bird the elusive Sombre Tit. Enisalu offered a castle much loved by film-makers – plus European Roller, European Bee-eater, Golden Oriole, and Turtle Dove; whilst Vadu combined the less scenic ruins of a uranium plant with the most overwhelming sequence of specialities imaginable – Red-footed Falcon, Levant Sparrowhawk, Stone-curlew, Broad-billed and Marsh and Curlew Sandpipers, Pied Avocet, Black-winged Stilt, Ruddy Shelduck, Little and Temminck's Stints, Spotted Redshank, Eurasian Hoopoe, Bluethroat, Red-necked Phalarope, Black-necked Grebe, Little Gull, Little Tern, and distant Collared Pratincoles.

Then came yet more new birds and more history at Histria, views of Red-rumped Swallow at the only breeding site in Romania, and finally some welcome action replays on our last day with Black Woodpecker, Common Kingfisher, Little Bittern, Great White and Dalmatian Pelicans, and Pygmy Cormorant at Calarasi.

If we had not sacrificed our circuit of Dobregia gorge and plateau in favour of a change of hotel and a good night's sleep (a popular choice that wasn't even put to the vote), we would certainly have finished with an all-time record number of species for this trip. As it was, we fell a few short of last year, but the selection and the views were probably the best ever. And certainly we saw a maximum number of monasteries and experienced many non-birding extras as we observed life in the fields and villages throughout the country. Our horse-and-cart count (including the aquatic form) was certainly a record.

16. *Star performers, a strong supporting cast, and a chorus-ending from Euripides*

Our one-week trips – whether to Majorca or Morocco, Slovakia or Lesvos – are always popular, probably because they don't use up too much of the holiday allowance yet so much living is packed into every day that in retrospect the holiday seems so much longer (more experiences to the pound). Northern Greece was a particular favourite, offering over 200 species (a good one-week tally for any location in Europe), a range of specialities from Eurasian Black Vulture and Dalmatian Pelican to Spur-winged Lapwing and Sombre Tit, and a spot of culture. Typical was the August 1995 tour, as summarized in this report.

> Despite the continued drainage of the deltas in northern Greece this trip gets better and better. This year we saw over 200 species in one week, including all the specialities perched for Questar views. These included Pygmy Cormorant, Dalmatian and Great White Pelicans, Black Stork, Eurasian Black Vulture, Spur-winged Lapwing, Masked Shrike and Sombre Tit.
>
> Of particular note was the parade of *Sylvia* warblers, text-book fashion, through one bush in the Avas Gorge (culminating in an adult Barred showing its name feature and glaring yellow iris) and the equally distinctive selection of 30 waders including the roadside puddle in the Evros Delta, with close comparisons of Temminck's and Little Stints, and Broad-billed Sandpiper, all dwarfed by a pair of Ruddy Shelducks. Other excellent comparisons for study purposes included Pied, Collared, and

Semicollared Flycatchers; Black, White-winged, and Whiskered Terns; Common and Long-legged Buzzards, and European Honey-buzzard; Levant and Eurasian Sparrowhawks; Golden, Eastern Imperial, and Lesser Spotted Eagles; Lanner and Peregrine Falcons, and Eurasian Hobby; and Willow, Wood, and Eastern Bonelli's Warblers.

Not exactly instructive but exciting as a spectacle was the swirling pink ribbon of 1,400 Greater Flamingos spiralling down to roost. Even so (thanks no doubt to a strong American representation), the first four places on the bird of the trip contest went to that most colourful classic foursome, European Bee-eater, European Roller, Eurasian Hoopoe and Common Kingfisher, which delighted us daily.

Although the tour was not officially a birds and history combination, the ruins of Philippi were always popular and one memorable year we were able to return to the 2,350-year-old amphitheatre in the evening to experience it being used for the purpose originally intended.

29 August – 5 September 1999

At its very eastern end the map of Greece seems to give a 'thumbs-up' sign where this narrow spur of Thrace is sandwiched between Bulgaria and Turkey. For birdwatchers this is symbolic. By any standards, a morning spent in these mountains followed by the afternoon in the Evros Delta immediately to the south must offer the best day's birding in Europe. With well over 100 species, including a succession of specialities, and with some species present in their thousands, the experience is overwhelming and difficult to match.

This year our day started with Questar views of Eurasian

Black, Griffon, and Egyptian Vultures (40 in all) on the ground, perched in trees, and in flight. The Golden, Booted, and Short-toed Eagles looked small by comparison, and the Eurasian and Levant Sparrowhawks positively tiny. It ended with equally exciting comparisons of herons – Squacco, Black-crowned Night, Grey, and Purple – plus Little Bittern, Little and Great White Egrets, both Black and White Storks, Eurasian Spoonbill, and Greater Flamingo. Pool after pool was thronged with vast numbers of wildfowl and waders, just like in the old days. This was like Bharatpur, not Europe. Black-winged Stilts, Pied Avocets, Spotted Redshanks, Common Greenshanks, Black-tailed Godwits, Wood and Green Sandpipers, Little and Temminck's Stints, Curlew Sandpipers, four plover species, and even more excitingly Broad-billed and Marsh Sandpipers and a flock of seven Red-necked Phalaropes, a new record for Greece. Gull-billed, Whiskered, and Caspian Terns hawked overhead; Tawny Pipits ran along the tracks; Montagu's and Western Marsh Harriers, Osprey, and Eurasian Hobby augmented the raptor list for the day; European Bee-eaters, Eurasian Hoopoes, European Rollers, Golden Oriole, and Red-rumped Swallows were showy bonuses; and Pygmy Cormorant and both Dalmatian and Great White Pelicans added further quality.

This was the climax of an increasingly impressive sequence of varied habitats and choice birds during a happy week – the lagoons and salt-pans at Porto Lagos with Slender-billed Gulls and Caspian Terns; the freshwater lakes of Volvi and Koronia not only alive with a selection of waterbirds, but also attracting Short-toed Eagle and Long-legged Buzzard; the Avos Gorge with a range of species from Masked Shrike and Cirl Bunting to Chukar Partridge and Lesser Spotted Eagle; the fields and olive

Eastern Black-eared Wheatear, Blue Rock Thrush, and Rock Nuthatch among the ruins at Philippi.

groves with ever-present Red-backed, Lesser Grey, and Woodchat Shrikes, Sardinian Warblers, Greater Short-toed Larks, and Red-rumped Swallows; and the attractive coast and coves with always the possibility of Yelkouan Shearwater beyond the Mediterranean and Yellow-legged Gulls.

But perhaps the most satisfying day to rival Dadia and the Evros was our trip to the Nestos Delta and Philippi – waking to the sounds of Rock Nuthatch, Blue Rock Thrush, and Eastern Black-eared Wheatear around our rooms at the attractive Tosca beach (birds that were to greet us also that afternoon as we wandered around ancient Greek and Roman ruins); continuing with Syrian and Middle Spotted Woodpeckers in the riverside woodland; peaking with 14 very close Spur-winged Lapwings, plus Stone-curlew and Collared Pratincole, near the little harbour of Keramoti where we enjoyed our daily taverna lunch of Greek salad, fish, calamari, taramasalata, aubergine, and cheese; and concluding after dinner in a 2,350-year-old amphitheatre for a striking performance of a 2,413-year-old play: Euripides' *Iphigenia in Tauris* (in Greek) with an impressively choreographed chorus which for two hours held us so spellbound that it never occurred to us that we couldn't understand a word.

Just when we're safest, there's a sunset touch,
A fancy from a flower-bell, someone's death,

A chorus-ending from Euripides,
And that's enough for fifty hopes and fears –
The grand Perhaps.

The ten participants in 2000 first met each other on my Northern India tour in 1990 and bonded so well that every year they enjoyed a reunion birdwatching in Norfolk. But for the tenth anniversary something special was required, so they were granted exclusive rights to the Greece trip. They were therefore a particularly happy group from the outset, and all the more so because one couple were celebrating their 37th wedding anniversary – as recorded in the tour report.

28 August–4 September 2000

The taverna lunches were even more convivial than usual, as were the alfresco evening meals overlooking Tosca and Alexandroupoli beaches and the final evening at Zorba's with the bouzouki playing and authentic dancing. But the feeding spectacles were not confined to the tavernas and hotels. A fresh carcass at the Dadia raptor station attracted 31 Eurasian Black Vultures, plus 38 Griffons and 11 Egyptians – a fascinating floorshow of interspecific relationship that must be unique in Europe, if not the world. Overhead a Levant Sparrowhawk circled for comparison with its commoner cousins, and European Honey-buzzards and Eastern Imperial, Booted, and Short-toed Eagles sailed across.

Although the core area of the Evros Delta was closed due to an outbreak of foot-and-mouth disease, exploration of the non-restricted areas yielded Little Bittern, Red-necked Phalarope, Marsh Sandpiper, and Stone-curlew, and the group was fortunate in finding the other specialities en route – Dalmatian Pelican and Terek and Broad-billed Sandpipers at Porto Lagos, Great White

Pelican at Mesi, Greater Flamingo at Lake Karonia, Spur-winged Lapwing at the Nestos Delta, and Collared Pratincole at the salt-pans. A few White Storks still lingered by the roadside, but the only Black Stork of the trip passed overhead whilst the group were scoping Grey-headed, Lesser Spotted, and Syrian Woodpeckers in the Nestos woodland. In the Avos Gorge both Sombre Tits and Masked Shrikes (sometimes very difficult species to locate at this time of year) appeared almost instantly, and the always-popular showy set of European Bee-eater, European Roller, Eurasian Hoopoe, Common Kingfisher, and Golden Oriole was seen on most days.

The roll-call of supporting cast was long and wide-ranging: Cory's and Yelkouan Shearwaters, Mediterranean Gull, Black, White-winged, and Whiskered Terns, Montagu's Harrier, Alpine Swift, Middle Spotted Woodpecker, Greater Short-toed and Calandra Larks, Eurasian Crag Martin, Red-rumped Swallow, Tawny Pipit, Isabelline and Eastern Black-eared Wheatears, Blue Rock Thrush, Collared and Red-breasted Flycatchers, Rock Nuthatch, and Lesser Grey and Woodchat Shrikes.

Yet despite the daily birding bonanzas and the time out for leisurely lunches, swimming, and admiring the ever-changing backdrops of dramatic mountains, rocky coves, clean beaches, meandering deltas, river gorges, cool woodland, and reed-fringed lakes, we still found time to experience some of the history that is such an essential aspect of Greece. This ranged from the Lion of Amfipolis to the 12th-century Byzantine church at Feres. But without doubt the most impressive ruins were those of Philippi with its amphitheatre, basilicas, palaces, market place, and mosaics evoking ancient Greece, classical Rome, and the early Christian era.

17. *The most unknown familiar place in Europe*

On the same reconnaissance visit to the Ukraine discussed in chapter 13, plans were laid for a tour to the Crimea. In fact, the proposed itinerary actually appeared in the 1994 brochure. But no sooner was that published than we heard that mafia control had spread to the peninsula so the trip was postponed. It did not take place until 2009. In the interim the Ukraine sorted itself out, independent and family-run hotels were established, and a good birding friend of some 35 years, Paul Goriup, had married Natasha, a Ukrainian national, and founded a travel agency there. The Ukraine (actually the largest country wholly in Europe) is now a fully democratic, stable, peaceful, and Western-leaning republic that is gaining more and more international recognition. The country offers an amazing range of habitats and a wealth of species due to its position between the Black Sea and Russian taiga, the Carpathians and Caucasus Mountains, and the Danube, Dneister, and Dneiper rivers.

The dichotomy of the Crimea is that it is arguably the most unknown familiar place in the Western Palearctic. Despite the proliferation of Sebastopol Roads and Inkerman Terraces thoughout Britain, and our national penchant for wearing balaclavas and reciting 'The Charge of the Light Brigade', many of us would probably pause for thought before pinpointing those original place-names on a map, and some might even need to think before allocating this oh-so-familiar peninsula to a country. In short, for most of us the Crimea means one thing – the war in the 1850s – and the only ornithological link so far has been a nurse called Florence.

The eventual launch of this tour, 15 years after it was first mooted, was therefore particularly satisfying.

5–13 May 2009

Eighteen years after I first reconnoitred the Ukraine and planned this tour, our new Crimea venture provided a happy and satisfying mix of history, scenery, and above all outstanding birding. This was thanks in no small measure to the excellent planning of our ground agents and the fact that the director of the company accompanied the tour together with his delightful Ukrainian wife. Paul and Natasha's knowledge of the country and their ability to adapt the itinerary according to the vagaries of weather and migration ensured that each day brought new delights and an understanding not only of the special avifauna but also of the culture of this little-known peninsula.

Natasha's picnics were a daily highlight, memorable for the varied buffet treats and for the birds at each location – Demoiselle Crane, Great Bustard, and Saker Falcon at one (the latter seemingly homing in on us from a distance and flying around low above our heads); Eastern Imperial Eagle, Barred and Eastern Orphean Warblers, and Chukar Partridge at another; Rufous-tailed Rock Thrush at a third; or Pallas's Gull, Pallid Harrier, and Caspian Tern; Siberian Stonechat; and hundreds of Great White Pelicans at the last en route to the airport (suitably celebrated with caviar and champagne).

Roadside birding was also outstanding – with literally thousands of Red-footed Falcons, marsh terns, Calandra Larks, Mediterranean Gulls, and a constant supply of Golden Orioles, Eurasian Hoopoes, Lesser Grey and Red-backed Shrikes, European Bee-eaters, European Rollers, Pied Wheatears, and

With or without Demoiselle Cranes overhead, the little harbour of Balaclava is remarkably beautiful.

Black-headed Buntings. Typical was a verge-hugging sentry line of spindly little trees that yielded in rapid succession not only the Golden Oriole which prompted our stop, but also Red-breasted and Pied Flycatchers, and Common Redstart. Or the lake shoreline with Temminck's and Little Stints, Kentish Plover, summer-plumaged Curlew Sandpiper, and displaying Ruffs alongside the coach. Or a seemingly unprepossessing phragmites-fringed pool with Paddyfield and Savi's Warblers, Bearded Tit, Red-necked Grebe, Red-crested Pochard, and Ferruginous Duck. And another that offered Eurasian Penduline Tits building a nest, Collared Pratincoles, and Eurasian Spoonbills. Other from-the-coach species included Eurasian Bittern, Purple Heron, Glossy Ibis, White Stork, Garganey, Montagu's Harrier, Griffon Vulture, Common Crane, Stone-curlew, Slender-billed Gull, Little and Short-eared Owls, Syrian Woodpecker, Tawny Pipit, Great Reed Warbler, Woodchat Shrike, and Ortolan Bunting. Plus (still from the roadside) Black-throated Diver, Peregrine Falcon, Alpine Swift, Firecrest, Eurasian Treecreeper,

Wood Warbler, and Common Crossbill. Indeed, it would have been possible to amass a magnificent tally without any walking at all. Even Pygmy Cormorant, White-tailed Eagle, and Eurasian Hobby were seen from the comfort of our silent electric boat gliding through the Dneiper tributaries from the very garden of our hotel.

Add to this wealth of birdlife the beauty of the little harbour of Balaclava and the many old palaces and fine houses from the 19th century, the fascination of the Odessa steps and the valley of the charge of the Light Brigade, the vastness of the steppe with such distant horizons contrasting with mountains higher than any point in Britain rising so close to the sea, the range of other life from the wild 'peony' anemones to Saiga, Asian Wild Ass, European Bison, and Przewalski's Horse, and of course the excellent company, and the Crimea was certainly a very good choice to spend eight days in May.

18. *The soul of the earth*

As alluded to on page 13 my first visit to Guatemala in 1979 was very brief – just long enough to be fumigated and sent back to Mexico.

In the early 1990s, co-leading with either Steve Howell or Jeff Kingery, I annually visited Tikal – the most spectacular Mayan ruins in the world (a city of 50,000 people in the 8th century AD) – but this was marketed as an adjunct to the Belize tour and the country's name was not highlighted in the heading as Guatemala was still perceived to be a dangerous country. Admittedly in the 1980s it was indeed plagued by political violence, coups, and guerrilla fighting. And roadside mugging was still a possibility in the 1990s (which we avoided by flying directly from Belize to Flores). So the tour had a definite Belize bias, as indicated in this report.

27 January–11 February 1994

The Central American country of Belize, together with the ancient Mayan city of Tikal in Guatemala, offers not only a superb introduction to the birds of the region, but also the chance to view some of the world's most intriguing ancient monuments.

Typifying this was our charmed day at Caracol in Belize on this year's trip. Only recently discovered and still largely unexcavated, Caracol dates from the Classic period. Following a war in AD562 this city-state dominated the area for at least a century, eclipsing even the mighty Tikal. We were lucky to get there, as for two weeks the access road had been closed. After even a brief shower the 80 kilometres of jungle track from San Ignacio alternate between a skid pan and a morass. The day we tried, only three vehicles reached Caracol – the two we hired and a British army helicopter checking the border. Our route took us past Crested Guans, Broad-winged Hawks, and Red-billed Pigeons, and on our arrival spectacular Ocellated Turkeys flashed metallic rainbow colours over the plain stones of the temples.

A jungle trail along an ancient Mayan sacred road led us beneath Slaty-tailed Trogons, Wedge-billed Woodcreepers and Thrush-like Manakins to a symbolic tapir skull marker and our goal: a sinkhole where, a month before, the almost mythical Keel-billed Motmot had been seen. At first the quest seemed impossible. Nothing stirred. Nothing called. Then suddenly it materialized – a Keel-billed Motmot sitting quietly nearby, long enough for everyone to have several views in both Questars. Then, just as magically, it vanished. It had not flown in. Nor had it flown out. And at no time did it call. The following day's quest was another near-impossible stake-out: the Orange-breasted Falcon at the Thousand-foot Falls in Hidden Valley, which again is only accessible in good weather. Unfortunately, we had to walk the last 5 kilometres, only to find the falls (and the falcon) shrouded in cloud. A deadline was set and right on cue, just as we were turning to leave, the mist cleared, and the Orange-breasted Falcon appeared. At first it could be seen in silhouette on the nearest tree – then a shaft of sunlight bathed the bird in glowing colour. Other specialities on this mountain-pine ridge walk included Azure-crowned Hummingbird, Grace's Warbler, White-winged Tanager, Rusty Sparrow, and Black-headed Siskin.

We were staying at duPlooy's Lodge, which has a bird list of some 200-plus species. This ensured that those who opted to take a rest day still had plenty of birds to enjoy, from Common

Potoo at dawn to Barn Owl at dusk with Red-capped Manakins and Yellow-throated Euphonias in between, and not forgetting the Sungrebe that gave close views in the river below our rooms. This was particularly welcome as it was the only target bird we had missed on our five-hour river trip at Crooked Tree Wildlife Sanctuary earlier in the tour. This boat trip did turn up lots of other species though, including Boat-billed Heron, Black-collared Hawk, Aplomado Falcon, Snail Kite, Limpkin, Grey-necked Wood Rail, and Glossy Ibis. DuPlooy's was so good that next year we are spending an extra day there.

Tikal is a great place to see birds of prey and the selection of raptors viewed from the tops of the temples – some of them at eye level – was overwhelming: American Swallow-tailed Kite, Hook-billed Kite, Crane Hawk, White Hawk, and Ornate Hawk-eagle to name but a few. In addition we saw a wide selection of parrots (six out of our trip total of eight), three species of toucan, four species of trogon, two more species of motmot, ten more species of woodpecker, five more species of woodcreeper, over 20 species of flycatcher, and over 20 warblers.

But above all (literally) was the sight from any temple top or pyramid of endless rainforest – in fact the largest tract of rainforest north of the Amazon. With nothing visible in any direction but the tops of giant forest trees, and not even one distant building in the whole 360-degree panorama, it was a bit like sitting on top of a giant broccoli. Surely no archaeological site anywhere can be quite so exciting, so atmospheric, or so satisfying as Tikal.

These encounters with ancient Mayan culture formed the central acts in our tour. But the prologue and epilogue were just as rewarding. Particular highlights included swimming in the Blue Hole (a limestone sinkhole in humid forest) surrounded by Sulphur-rumped Flycatchers, Scaly-breasted Hummingbirds, and Rufous-tailed Jacamars; snorkelling in the Hol Chan marine reserve surrounded by Stoplight Parrotfish, Blue-striped Grunt, and Great Barracuda; birding along the Hummingbird Highway with three species of hawk-eagle in view at once, including an unforgettable moment when Black-and-white stooped on Black and talon-grappled in the Questar; Monkey Bay with Short-billed Pigeon, Yellow-headed Parrot, Rufous-breasted Spinetail, Rose-throated Becard and that elusive bamboo-specialist Blue Seedeater; the White-necked Jacobin, White-necked Puffbird, White-collared Manakin, and Crimson-collared and Scarlet-rumped Tanagers at Cockscomb Basin Jaguar reserve; Ambergris Caye with Reddish Egret, Roseate Spoonbill, Black Catbird, Yucatán Vireo, and Yellow-backed Oriole – the highlights go on and on and it really is very difficult to pick out a few good bits from what was a wonderful tour.

Mention of duPlooy's Lodge evokes a potentially embarrassing incident. Steve and I had vacated our cabin so that the clients in the adjacent quarters did not have to share facilities. We were allocated a room in the original lodge, which had no en-suite rooms and was used as accommodation for students and backpackers. As it happened the communal toilet was immediately opposite our room. On our second night, arriving back late from our day in the Hidden Valley, we were moved to a different room. Taken short in the middle of the night and still only half awake, I crossed the corridor for instant relief. The building was in complete darkness but I didn't need visual clues to realize that my feet were on carpet, not tiles. Of course: we had moved rooms and this wasn't the toilet; it was someone's bedroom. I then realized I had no idea where I was in relation to what suddenly became the most vital destination in the world. And I had never known such pitch blackness. Not only was the generator not operating, but also there was absolutely no glimmer of moonlight or starlight. In the maze of corridors I didn't even know which way led to the garden. Immediately my bladder threatened to burst so, completely naked, I had to enter every room hoping that no one had a handy torch. At last I felt tiles and cold porcelain. Blessed relief. But then I realized I was so disorientated that I didn't know the way back to our room. I listened at every door until I detected heavy breathing, which I thought sounded Welsh with a slight North American influence. I hoped it was Steve. At least there was an empty bed. In the morning Steve told me he had heard an interesting conversation between a group of young ladies. One recounted that in the middle of the night someone had entered her room and, terrified, she had held her breath as long as possible. 'The same thing happened to me' gasped another. 'And to me.' And apparently to every young lady in the building.

When we transferred to Guatemala and set out on our first walk around Tikal, Steve and I pointed out a Sungrebe on the pool near our hotel and mentioned that after a short incubation period the naked young are carried in the pockets of skin under the male's wings. On entering the forest we heard the low throaty croak of a Keel-billed Toucan and discussed the symbiotic relationship between bird and frog. We explained that the toucan has no syrinx and is therefore voiceless. Another denizen of the treetops – a small frog – is also disadvantaged by the dearth of pools up there. So the two species teamed up. The toucan carries a reservoir of water in its huge bill to provide a home for the frog, and in return the frog provides a voice for the toucan. We proved this by pointing out that whenever a frog-like croaking was audible above us a toucan could be seen opening its bill to allow its little lodger to take the air. The sudden appearance of a Northern Royal Flycatcher then distracted us before we had time to confirm that this fantasy was, of course, quite ridiculous. (But on reflection no more ridiculous than the perfectly true scenario of naked young being carried in pockets of skin under a male Sungrebe's wings. I would have believed it myself if voiced by Sir David Attenborough.) Embarrassingly, years later, one of the participants revealed that he had been relaying the toucan/frog partnership in all sincerity to interested parties around the world, and at an art exhibition in Britain had even discovered corroborative evidence: a sculpture of a toucan with a frog in its bill.

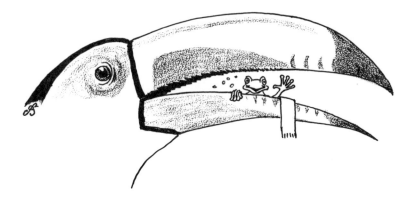

I should have learned by then that nature is so incredible that it can always top a tour leader's wildest imaginings but that, even so, a tour leader's wild imaginings must be kept in check. On the 1980 Great British Experience, as we arrived at Aviemore in Scotland, I pointed out a sign declaring 'Osprey Fishing School' and observed how splendid it was that the young RSPB wardens devoted their summers to teaching the birds how to fish. 'If you go down to the loch at dawn,' I explained, 'you'll see these volunteers sitting on the overhanging Scots Pine branches and diving into the cold waters until the birds get the hang of it.' It never occurred to me that anyone was taking this seriously, but the next day one of the participants commented that he hadn't realized Ospreys have to be taught how to fish. 'Do they hackle them?' he enquired. My running commentary on the coach microphone over the past week was then reviewed in detail by reference to the notes that had been taken. It was even discovered that the road signs showing a man struggling to open his umbrella were not council warnings of impending rainshowers but referred to roadworks ahead. Thereafter, to ensure the veracity of imparted information, the Americans devised a simple solution. I could be taken seriously if I was wearing my bowler hat. (I happened to have it with me as protection against Arctic Tern attacks on the Farne Islands.) 'Say that again with your hat on,' became a regular request.

After 35 years of civil war Guatemala eventually acquired a stable government and became ready and eager for tourism. A series of annual International Birdwatching Encounters was launched. In 2007 Steve Gantlett and I were the first Old World birders to be invited and were impressed by the country's commitment to ecotourism. As I wrote in an article for the estimable *Birding World* (volume 20, no 5):

> Most wonderfully, the whole country seems to have embraced ecotourism, from the enlightened Director of the Guatemala Tourism Board and a proliferation of birding-oriented tourist agencies to the many private individuals who are creating reserves and comfortable lodges. Wisely, some of the reserves and lodges are being developed by communities so that the local population benefits from the profits – a long-term financial return instead of the one-off cash crop from logging.
>
> This environmental awareness has been snow-balling since the government passed the Ley de Areas Protegidas (Protected Areas

Law) in February 1989 in a move to protect the nation's rapidly dwindling forests. This designated 44 new conservation areas and now all of Guatemala north of latitude 17°10'N (about a million hectares) has been declared as the Mayan Biosphere Reserve. Over 15 per cent of Guatemala's territory is now under protection. The areas include many 'islands' of cloud forest on peaks throughout the country, all of which constitute important watersheds that are among the most threatened habitats in Central America. All of this is good news for the birds. And, for the birdwatcher, Guatemala has much to offer: over 700 species, representing 80 families, all concentrated in a country a little larger than Scotland and significantly smaller than England. Guatemala has both a Pacific and Caribbean coastline and contains many diverse ecosystems and habitats, including tropical humid forest, tropical rainforest, cloud forest, dry scrub, mountain forest, subtropical humid forest, and tropical humid savanna – yet it is possible to drive through three or four of these regions within three hours and see a cross-section of several different bird groups. This makes the country an ideal destination for a small group of birders intent on seeing as many different species as possible in a limited amount of time, including a sequence of outstanding target birds. A good birder – particularly if accompanied by a local guide – could expect to see 300 species in a week. This was confirmed at the Third International Birdwatching Encounter at Alta Verapaz, Guatemala, on 19–24 February 2007, when, before, between, and after the lectures, delegates were shown over 300 species, including a high percentage of regional endemics and such star attractions as the Resplendent Quetzal, Ocellated Turkey, Horned Guan, Pink-headed Warbler, and Blue-throated Motmot.

Besides these and other such regional endemics as Belted Flycatcher and Cabanis's Tanager, many other tropical species such as parrots, other motmots, and cracids are also present in Guatemala, plus one of the highest concentrations of hummingbird species in Central America. A bonus is the huge number of North American warblers wintering there – including species such as Golden-cheeked that are restricted in range or difficult to see on the breeding grounds.

True, it is possible to see many of these species in neighbouring Central American countries. Even Guatemala's stunning national bird (Resplendent Quetzal) can be seen in Costa Rica or Panama, for instance. But Guatemala has a magnificent trump card: the archaeology. For a couple or a party of friends where one is less than obsessional about the birds, the added attraction of so many Mayan ruins throughout the country (many of them in superb birding habitat) cannot be over-emphasized. What is more, this country is astonishingly beautiful, the culture colourful and instantly accessible, and the people welcoming and friendly. Spanish is the main language, but English is spoken widely.

There is no doubt that Guatemala is the new Central American destination and will soon be featuring in British and American bird-tour brochures. Meanwhile, nothing is simpler than for a group of friends to contact one of the many knowledgable indigenous ground agents and request a tailor-made tour to experience as many as possible of the wonders on offer. A satisfying series of ornithological encounters is guaranteed, along with spectacular scenery, absorbing archaeology, and a warm welcome.

I have been happy to assist in Guatemala's ecotourism programme, lecturing at subsequent Encounters, inspecting new ecotourism facilities, and hosting Guatemalan teams on their visits to the British Birdfair. One most encouraging development is the plan by the private coffee fincas to create a continuous Meso-American biological corridor on the volcanic slopes from Mexico to Colombia. I detailed this in another *Birding World* article:

Guatemala's sixth International Birdwatching Encounter – held in 2010 at Los Tarrales and San Juan La Laguna, Solola (Lake Atitlán) on 4–7 February – continued to showcase the many birdwatching opportunities offered by this increasingly conservation-conscious country. It was significant that, before the lectures at San Juan, the mayor of this delightful town, renowned for its colourful murals, unveiled the latest work of art which featured not only one of the iconic birds of the area (Blue-and-white Mockingbird), but also a birdwatcher being shown this speciality. In short, birdwatching has found its place in popular culture. Happily, delegates to the Encounter had already seen the real thing on their early-morning walk.

San Pedro volcano, for the first time, did not deliver Horned Guan, but other Atitlán species seen included Spotted Wood-quail, Black-and-white Owl, Yellow-naped Parrot, Belted Flycatcher (above the luxurious Laguna Lodge), Orange-billed Nightingale-thrush, Wine-throated Hummingbird, Long-tailed Manakin, White-throated Magpie-jay, and Blue-winged Warbler.

Post-Encounter mini-tours produced Pink-headed, Red-faced, and Crescent-chested Warblers at Rincon Suizo; Azure-crowned and Magnificent Hummingbirds, Guatemalan Flicker, Blue-throated Motmot, Bushy-crested Jay, and Hooded Grosbeak at El Pilar; Highland Guan, Green-throated Mountain-gem, and Blue-tailed Hummingbird at Las Nubes; and Black Hawk-eagle,

Barred Parakeet, Scaled Antpitta, Golden-browed Warbler, and Azure-rumped Tanager at Los Andes plus, most of all, Resplendent Quetzal – what gasps of wonder when those shimmering, ultra-long uppertail-coverts (spectacularly so in the Guatemalan race) were first seen trailing down through the vegetation.

The Private Nature Reserve Scheme

Most of the sites itemized above – Los Tarrales, Los Andes and El Pilar – will be familiar to readers of previous reports on Guatemala (*Birding World* 20: 210–215 and 21: 128 and 484). The new one is Las Nubes. All these are coffee fincas which are providing facilities for ecotourists, in particular birdwatchers. This inspired scheme is one of the great success stories of conservation and ecotourism. In *Birding World* 20: 210–215, it was reported how environmental awareness has been snowballing in Guatemala since the government passed the Ley de Areas Protegidas (Protected Areas Law) in February 1989 in a move to protect the nation's forests. A million-hectare area in the north was declared the Mayan Biosphere Reserve. But national parks (the locals often assume that means 'belonging to us') and appropriate legislation are one thing; enforcing the law in remote areas is another. Which is why the Private Nature Reserve Scheme is so important.

Shade-grown coffee excels in taste, so most coffee fincas have retained areas of primary forest. To encourage the owners to conserve (and even develop) these, the government introduced a fiscal incentive and schemes by which they can become certified private nature reserves (with facilities for birdwatchers and ecotourists) and Rainforest Alliance certified. The first was the Santo Tomas Pachuj Reserve in 1996. Two years later, the six reserves in the scheme formed an association. One neighbour persuaded another. Now there are over 40 in the Atitlán Chapter alone and 140 in the country as a whole, ensuring the protection of some 60,000 hectares of forest. Since these coffee fincas on the volcanic slopes are not isolated but contiguous, this means that long biological corridors are now protected (and, as the land is private, the owners really can enforce the law). The fincas have now convinced the environment minister that it is possible to create a 'coffee' biological corridor along 275,000ha of protected forest. Their aim is eventually to create a continous Meso-American corridor from Mexico to Colombia. In 2008, an agreement was signed with the government to that effect and made public last year. It is inspiring to realize that one of the most significant conservation projects in Central America is driven by enlightened private commercial enterprise. And it is reassuring to reflect that the money birders spend in indulging their passion is not swelling the coffers of big business or some faceless hotel chain, but is being invested directly back into conservation and helping the local community – a win-win situation.

Las Nubes

Under this scheme, Las Nubes welcomed its first group of visitors in January 2009 and, by the end of the year, had hosted a remarkable 377 ecotourists. The extra profit generated is being spent on a reafforestation programme on the finca and on improving the lot of the 40-plus families living on the estate (just as Los Tarrales provides income to 60 Maya Kaqchikel families living within their protected area). In common with all the fincas, Las Nubes provides a school, a clinic, and a nursery, and is now introducing a scholarship programme for the locals to learn a trade. The estate employs 900 registered pickers (each assisted by two or three family helpers), so is essential to the local economy. Manager of the ecotourism department Mario Castillo sees ecotourism as 'the industry without chimneys' and is committed to maintaining and increasing the natural forest and improving facilities for birdwatchers. Already, accommodation is provided in the finca's original 1860s house and an attractive complex just above. New rooms overlooking a bird-filled valley are planned. And, in February 2010, they were busy building a viewing platform so that birders will be able to obtain even better looks at Highland Guan, Resplendent Quetzal (which is probably better seen here than anywhere else in the country), and Azure-rumped Tanager. This is situated more than 300m above the comfortable tourist accommodation at an elevation of nearly 1,600m, but is easily accessed by the reserve's four-wheel-drive vehicles (see Plate 13, page 245). Intriguingly, one of the estate workers recently reported seeing a turkey-sized bird with a red lump growing out of its head, just 40 minutes walk from this point. A team is being arranged to clear the trail and investigate this report. If Horned Guan is confirmed, Las Nubes will surely take its place alongside Los Tarrales and Los Andes as a must-stay destination.

After the 2007 Encounter I took the opportunity of searching for Horned Guan, the most wanted of the Chiapas – Guatemala highlands endemics. This bizarre and endangered cracid is restricted to remote cloud forest at 2,000–3,000m and threatened by habitat destruction. It is possible to see it in the Sierra Madre de Chiapas, Mexico, but the hike up El Triunfo is a two-day expedition requiring an overnight stay on the mountain. Guatemala offers easier options to see this enigmatic species. Even so, it is no roadside tick and the quest calls for a satisfying degree of effort involving a long uphill climb. In fact, listening to

*Horned Guan: the most wanted of the
Chiapas-Guatemala highlands endemics.*

the young American tour leaders describe the expedition up San
Pedro volcano as the most exhausting walk they had ever attempted,
I began to wonder whether it was a suitable outing for someone on
the count-down to his allotted three-score years and ten. But in fact,
although relentlessly uphill and consistently steep (it was necessary to
reach 2,500m from a starting altitude of 1,700m) the climb did not
seem at all gruelling. Fortunately there were many birds at the lower
elevations and the frequent pauses to search through the flocks provided
opportunities for resting. These included Chestnut-sided Shrike-vireo,
Blue-throated Motmot, Provost's Ground-sparrow, Lesser Roadrunner,
Wine-throated Hummingbird, Sparkling-tailed Woodstar, Magnificent
Hummingbird, Rufous Sabrewing, Collared Forest-falcon, Emerald
Toucanet, Mountain Trogon, Rufous-collared Thrush, and Azure-
hooded and Bushy-crested Jays – plus more than 100 other species.

The Horned Guans have a particular association with the Canak tree, eating both the flowers and the fruits, so if you attempt this expedition look for fallen flowers on the path: their distinctive form has earned them the local name of *mano de leon* (lion's hand). Alternatively, carry on to a sign depicting the guan and a pair of binoculars with a red arrow connecting the two. We were assured that this meant 'raise your binoculars and look at the bird'. So we did. It was in the very crown of a tree to the right of the sign. Whilst we were scoping this splendid adult, a younger individual flew in and perched on a low branch to the left of the sign. Two more birds were seen a little higher up the trail.

The following year several friends repeated the experience with equal success. So after the 2010 Encounter I assured my room-mate Bill Oddie that the climb was not so bad and the rewards well worth the effort. I was lecturing at San Juan La Laguna that day so I did not accompany the group. I assumed that when they did not return until well after dark it was because they were having such a wonderful time up there. 'Well, was that the best birding day you have ever had?' I asked Bill when he eventually entered the bedroom. 'No, the worst,' replied the mud-splattered figure. I had overlooked the fact that this was Bill's first walk after 18 months in hospital. The quest had taken them six hours up and six hours down. What's more the Horned Guan had not obliged. I felt acutely embarrassed. Apparently the climb is as bad as first described to me. Yet to Bill's credit the next day he was climbing up another near-vertical slope above the luxurious Laguna Lodge on Lake Atitlán to see Belted Flycatcher. However, my tour following that Encounter saw some spectacular birds without too much effort, a far cry from the 1994 tour which began this chapter.

10–19 February 2010

In the last two decades of stable government and insurgent-free existence, Guatemala has made great strides in ecotourism and is rapidly becoming the new birding Mecca in Central America. This comparatively small country embraces seven main ecosystems and accordingly a remarkably varied selection of birds (over 700 species, many of them iconic) including many regional endemics (of which we tallied 30).

The new tour visited as many sites as possible in ten relaxed days and enjoyed vistas of outstanding natural beauty, the breathtakingly scenic volcano-fringed Lake Atitlán, the charm of 16th- and 17th-century Antigua, a sequence of private nature reserves created on the coffee fincas offering comfortable accommodation and good food, and the world-famous Tikal National Park. Daily dazzles included orioles, euphonias, hummingbirds, tanagers, trogans, toucans, araçaris, motmots, parrots, and parakeets – the very epitome of tropical birds – complemented by a showy selection of wintering North American warblers (28 species, including the highly sought-after Golden-cheeked).

Abiding images include a sunlit tree at Rincon Suizo decorated as if for Christmas with a profusion of warblers (Pink-headed, Red-faced, Crescent-chested, Wilson's, Townsend's, Olive, Yellow, Tennessee, Hermit, and Black-and-white) plus Bushtit, Hutton's Vireo, Brown Creeper, Tufted Flycatcher, Slate-throated Redstart, and other baubles. A stunning, unreal selection. Or Red-capped Manakins outblossoming the brightest bromeliad. Or parrots and parakeets not just as fly-bys but also perched to reveal how they earned their names – red lores, white crowns, white foreheads, yellow napes, olive throats, orange foreheads, orange chins. Or trogans as lusciously ripe and motionless as fruits in the foliage. Or hummingbirds (Azure-crowned, Magnificent, and Rufous Sabrewing) on the feeders as we too enjoyed an elegant buffet lunch. But the grand climax was surely Tikal – sitting atop Temple IV with a pair of Orange-breasted Falcons on the scaffolding just above us and a Crested Guan on a treetop below us; the army ants with the accompanying fearless feeding frenzies of acrobatic leapfrogging woodcreepers interspersed with Grey-headed Tanagers and Red-crowned and Red-throated

Endemic 'elusive and wary' Ocellated Turkeys wander around the ruins at Tikal like chickens in a farmyard.

Ant-tanagers; the 'rare and elusive' Ocellated Turkeys wandering around the ruins like chickens in a farmyard; or just quiet walks along the forest trails to come across yet another temple, row of stellae, or limestone slab recording the capture of the ruler Wilan Tok Wayib by the Tikal ruler Yik'in Chan Kawil on 8 December AD748. And all this while encountering one exciting avian speciality after another: Great Curassow, King Vulture, Ruddy Quail-dove, Yucatán Nightjar, White-bellied Emerald, Violaceous Trogan, Keel-billed Toucan, Pale-billed and Lineated

Woodpeckers, Eye-ringed Flatbill, Royal and Sulphur-rumped Flycatchers, Rufous Mourner, Tawny-crowned and Lesser Greenlets, White-bellied Wren, Yellow-breasted Chat, Black-throated Shrike-tanager, Green-backed Sparrow, Black-cowled Oriole, Olive-backed Euphonia... This must be one of the world's best birding sites.

In itemizing a score or more species like that, it is significant to recall how each site on our itinerary yielded a different set of specialities. El Pilar gave us Collared Trogan, Guatemalan (Northern) Flicker, Blue-headed Vireo, Bushy-crested Jay, Eastern Bluebird, Black and Rufous-collared Robins, Blue-and-white Mockingbird, Grey Silky-flycatcher, Chestnut-sided and Golden-cheeked Warblers, Elegant Euphonia, Black-headed Siskin, Lesser Goldfinch, and the easily overlooked endemic Hooded Grosbeak. Rincon Suizo, in addition to our bauble tree, offered Band-tailed Pigeon, White-eared Hummingbird, Mountain Trogan, Spot-crowned Woodcreeper, Steller's Jay, Rufous-browed Wren, and a proliferation of Acorn Woodpeckers. Los Andes, most remembered for the Blue-tailed Hummingbirds and Provost's Ground-sparrows outside our rooms, added Highland Guan, Broad-winged and Short-tailed Hawks, Crested Caracara, Red-billed Pigeon, Pacific Parakeet, Emerald Toucanet, Common Tody-Flycatcher, and Yellow-throated Euphonia. Our day around Lake Atitlán produced Ruddy Duck (a target bird for the Brit), Brown Pelican ('rare far off-shore'), Yellow-naped Parrot, Lesser Roadrunner, Sparkling-tailed Hummingbird, Black Phoebe, a Brown-backed Solitaire finally perched in the open, White-throated Magpie-Jay, MacGillivray's and Rufous-capped Warblers, and Black-vented Oriole. Los Tarrales overwhelmed us with White-bellied Chachalaca, Orange-chinned and Orange-fronted Parakeets, Squirrel Cuckoo, Long-billed Starthroat, Cinnamon Hummingbird, Blue-crowned and Turquoise-browed Motmots, Collared Araçari, Barred Antshrike, Rufous-breasted Spinetail, Northern Bentbill, Paltry Tyrannulet, Rose-throated Becard, Rufous-naped Wren, Golden-crowned Warbler, White-winged Tanager, Scrub Euphonia, Red-legged Honeycreeper, Spot-breasted and Altamira Orioles – but most of all Long-tailed Manakin, Tody Motmot, and Blue-throated Goldentail. Even Yaxha, the impressive Mayan site that gave us a foretaste of Tikal, offered different birds: Laughing Falcon, Ornate Hawk-eagle, Scaly-breasted Hummingbird, Purple-crowned Fairy, White-whiskered Puffbird, Buff-throated Foliage-gleaner, Bright-rumped Attila, and Blue Bunting.

Yet the lasting impression is not merely of a sequence of colourful and exotic species, but of a beautiful country with a warm and welcoming population anxious to protect the environment and provide a happy and satisfying experience for visiting birdwatchers and ecotourists in general. The Guatemala Tourism Board promotes the slogan 'Guatemala, soul of the earth'. That's a good summary.

19. *No profit grows where is no pleasure ta'en*

There are so many other destinations I could have featured in these reminiscences. Costa Rica, for instance, as in this report extract.

18 March–4 April 1994

The Costa Rica tour this year was very alliterative. Led by the two BBs (Bob Behrstock and Bryan Bland), it was a triple-ten trogon trip. All ten Costa Rican trogons were seen within ten days, with a total of ten of the most significant – the Resplendent Quetzal – on one day. And all of them frame-filling in the Questar to reveal the notched bill that gives them their name (from a Greek word meaning to gnaw). Statistics apart, a pair of these magnificent birds nesting by a waterfall in the lush tropical foliage was a sight never to be forgotten. Other T-shirt images that were brought vividly to life included Black-chested Hawk, Scarlet Macaws, and Three-wattled Bellbird.

There were many other memorable images from the same two weeks. For some it was a Spectacled Antpitta filling the Questar as it reiterated its fluty notes in the forest understorey; for others it was the smallest passerine in the world (Black-capped Pygmy-Tyrant) hovering in front of our eyes like a hummingbird, or the female Great Curassow treading silently and stealthily over the forest floor just metres from the trail, yet so melting into invisibility on our passing that, despite her huge chestnut body, black-and-white striped tail, and crested head, one client had to query her whereabouts 'in relation to that sandy bank with the branch across it' (the sandy bank being the body of the bird). Then there were Great Tinamou, Black-and-white Owl, Purple-throated Fruitcrow, Long-tailed Manakin, Buffy Tuftedcheek, and all those antbirds and all those hummingbirds. If you don't already have mental pictures of them look them up in a field guide and you'll understand why Costa Rica is such a colourful and richly rewarding experience.

Or Oregon, a birds and the bard tour centred on the Shakespeare Festival at Ashland, as outlined in this report penned by American co-leader Rich Hoyer who, inspired by Sunbird's birds and history and birds and music tours, devised this particular pairing.

18–28 July 2007

Despite the binary nature of this tour's title, it was a complete experience – much more than seeing a few birds and then watching a play. Each morning began with a copious picnic breakfast in idyllic settings with fresh mountain air, forest scents abounding, and birds singing. The backdrops for the birds were no less stunning, with coastal vistas, looming Cascade peaks, rich and wild coniferous forests, craggy mountain tops, and wildflower-drenched meadows framing great birds such as Northern Pygmy Owl, voted trip favourite, and amazing views of Lazuli Bunting, Wrentit, and Rhinoceros Auklet. The picnic lunches were equally resplendent, and even the restaurant dinners were fantastic, from French to Eastern Fusion to a down-home grilled dinner in the forest. Then the plays! Particularly enchanting were topnotch performances of *Tartuffe* (a premier translation, destined to become the standard for American audiences) and *As You Like It*, with *Taming of the Shrew*,

The Tempest, and the newcomer *Distracted*, gaining high marks.

The highlight of the first day, after plunging Bryan headfirst into American driving by navigating Portland rush-hour traffic, was a pair of American Dippers at a bridge not far out of the city. We also saw our only Evening Grosbeaks at this quick roadside stop before heading to the coastal headlands where swarms of Common and Pigeon Guillemots, Western Gulls, and cormorants filled the air. One stop yielded great views of several Marbled Murrelets and a rare summer Red-throated Diver, while another had closer Surf Scoters. Our next morning on the coast yielded the stakeout Grey Catbird (hundreds of kilometres out of range), but a total surprise was the Northern Mockingbird that came to perch right above it. It was on this morning that we had our best Rhinoceros Auklet views, and we lucked out with the 'rockpeckers' here: Wandering Tattler, Black and Ruddy Turnstones, and Surfbird.

Our time spent in the mountains surrounding Ashland was productive. Sandhill Cranes by the road, Dusky Flycatcher and

Black Oystercatchers and Black Turnstones on the west coast.

gorgeous Western Tanagers in the woods, and Green-tailed Towhees and Rufous Hummingbirds in the brushy wildflower slopes were highlights. Then came our side trip to the different world on the other side of the mountains, where we saw Sage Thrasher, Brewer's Sparrow, Tricoloured Blackbird, countless ducks and coots, White-faced Ibis, and Black-necked Grebes carrying their adorable chicks. Our outdoor grilled dinner here was our most pleasurable meal of the trip, as the Pandora Moths (in the midst of a 20- to 30-year outbreak) and Pygmy Nuthatches adorned the trees nearby. After some morning birding that included MacGillivray's Warbler and some lovely butterflies and dragonflies (Great Spangled Fritillary, Sonoran Skipper, Twelve-spotted Skimmer, and Band-winged Meadowhawk), Crater Lake offered an impressive vista before we had to head back to Ashland, stopping for a picnic lunch to be shared with Grey Jays coming to our hands.

We spent our last birding days in the valley near Grants Pass (great views of Wrentit and countless Black-headed Grosbeaks) and in the mountains near Ashland, where we experienced fly-by views of Great Grey Owl, a very co-operative pair of Mountain Quail, Olive-sided Flycatchers singing, Fox Sparrow of the thick-billed subspecies, and colourful Mountain Bluebirds.

Thanks to a fabulous group of people who know how to enjoy themselves, we all made full use of the pleasures offered by this little-known corner of the world.

Or Trinidad and Tobago, Bermuda (little more than one huge golf course), the Galápagos, Antarctica, Tristan da Cunha, Venezuela, Ecuador, Peru, Argentina, Texas, Arizona, California, Ethiopia, Kenya, South Africa, Thailand, Japan, China, Tahiti... the world really is a

Steller's Jay is always a popular bird on tours to the western United States.

global village for the average birdwatcher. But enough is enough. The arbitrary destinations selected for detailed examination in the foregoing pages are already sufficient to have suggested by now the profit of birding. It provides a vital lifeline to the whole of Creation and beyond, as implied in the final paragraph of chapter one. It gives you a feeling for world politics. It is the common denominator for providing a lifetime of compatible company and a constant reminder that there are some wonderful people out there, even the non-birders.

Green Exercise and Green Care, a 2009 report by researchers at the Centre for Environment and Society at the University of Essex, stated 'There is growing... empirical evidence to show that exposure to nature brings substantial mental health benefits... Our findings suggest that priority should be given to developing the use of green exercise as a therapeutic intervention (green care).' In 2010 Jules Petty and Jo Barton of the University of Essex published results in the journal *Environmental Science & Technology* suggesting the proper minimum dosage. 'For the first time in scientific literature, we have been able to show dose-response relationships for the positive effects of nature on human mental health.' A five-minute dose is sufficient to improve mood and self-esteem. 'Exposure to nature via green exercise can thus be conceived of as a readily available therapy with no obvious side effects.' Blue-green exercise is even better: the study found that a walk in a natural area adjacent to water offered people the most improvement. What price a Great Crested Grebe or Common Kingfisher census?

Researchers suggest we are still hunter-gatherers at heart. Harvard's E. O. Wilson hypothesized that biophilia is our 'innately emotional affiliation to... other living organisms'. Dr William Bird, Chief Health Advisor for Natural England, has explained at length why exposure to and experience of nature is so important to our mental and physical health. 'The fight or flight reflex is a normal response to stress caused by the release of catecholamines (including adrenaline) and results in muscle tension, raised blood pressure, faster pulse, diversion of blood away from the skin to muscle and sweating. All of these factors help the body to cope with a dangerous situation. However, without rapid recovery this stress response would cause damage and exhaustion with limited response to a repeat dangerous situation.' It would seem that those of our ancestors who survived were the ones who could recover from the stress of natural threats by using the restorative powers of nature.

And even the much-derided lowest-common-denominator anorak aspect of birding – the tick list – is an inevitable legacy of the survival of the fittest, not to be scorned. Those of our ancestors who had this penchant for listing (i.e. pigeon-holing, categorizing, comparing and contrasting) were those who could best evaluate every new situation and assess (and evade) potential danger. Hence the human desire to collect – whether it be train numbers, Meissen china, sporting prints, books, creamers, Beatles memorabilia, or species.

As observed by American author Richard Louv in his timely book

Last Child in the Woods: Saving our children from nature-deficit disorder we are paying a high price for our increasing alienation from the natural world. Watching TV and playing computer games are poor substitutes for such green activities as birdwatching. Sir David Attenbourgh, in an interview at the tenth anniversary of the Wildfowl and Wetlands Trust's London Wetland Centre in 2010, highlighted the current paradoxical situation '... whereas over half the world's population is becoming urbanized and knowing less and less, oddly – through the television – they know more and more about exotic places... I dare say they know more about East African lions and game that they do about foxes.'

So what is the profit of birding? It gets you out of the house.

Other Bird Books by New Holland Publishers

Advanced Bird ID Handbook: the Western Palearctic

Nils van Duivendijk. Award-winning and innovative field guide listing every key character of every distinct plumage of all 1,350 species and subspecies that have ever occurred in Britain, Europe, North Africa and the Middle East. Includes 23 tables comparing similar species. Published in association with the journal *British Birds*.

£24.99 ISBN 978 1 78009 022 1

Also available: *Advanced Bird ID Guide: the Western Palearctic* (£14.99, ISBN 978 1 84773 607 9).

The Birdman Abroad

Stuart Winter. A gripping account of the overseas escapades of Britain's best-known birding journalist, from showdowns with illegal bird-trappers in Malta to heart-warming tales of conservation in Africa and meetings with big names in birding.

£7.99 ISBN 978 1 84773 692 5

Bird Songs and Calls

Hannu Jännes and Owen Roberts. Perfect for the dawn chorus. CD containing the bird sounds of 96 common species and an accompanying book explaining the songs and calls and illustrating each bird with colour photos.

£9.99 ISBN 978 1 84773 779 3

Birds of Africa South of the Sahara

Ian Sinclair and Peter Ryan. Fully updated edition covering more than 2,100 species in full colour over 359 beautifully illustrated artwork plates. The text and distribution map for each species are on the page facing the relevant plate. The most comprehensive field guide to the continent's birds.

£29.99 ISBN 978 1 77007 623 5

Birds of Indian Ocean Islands

Ian Sinclair and Olivier Langrand. The first comprehensive field guide to the birds of Madagascar, the Seychelles, Mauritius, Reunion and Rodrigues. Covers 359 species in full colour.

£18.99 ISBN 978 1 86872 956 2

Birds: Magic Moments

Markus Varesvuo. Bringing together the work of one of the world's best bird photographers, this is a celebration of the avian world, illustrating rarely observed scenes from courtship, nest-building, hunting and raising young. The author's stunning images cover species ranging from colourful bee-eaters to majestic eagles.

£20 ISBN 978 1 78009 075 7

Chris Packham's Back Garden Nature Reserve

Chris Packham. A complete guide explaining the best ways to attract wildlife into your garden, and how to encourage it to stay there. Packed with practical advice on gardening for wildlife and the identification of birds, animals and plants.

£12.99 ISBN 978 1 84773 698 7

Colouring Birds

Sally MacLarty. Ideal gift to help develop a child's interest in birds. Features 40 species outlines – including such favourites as Robin, Blue Tit, Chaffinch and Green Woodpecker – and a colour section depicting the birds as they appear in life.

£2.99 ISBN 978 184773 526 3

Also available: *Colouring Bugs* (£2.99, ISBN 978 1 84773 525 6).

Common Garden Bird Calls

Hannu Jännes and Owen Roberts. Invaluable book and CD featuring the songs and calls of 60 species likely to be encountered in gardens and parks. Each is illustrated with at least one photo and a distribution map.

£6.99 ISBN 978 1 84773 517 1

The Complete Garden Bird Book

Mark Golley and Stephen Moss. New edition of a best-selling book which explains how to attract birds to your garden and how to identify them. Packed with more than 500 colour artworks of 70 of the most common and widespread garden bird species.

£9.99 ISBN 978 1 84773 980 3

Creative Bird Photography

Bill Coster. Illustrated with the author's inspirational images. An indispensable guide to all aspects of the subject, covering bird portraits, activities such as flight and courtship, and taking 'mood' shots at dawn and dusk.

£19.99 ISBN 978 1 84773 509 6

Also available: *Creative Nature Photography* (£19.99, ISBN 978 1 84773 784 7).

Fascinating Birds

Markus Varesvuo. Bird photographer extraordinaire Markus Varesvuo has selected 100 favourite species from Britain and Europe. One or more photos of each are accompanied by text explaining why the bird has been chosen, and interesting facts about it and how the image or images were taken.

£20 ISBN 978 1 78009 178 5

A Field Guide to the Birds of Borneo

Susan Myers. Features more than 630 species. The only comprehensive and accurate field guide to the varied avifauna of this island biodiversity hot-spot, which comprises Brunei, the Malaysian states of Sabah and Sarawak, and the Indonesian states of Kalimantan.

£24.99 ISBN 978 1 84773 381 8

A Field Guide to the Birds of South-East Asia

Craig Robson. New flexi-cover edition of the region's only comprehensive field guide. Fully illustrated in colour. Covers all 1,300 species recorded in Thailand, Vietnam, Singapore, Peninsular Malaysia, Myanmar, Laos and Cambodia.

£24.99 ISBN 978 1 78009 049 8

The Garden Bird Year

Roy Beddard. Gives both birdwatchers and gardeners insights into how to attract resident and migrant birds to the garden, and how to manage this precious space as a vital resource for wildlife. Includes many tips on feeding, planting, nestboxes and identification.

£9.99 ISBN 978 184773 503 4

The History of Ornithology

Valerie Chansigaud. The story of more than two millennia of the study of birds. Richly illustrated with numerous artworks, photographs and diagrams, including a detailed timeline of ornithological events.
£17.99 ISBN 978 1 84773 433 4

Kingfisher

David Chandler. Beautifully illustrated book detailing the life of the Common Kingfisher, including feeding, courtship, tunnel-building and raising young. Contains more than 80 outstanding colour photographs.
£12.99 ISBN 978 1 84773 524 9
Also available in the same series: *Barn Owl* (£12.99, ISBN 978 1 84773 768 7), *Peregrine Falcon* (£14.99, ISBN 978 1 84773 769 4).

The Naturalized Animals of Britain and Ireland

Christopher Lever. Authoritative and eminently readable account of how alien species were introduced and naturalized, their status and distribution, and their impact. Includes everything from the Ruddy Duck to the Red-necked Wallaby.
£35.00 ISBN 978 1 84773 454 9

New Holland Concise Bird Guide

An ideal first field guide to British birds for adults and children. Covers more than 250 species in full colour, contains more than 800 colour artworks, comes in protective plastic wallet and includes a fold-out insert comparing species in flight. Published in association with The Wildlife Trusts.
£4.99 ISBN 978 1 84773 601 7

Other titles in the *Concise Guide* series (all £4.99):

Butterfly and Moth (ISBN 978 1 84773 602 4),

Garden Bird (ISBN 978 1 84773 978 0),

Garden Wildlife (ISBN 978 1 84773 606 2),

Herb (ISBN 978 1 84773 976 6),

Insect (ISBN 978 1 84773 604 8),

Mushroom (ISBN 978 1 84773 785 4),

Pond Wildlife (ISBN 978 1 84773 977 3),

Seashore Wildlife (ISBN 978 1 84773 786 1),

Tree (ISBN 978 1 84773 605 5) and

Wild Flower (ISBN 978 1 84773 603 1).

New Holland European Bird Guide

Peter H. Barthel. The only truly pocket-sized comprehensive field guide to all the birds of Britain and Europe. Features more than 1,700 beautiful and accurate artworks of over 500 species, plus more than 500 distribution maps and a chapter on recognizing bird sounds.

£10.99 ISBN 978 1 84773 110 4

Newman's Birds of Southern Africa

Kenneth Newman, updated by Vanessa Newman. Revised, updated and expanded edition of the classic field guide. Covers more than 900 species and includes 3,500 colour artworks.

£19.99 ISBN 978 1 77007 876 5

SASOL Birds of Southern Africa

Ian Sinclair, Phil Hockey and Warwick Tarboton. Fully updated edition of the world's leading guide to southern Africa's 950 bird species. Each is illustrated in full colour and has a distribution map.

£19.99 ISBN 978 1 77007 925 0

The Slater Field Guide to Australian Birds

Peter Slater, Pat Slater and Raoul Slater. Fully updated edition of the classic comprehensive field guide. Features more than 750 species depicted over 150 colour artwork plates. The most portable complete guide to the country's birds available anywhere.
£17.99 ISBN 978 1 87706 963 5

Tales of a Tabloid Twitcher

Stuart Winter. The key birding events and personalities, scandal and gossip of the past two decades and beyond seen through the eyes of a birding journalist. A 'must-read' book for all birdwatchers.
£7.99 ISBN 978 1 84773 693 2

Top Birding Sites of Europe

Dominic Couzens. A site-by-site guide to the best birding destinations on the continent, from Svalbard to the Azores via north Norfolk and the Black Sea coast of Bulgaria. Includes 175 photos, more than 30 locator maps and a CD of bird sounds likely to be heard at each site.
£22.99 ISBN 978 1 84773 767 0
Also available: *Top 100 Birding Sites of the World* (£35, ISBN 978 1 84773 109 8).

The Urban Birder

David Lindo. Even the most unpromising cityscapes can be havens for birds, and *The Urban Birder* shows you how via a series of remarkable stories, from run-ins with gun-toting youths in London to migration-watching from skyscrapers.
£9.99 ISBN 978 1 84773 950 6

See www.newhollandpublishers.com for details and special offers